Library of
Davidson College

The politics of French trade unionism

for Ilona

The Politics of French Trade unionism
Party—union relations at the time of the Union of the Left

Jeff Bridgford
Heriot-Watt University Edinburgh

Leicester University Press
Leicester, London and New York

© Jeff Bridgford 1991

First published in Great Britain in 1991 by Leicester University Press (a division of Pinter Publishers Ltd)

All rights reserved. No part of this publication may be reproduced, stored in a retrieval system, or transmitted, in any form or by any means, electronic, mechanical, photocopying, recording or otherwise, without the prior permission of the Leicester University Press.

Editorial offices
Fielding Johnson Building, University of Leicester
University Road, Leicester, LE1 7RH

Trade and other enquiries
25 Floral Street, London, WC2E 9DS

British Library Cataloguing in Publication Data
A CIP cataloguing record for this book is available from the British Library.

ISBN 0 7185 1350 9

For enquiries in North America please contact PO Box 197, Irvington, NY 10533

Library of Congress Cataloging-in-Publication Data
Bridgford, Jeff.
    The politics of French trade unionism : party-union relations at the time of the union of the left / by Jeff Bridgford.
        p. cm.
    Includes bibliographical references and index.
    ISBN 0-7185-1350-9
        1. Trade-unions--France--Political activity. 2. Socialism--France. 3. France--Politics and government--1958- I. Title.
HD6687.B74 1991   90-28740
322′.2′0944--dc20   CIP

Typeset in 10/11.5 point Baskerville by
The Castlefield Press Ltd, Wellingborough, Northants
Printed and bound in Great Britain by
Biddles Ltd, Guildford and King's Lynn

Contents

List of tables		vi
Preface		viii
Abbreviations		ix
Introduction		1
Chapter 1	Party–union relations	7
Chapter 2	Trade union confederations and the Common Programme of Government	33
Chapter 3	Trade union confederations and elections	58
Chapter 4	The consequences of party–union relations for inter-confederal unity: CGT–CFDT	82
Chapter 5	The consequences of party–union relations for intra-confederal factionalism	104
Chapter 6	Strikes, trade union confederations and the Union of the Left	129
Chapter 7	Collective bargaining, trade union confederations and the Union of the Left	153
Conclusions		175
Appendix	Union and party structures	182
Bibliography		186
Index		194

List of Tables

1.1	French Communist Party workplace branches (1970–75)	10
1.2	French Communist Party workplace branches (workplaces with more than 5,000 employees)	12
1.3	French Socialist Party workplace branches (1973–76)	13
1.4	Geographical distribution of PS workplace branches	14
1.5	Sectoral distribution of PS workplace branches	15
1.6	Trade union membership among PS members in the Bas-Rhin	20
1.7	Trade union membership among PS members in the Bordeaux area	21
1.8	Trade union membership among PS conference delegates (1973)	21
1.9	Trade union membership among PS conference delegates (1977) with age variables	22
1.10	Trade union and PS faction membership among PS members in the Bas-Rhin (1975)	23
1.11	Party membership of CFDT conference delegates (1973–79)	27
3.1	Results of the 1st round of the 1973 and 1978 legislative elections in St-Pierre des Corps	70
3.2	Results of the 1973 and 1978 elections for the works committee (Comité Mixte) of the SNCF Depot in St-Pierre des Corps	71
3.3	Voting preference according to trade union membership 1st round, 1973 legislative elections	73
3.4	Voting intentions according to trade union membership 1st round, 1974 Presidential election	73
3.5	Voting preference according to trade union membership 2nd round, 1974 Presidential election	74
3.6	Voting intentions according to trade union membership 1st round, 1978 legislative elections	75
3.7	Voting preference according to trade union membership 1st round, 1978 legislative elections	76
4.1	Unemployment in France 1970–80	85
6.1	General strike statistics – France (1970–79)	133

6.2	Frequency of strike grievances I	134
6.3	Frequency of strike grievances II	135
6.4	Monthly strike statistics (1970–73)	136
6.5	Monthly strike statistics (1975–78)	137
7.1	Industry-wide collective bargaining agreements – France (1970–79)	158

Preface

It would have been impossible to complete this book without the support and assistance of many others. I am endebted to the many trade unionists and political activisits who agreed to explain their views and who were prepared to provide access to important primary source materials. I would like to acknowledge the guidance and encouragement of Ella Ritchie, David Bell, Tim Gray, Rod Hague, Peter Morris, Chris Ross and Vincent Wright, all of whom commented on earlier versions of this work. In addition, I owe a particular intellectual debt to René Mouriaux who has provided regular advice on various aspects of trade unionism and industrial relations in France. Essential material support for this research was provided by Newcastle upon Tyne Polytechnic, and Peter Hubsch, the Head of the School of Modern Languages, is to be particularly thanked. Marie-Claude Guin, Yannick Guin, Roger Lemaistre, Jacqueline Chatelet and Frédéric Schuller have all provided generous hospitality in France. Finally, I would like to acknowledge the support and forbearance of Ilona Buchroth to whom this book is dedicated.

Jeff Bridgford
Newcastle upon Tyne
May 1990

Abbreviations

BRAEC	Bureau de Recherches, d'Analyses et d'Etudes Coordonnées
CDS	Centre des Democrates Sociaux
CERC	Centre d'Etude des Revenus et des Coûts
CERES	Centre d'Etudes, de Recherches et d'Education Socialistes
CFDT	Confédération Française Démocratique du Travail
CFTC	Confédération Française des Travailleurs Chrétiens
CGC	Confédération Générale des Cadres
CGT	Confédération Générale du Travail
CGTU	Confédération Générale du Travail Unitaire
CNPF	Conseil National du Patronat Français
ETUC	European Trade Union Confederation
FEN	Fédération de la Gauche Démocrate et Socialiste
FO	Confédération Générale du Travail-Force Ouvrière
INSEE	Institut National d'Etudes Statistiques et Economiques
MRG	Mouvement des Radicaux de Gauche
PCF	Parti Communiste Français
PR	Parti Républicain
PS	Parti Socialiste
PSU	Parti Socialiste Unifié
RPR	Rassemblement pour la République
SFIO	Section Française de l'Internationale Ouvrière
SGEN	Syndicat Général de l'Education Nationale
SMIG	Salaire Minimum Interprofessionel Garanti

Introduction

Party–union relations form an integral part of West European political systems. Most trade union organisations pursue key goals in the political sphere through their links with political parties, who for the most part take trade union concerns into consideration when formulating their own strategies. Many areas of public policy are of direct interest to trade unions and their members, and they attempt to use their links with political parties to influence the policy making process. Political parties need to attract the support of a wide constituency, which, on the industrial Left, is dominated by the trade union organisations. They cannot afford to neglect the interests of trade unions, any more than the latter can afford to abstract themselves from the political sphere. From this emerges a pattern of party–union relations which is undoubtedly complex in all liberal democracies, but more so in France for a number of reasons.

Firstly, relations between trade unions and political parties in France are multi-dimensional. French trade unionism is fragmented, not according to crafts, as has traditionally been the case in Great Britain, but along ideological, confessional and political lines, with the result that three major trade union confederations have been established, the *Confédération Générale du Travail* (CGT), the *Confédération Française Démocratique du Travail* (CFDT) and *Confédération Générale du Travail – Force Ouvrière* normally known as *Force Ouvrière* (FO), along with a number of smaller groupings. The French party system is also fragmented, and two major political formations on the Left advocating differing ideological and political perspectives have, in part at least, competed for the same working class support; on the one hand an important and tenacious French Communist Party – *Parti Communiste Français* (PCF), historically one of the largest and most influential in Western Europe, and on the other a non–communist Left, which has traditionally been dominated by the *Section Française de l'Internationale Ouvrière* (SFIO), and since 1969 by the Socialist Party – *Parti Socialiste* (PS). Secondly, French trade unionism has an anarcho–syndicalist strand which has traditionally rejected links with political parties. In this context it is customary to refer to the Charter of Amiens (1906), the first universally recognised definition of the aims and methods of French trade unionism, which underlines trade union independence from the State and also political parties. As a result of this, structural and financial links between trade unions and political parties have not been established in France. Consequently, any relations between trade unions and political parties are veiled and mediated through a convention which has denied, superficially at least, the very existence of this relationship.

Trade unions and political parties perform a variety of different functions, although, as will be shown in this book, there is a certain overlap. In the political sphere, political parties select candidates and contest elections, and they attempt to organise the elected decision–makers in government. However, they are also interested in aspects of the industrial sphere. It provides an arena for potential support, and, because of this, political parties have striven to establish a presence in the workplace. Moreover, certain features of the regulation of employment, particularly wage bargaining, are central to the success or failure of the macro–economic policy of any potential government. Trade unions are clearly important actors in the industrial sphere. They are engaged in most aspects of the regulation of employment, through their participation in the collective bargaining process and, when this fails, through their use of industrial conflict. In the political sphere, they are not indifferent to the outcome of elections and the activities of government and, although they do not participate directly in the acquisition of power or in its exercise, they aim to influence the political process. However, because of their general weakness in the industrial sphere, French trade unions are for the most part anxious to play a significant role in the political sphere. They are to be found at the interface between the industrial and the political, and there is a manifest tension between these differing functions. To concentrate solely on the functions of trade unions in the industrial sphere or on the functions of political parties in the political sphere would misrepresent the activities of both sets of organisations. It is the contention of this book that it is only possible to understand the relations between political parties and trade unions in France if both the political and industrial elements of this tension are investigated.

This book will concentrate on the relations between trade union confederations, CGT and CFDT, and the political parties of the Union of the Left, PCF and PS. The CGT and the CFDT were chosen for two sets of reasons. At the beginning of the period under investigation they were the two most important trade union confederations, whether measured in terms of members, activists or supporters; FO lagged some way behind. At the beginning of the 1970s, the CGT claimed just over two million working members and a quarter of a million retired members, while the CFDT claimed nearly 900,000 (FO was claiming 600,000–700,000 at that time). The CGT accounted for over 40% of all trade union branches, whilst the CFDT was credited with around 25% (10% were affiliated to FO). At the 1970 elections for entreprise committees, the CGT obtained 46 per cent of the vote; the CFDT 20 per cent (FO 7 per cent). Secondly, unlike the other French trade union confederations, the CGT and the CFDT saw themselves as actors in the political sphere. Although their roots were to be found in differing trade union traditions (the CGT inherited an uneasy mixture of reformism and marxism, while the CFDT inherited an equally uneasy mixture of Christian socialism and anarcho-syndicalism), they had developed such that at the beginning of the 1970s they both considered themselves to be 'revolutionary' trade unions, intent on putting an end to capitalist exploitation and on ushering in a socialist economic and political system. As a result, the CGT and the CFDT were drawn into a situation which required some form of relationship with political parties, in spite of their claims to the contrary. This does not mean however that they could afford to neglect their responsibilities in the industrial sphere. Gallie has drawn a distinction between the ideological mobilisation of the French unions and the interest representation of their British counterparts. However, if these two positions were represented along a continuum, 'neither the French nor the British could be placed fully at one extreme or another ... the French unions saw themselves as having a responsibility to take into account the existing views of the workforce – indeed if they had failed to do so, they would have quickly been eliminated' (Gallie, 1978, p. 246). While the other trade union confederations, particularly FO, made a positive virtue of eschewing links with the political sphere, the CGT and the CFDT saw their activities in the political and industrial spheres as complementary.

The French Communist Party and the Socialist Party were chosen because they represent the two most important political parties on the Left, whether measured in quantifiable terms of members, voters or elected representatives or in more qualitative terms of political presence. Since it was set up in 1920, the Communist Party has historically been a major force on the Left in French politics, albeit with varying fortunes.

By the beginning of the 1970s it was the most important political party on the Left, claiming just over a quarter of a million members, a particularly high figure for French political parties. In the 1968 legislative elections, it polled 20 per cent of the vote at the first round, and in the 1969 Presidential elections, its candidate Jacques Duclos obtained 21.5 per cent of the vote. The non–Communist Left has also had a chequered history. By the beginning of the 1970s its political stock stood at an all–time low. Its membership had slumped to 70,000. In the 1968 legislative elections, it only managed to obtain 16.5 per cent of the vote at the first round, and in the 1969 Presidential elections, Gaston Defferre, the candidate most closely identified with the Socialists, only obtained 5 per cent of the vote. However, the early 1970s saw a renaissance of the non–communist Left. The Socialist Party was founded at Issy-les-Moulineaux, and in 1971 at its Epinay Conference François Mitterrand became its First Secretary. Relations between the two parties of the French Left have waxed, and more often waned, in line with varying ideological positions and strategic options. After months of negotiations and, before that, years of ritual courtship, the PCF and the PS managed to overcome their differences and to seal their 'union' with the signing of the Common Programme of Government on 27 June 1972. Indeed it was from this moment that they gained in political presence. For the first time for many years, they appeared as a realistic alternative government. There are, however, other reasons for choosing these two political parties for this particular study. They were the 'natural' allies of the trade unions, and they needed the support of the trade unions confederations to further their own objectives in the political sphere. In addition, they strove, with differing levels of aptitude and success, to consolidate their support within the trade union movement, both at the national and local levels.

This book focuses specifically on the 1970s, and more precisely on the period of the Union of the Left (1972–77), so is an analysis of the relations between trade unions and political parties in opposition. This time scale has been chosen, because it provides an excellent case study for the investigation of party–union relations. Firstly, it forms a significant period in the development of the Left in France and, above all, in the development of the non–Communist Left, an issue which has been neglected in terms of party–union relations. Secondly, it is a period in which, for the first time in the Fifth Republic, the Left was seriously expecting to obtain a majority in the National Assembly and thus to form a government. The parties of the Union of the Left required allies to assist in this process, and it could reasonably be expected that trade unions would barter their support for influence over the political parties' policy proposals. Finally, during this period the dynamics of the politics of the Left were fascinating, demonstrating moments of unity and also disunity. Once the trade union confederations embarked on a policy of support for a united Left, they were also drawn inexorably into the politics of the disunity of the Left, both processes providing valuable data for an analysis of party–union relations.

This book builds on the work of other writers in the field of party–union relations, particularly that of Ross, who has chronicled the changes in the relationship between the French Communist Party and the CGT during the post–war period. He has noted a move from the 'transmission beltism' of the 1950s to the 'relative autonomy' of the 1970s. In the first instance, the PCF saw the CGT as a 'quasi–direct conduit for mobilising workers around political goals', whereas in the second 'the party recognizes that the dynamics of the labor market ought to be the primary focus of labor mass-organisational activity'. In both cases the union is subordinate to party strategy, whether directly or indirectly (Ross, 1982, p.xv). It is a matter of some debate as to whether the party did have a coherent and unified position on party–union relations, particularly during the mid and latter parts of the 1970s. Furthermore, the PCF and the CGT did not act in a political and industrial vacuum. Although undoubtedly powerful on the political Left and in the trade union world, they merely formed part of an overall pattern of party–union relations which also included the CFDT and the PS. In this context notions such as 'transmission–beltism' and 'relative autonomy' are inappropriate, and this relationship also requires close investigation . In addition, given that trade unions are by definition active in the industrial sphere, it is necessary to place the issue of party–union relations in a wider context and to analyse the consequences of this for broader issues of trade unionism and industrial relations in France.

Chapter 1 provides a framework of analysis for the relationship between political parties and trade unions. An investigation of functional and personnel linkages makes it possible to establish patterns of dependance and influence which run counter to formal statements of autonomy. Some of the activities of the trade unions and political parties at national and local level compromise functional differentiation, which is further blurred by the existence of a network of personnel linkages. Chapters 2 and 3 focus on the political sphere. They analyse the ways in which the CGT and the CFDT were drawn into the political debate surrounding the Common Programme of Government and the ways in which they provided the political parties of the Union of the Left with considerable, although differing, levels of support at election time. Chapters 4 and 5 analyse the consequences of party–union relations for

French trade unionism. CGT-CFDT relations are studied to see whether they were determined by developments within the political sphere, and more specifically by the state of PCF-PS relations, or whether other factors inherent in the industrial sphere played a significant role. Factionalism was rife in the CGT and the CFDT at certain periods during the 1970s and is investigated to see whether its origins lay in the political or industrial spheres. Party–union relations had major consequences for certain aspects of industrial relations in France and the decision to participate in the political sphere had consequences for the trade unions' ability to act in the industrial sphere. Chapters 6 and 7 investigate the pattern of strike activity and collective bargaining during the 1970s and assess the relative significance of industrial and political factors as explanatory variables. This book aims to examine the evolution of party–union relations in the 1970s. It concentrates on the form they took and on their consequences for trade unionism and industrial relations. The picture is complex and changing and thus requires an extension and re–formulation of previous interpretations of party–union relations in France.

Chapter 1

Party–Union Relations

There is a tradition of referring the question of French party–union relations directly to the Charter of Amiens, the first national definition of trade unionism in France signed in 1906 by all major strands of the trade union movement. It stated:

In the case of individuals, the conference maintains the right of trade union members to participate outside the union in those forms of struggle which correspond to their political or philosophical opinions. In return it asks that they should not introduce those opinions held elsewhere into the union.

In the case of institutions, the conference considers that for trade unionism to fulfill its true potential, activities in the economic sphere should be directed against the employers. Confederal organisations are unions and should not have dealings with parties and organisations which may elsewhere freely pursue the goal of social change.

This has been repeatedly interpreted by trade union confederations and political parties as meaning that they should act independently of each other; a disingenuous interpretation given the number of times that they have in fact acted in concert over the years. During the period of the Union of the Left this article of faith was reiterated by leaders of both trade union confederations and political parties of the Left. However beneath the level of public statements, a complex set of relations has been established between trade unions and political parties and this chapter aims to provide a framework for the analysis of party–union relations which will demonstrate patterns of convergence and divergence between the different organisations.

In contrast to the British case, financial and institutional links do not represent fruitful areas of study. Unlike their British counterparts, French trade unions do not make major contributions to the coffers of political parties, and political parties do not make any systematic attempt to subsidise the activities of trade unions. French trade unions are not represented on the governmental and administrative bodies of political parties, nor do they wield a block vote at party conference, which would grant them a preponderant role in policy–making and in the election of the leader of the party. Nor do they have the opportunity to exercise some tenuous control over political parties through the sponsoring of individual Members of Parliament. In France there has been no attempt recently to establish a permanent bridging committee such as the Liaison Committee, with the aim of coordinating union and party policy–making. Nor is there a French equivalent of the cross–representation which exists between the Labour Party National Executive Committee's Home Policy Committee and the Economic Committee of the Trades Union Congress. Nor has there been any attempt to establish a joint campaigning body for election purposes, such as Trade Unions for Labour (later known as Trade Unions for Labour Victory). Indeed, any exposition of British party–union financial or organisational links is met in France with open–mouthed incredulity.

There is however clear evidence of formal and informal contacts. At the formal level, delegations from both the CFDT and the CGT visited the PS conference at Nantes in 1977.[1] An official PCF delegation visited the CGT conference in 1973.[2] Numerous meetings at other levels took place. The PCF and the CFDT met for the first time in November 1971 and published a restrained joint declaration[3] – a meeting described later by the CFDT as difficult and lacking in spontaneity.[4] The most significant meetings occurred when representatives from trade union confederations and from political parties all met together, as in July 1973, or in December 1975 when they agreed to take part in joint demonstrations condemning the government's economic policies.[5] These formal meetings provided a clear signal of official positions to members, supporters, would-be supporters and, of course, rivals. This was particularly the case at the time of the initial negotiations preceding the signing of the Common Programme of Government, when the CFDT met the PCF and the CGT met both the PCF and the PS[6] and perhaps more importantly at the time of the breakdown of the renegotiation of the Common Programme of Government in Autumn 1977, when the CGT and the CFDT both met the PCF and the PS.[7] Informal meetings are more significant but clearly, given their very nature, it is difficult for outside observers to estimate their impact. It is known that Georges Séguy, the general secretary of the CGT, met François Mitterrand just prior to the 1974 Presidential elections, but it is not known what was discussed or what possible deals were struck. It is clear that Georges Séguy would have had ample opportunity to liaise with Georges Marchais, before, during and after Communist Party meetings, and, although it is impossible for the outsider to know what was discussed, it can be presumed that these occasions provided the leaders of the CGT and PCF with optimal conditions for informal contact. Of course, the potential benefit of informal meetings may be lost because of personality differences. Encounters between François Mitterrand and Edmond Maire, the general secretary of the CFDT, were frosty affairs and compared to meetings between 'the Queen of England and the Maharajah of India' (Hamon & Rotman, 1982, p. 336). André Salomon described the dinners he arranged between François Mitterrand, Gérard Jacquet and Pierre Bérégovoy of the PS on the one hand, and Edmond Maire, Jacques Moreau and Jacques Chérèque of the CFDT on the other, as 'a fiasco' (Salomon, 1980, p. 177).

Functional differentiation between trade unions and political parties

Drawing a neat financial distinction between political parties and trade unions is fraught with difficulties. The political and industrial spheres do not separate out easily in practice. The PS itself has pointed out, 'there is no such thing as apolitical trade union activity'. As the State becomes increasingly involved in socio-economic affairs, trade unions need to negotiate with government to satisfy their demands. Industrial demands, such as wage claims for instance, relate to a basic element of government policy. Trade union activities encompass all aspects of political and social life in France.[8] The trade union confederations themselves had clear views on the political nature of their activities. According to René Duhamel, one of the CGT national secretaries, the CGT had always spoken out on political affairs, both domestic and international, and not to do so would 'make the CGT an impotent, paralysed and mutilated organisation dependent on what the parties said and did'.[9] According to the CFDT, 'trade union activity has inevitable political consequences, since any modification of the power relations in society is, by its very nature, political'. The CFDT expected to express its views on all aspects of political life.[10] The CFDT had a vision of trade unionism which was firmly opposed to those who wanted to reject the role of 'managing workers' immediate demands and in this way granting the political parties the principal role in the construction of socialism.[11] In a special issue of *CFDT Aujourd'hui*, the CFDT stated that it was opposed to the idea of 'job demarcation' between union and party activities, while still nevertheless insisting on some form of functional differentiation between unions and parties. Parties exist to govern society at large and the political institutions of the State. Trade unions exist to rally workers in the workplace. This said, trade unions should be able to deal with everything of concern to workers and with an influence on their existence.[12]

For their part, the political parties did not want to remain outside the industrial sphere. They were keen to have a presence in the workplace, an area which, as was seen above, the CFDT claimed was the sole responsibility of trade unions. In this respect, the legal position on workplace representation is worth noting. Although trade unions had been originally legalised in 1884, it was not until 1968, as a result of the negotiations and legislation issuing from the Events of May, that trade unions had legal authority to exist within the workplace. This did not mean that they had not existed previously, but that their right to exist was henceforth protected by law. For political parties, the situation was less clear. In January 1977 an official communiqué from the Council of Ministers stated that political parties should not be active within the workplace and that the government would do all it could to ensure the political neutrality of the firm. An anonymous editorialist from *Le Monde* questioned the validity of the Minister's interpretation of the law and in the same issue the views of representatives of a wide spectrum of political opinion were sought.[13] A lively academic debate ensued, with Savatier questioning the legality of party workplace branches, and Cohen defending their existence (Savatier, 1977, p. 231–36. Cohen, 1977, p. 361–76). In the event, there was no attempt to curb the activities of workplace branches. The parties of the Union of the Left were nevertheless aware of this precarious legal position, because in the Common Programme of Government they demanded the right to set them up.

Table 1.1 French Communist Party workplace branches (1970–75)

1970	5050
1972	5348
1973	5680
1974	6575
1975	**8042**

Source: Elleinstein, 1976, p. 44.[15]

The PCF had long been aware of the strategic importance of the workplace and had been organising workplace branches since 1924. At the 21st Conference of the PCF held in October 1974 in Vitry, Georges Marchais stated that it was above all in the workplace that the battle need to be won, so that the PCF would be granted its due place in national politics.[14] As Table 1.1 shows, there was a considerable increase in the number of PCF workplace branches in the first half of the 1970s. This could be explained by a shift in party priorities but also by the problem of monitoring. Only three PCF members were needed to set up a workplace branch, and the party tended to err on the side of generosity so as to out-distance the efforts of the Socialist Party. In fact, establishing workplace branches has always proved very difficult. The PCF has been more successful in large companies and the figures in Table 1.2 show the number of workplace branches existing in a selection of workplaces with more than 5,000 employees, broken down on a geographical basis. In certain firms, there was a significant PCF presence, notably Renault in Boulogne-Billancourt (Hauts-de-Seine). Over two thousand members in a workplace branch would clearly make a significant impact on industrial and political activities within the firm. In other workplaces, the Berliet commercial vehicle plant (Rhône) and Orly Airport (Val-de-Marne), the PCF also had a significant presence. However, the PCF would not make much impact in other workplaces, such as the Simca or Citroën car manufacturing plants. Moreover, it can be assumed that in smaller firms, PCF workplace branches were less numerous and less effective. The importance of workplace branches, and particularly those in larger firms – where the greatest concentration of the working class was to be found[16] – is reflected in the fact that they were extracted from normal party structures and linked directly to the Party's Central Committee via a 'national committee for the party's political and ideological activities in large firms', which was set up in March 1973. This body became the direct responsibility of André Vieuguet and then Jean Colpin, a high-ranking member of the Political Bureau and also of the party's Secretariat, which is a measure of the importance of workplace organisation to the PCF at that time (Jourdain, 1982, p. 182). National meetings of PCF representatives from different industrial sectors were arranged. It was not however until 1975, after the realisation that the PS were attempting to move in on a PCF preserve that a 'national workplace section' was established. Each month in Paris a 'national committee' brought together representatives of the 'national workplace sections' and representatives from different industrial sectors participated regularly in national conferences in Paris (Evin & Cayrol, 1976, p 638, 641). There is no evidence to suggest that these

Table 1.2 French Communist Party workplace branches (workplaces with more than 5,000 employees)

Départment	Firm	Employees	Members	Cells	Section
Bouches-du-Rhône	Sud Aviation	6,580	116	6	
	La Ciotat	5,000	170	9	
Calvados	Saviem	6,600	54	4	1
	SMN	6,200	55	7	
Doubs	Peugeot	34,585	350	21	1
Finistère Nord	Arsenal	8,000	100	8	
Haute-Garonne	SNIAS	8,000	230	13	1
Ille-et-Vilaine	Citroën	11,545	8	1	
Isère	Merlin Gerin	7,713	149	10	1
Loire	Creusot	5,117	190	12	1
Loire-Atlantique	Chantiers	9,774	74	4	1
Manche	Arsenal	5,000	52	4	
Meurthe/Moselle	Usinor	7,600	220	20	1
Moselle	Sacilor G	14,000	75	4	1
Nord	Usinor DK	12,300	79	11	1
	Usinor Denain	8,000	45	1	
Puy-de-Dôme	Michelin	27,000	230	27	1
Saône-et-Loire	Creusot	8,753	214	13	1
Haut-Rhin	Peugeot	11,000	54	10	1
Rhône	Berliet	15,000	430	32	1
Sarthe	Renault	9,494	250	18	1
Seine-Maritime	Sandouville	9,350	80	6	1
	Cléon	7,600	120	7	1
Var	Arsenal	8,800	268	17	1
	CNIM	5,200	230	11	1
Belfort	Alsthom	8,518	121	7	1
Essonne	CEA	8,000	132	10	1
	SNECMA	5,180	180	12	1
Seine-St-Denis	Citroën	5,000	9		1
Yvelines	Simca	22,500	14	1	
	Renault	20,800	197	15	1
Val-de-Marne	Orly	25,000	525	45	1
Hauts-de-Seine	Citroën	5,000	25	1	
	Renault	30,000	2,108	87	1
Paris	Crédit Lyonnais	6,000	86	4	1
	Printemps	8,000	65	2	
	Bull	5,000	14	1	
	Banque de France	5,000	33	2	
	BNP	5,000	75	5	
	Métro	12,500	429	33	

Source: adapted from Evin & Cayrol, 1976, p. 640.

organisations within the PCF met and liaised with organisations from the trade union confederations. However, given the personnel overlap existing between the PCF and the CGT, which will be studied below, close informal links would certainly have been established.

The Socialist Party had more tenuous links with the world of work and was slower to develop a network of workplace branches. By the time of the Pau conference in 1975 however it had been decided that 'priority would be given to the development of workplace branches, the manifestation of the party's roots in a working class environment'.[17] Only 54 workplace branches existed in 1970 but growth developed apace, as the figures in Table 1.3 illustrate. There were two types of workplace branch organisation, entreprise sections, *sections d'entreprise* (SE) and socialist entreprise groups, *groupes socialistes d'entreprise* (GSE), differing mainly as to their status within the structures of the party. The former had the same political status as ordinary sections; they were linked into the party structure and had normal voting rights: the latter had no official status as such; they merely provided a forum within the workplace for PS activities. The decline in the number of the former from 1974 to 1976 can be explained by more rigorous monitoring practices.[18]

Table 1.3 French Socialist Party workplace branches (1973–76)

Year	Sections d'entreprise (SE)	Groupes socialistes d'entreprise (GSE)
1973	66	129
1974	237	494
1976	211	545

Source: Cayrol, 1978b, p. 298.

Table 1.4 shows the geographical distribution of PS workplace branches. In many *départements* there were no workplace branches at all, which perhaps would not be surprising for areas with small populations and little industry, but would be for other regions such as Lorraine. Enterprise sections (SE) were particularly numerous in Paris, whereas socialist entreprise groups (GSE) were most numerous in the Pas-de-Calais. This can be explained by the interplay of factional politics within the Socialist Party. The *Centre d'Etudes, de Recherches et d'Education Socialistes* (CERES), a left-wing faction, was strong in Paris at that time and was committed to workplace organisation. It favoured enterprise sections with their real, albeit limited, rights,[19] hoping also to use them as a powerbase for reinforcing its position within the party. Other factions preferred socialist enterprise groups, which would not detract from the activities of the normal party sections and moreover would not cause activists to be spread too thinly – a major concern for a party with relatively few activists.

Table 1.4 Geographical distribution of PS workplace branches

	SE	GSE	Total
Ariège	1	9	10
Calvados	4	13	17
Haute-Garonne	1	15	16
Gironde	6	9	15
Isère	8	11	19
Nord	1	13	14
Pas-de-Calais	0	112	112
Puy-de-Dôme	4	9	13
Rhône	3	13	16
Paris	97	69	166
Seine-Maritime	0	14	14
Hauts-de-Seine	16	7	23

Source: Evin & Cayrol, 1976, p. 637.

Table 1.5 shows that PS workplace branches were most numerous in the public sector (71 per cent). The largest number of sections was in education (160), post and telecommunications (82), health (54), transport-SNCF (52) and the metalworking industries (44). Workplace branches were organised into national organisations corresponding to particular industrial sectors, National Socialist Enterprise Groups (GSEN), whose function within the party was 'to organise activities and to set up branches in the appropriate industrial sectors', and 'to participate in working parties preparing policy documents on the appropriate industrial sector', a feature which was generally neglected. In addition, a National Enterprise Commission, elected proportionately to the vote taken at Conference, was responsible for advising the leadership of the party on workplace affairs. At the top of the party's structure, a National Secretariat for Enterprises 'coordinated all the workplace activities of the Party'. The first National Secretary was Georges Sarre, but, when CERES fell from favour at the Pau Conference in 1975, he was replaced by Louis Mermaz.[20] A full-time organiser, Alain Rannou, was also appointed in 1975.[21] Finally a national conference of workplace branches, bringing together grass-roots activists was held every two years, in Pantin (13 January 1973). Alfortville (15 December 1974) and Massy (25–26 April 1976). As with the PCF, there is no evidence to suggest that these organisations met formally with delegations from the different trade union confederations.

Table 1.5 Sectoral distribution of PS workplace branches (%)

Nationalised companies, SNCF, EDF-GDF	29
Civil service, health, PTT	25
Education, research	11
Local government	6
Private sector	28
Others	1

Source: Evin & Cayrol, 1976, p. 637.

In theory, the workplace branches of the political parties did not engage in the regulation of employment and so did not impinge upon the functions of the trade unions. The workplace branches were supposed to concentrate on political activities. According to André Vieuguet. PCF workplace branches had the following functions. Firstly, they were 'to combat the ideas and policies of the employers and the government with the ideas and the policies of the party, and they were to contribute to ensuring the success of the workers' struggle for better living and working conditions'. Secondly, they were to combat class collaboration, in part by explaining the proposals of the Common Programme of Government. They were to demonstrate on all occasions the superiority of the socialist system over the capitalist system. Thirdly, they were to organise mass grass-roots political activities. Finally, they were to accomplish the international tasks of the party, by campaigning for peace and by participating in solidarity activities with those populations who were fighting against imperialism and fascism.[22] According to the PS, workplace branches were to:

encourage as many workers as possible to take an interest in the activities of the party ... the aim of our political activities in the workplace is to encourage workers to become aware of the political nature of the problems they are faced with, of the political solutions available and of the need to engage in mass political activities within the workplace for the defence of their immediate interests.[23]

Functions, such as ensuring the success of the workers' struggle for better living and working conditions and engaging in mass activities within the workplace for the defence of the workers' immediate interests, would however, clash with the industrial functions of the trade unions. The political parties claimed that this was not the case. According to Henri Jourdain, PCF workplace branches were not to decide on industrial demands nor the means for obtaining them: 'The specific role of the party should be to give these demands a political dimension and a theoretical explanation'.[24] The PS claimed that 'the party should not encroach upon the role of the trade unions, by defining the content of industrial demands and the methods and conduct of industrial action, but that this would not stop us from making our positions known'.[25] However, in the same document, the PS claimed that workplace branches should analyse concrete problems such as employment, work organisation and working conditions. They should also attempt to extract information from management concerning the running of the firm, its economic, social and financial plans. They should denounce the increase in sub-contracting work, the unnecessary creation of subsidiaries and the dismantling of economic activities. They should act against the arbitrary decisions of management concerning work organisation, hours of work, workrates, conditions of hiring and firing, wages and wage differentials.

This full catalogue of industrial activities clearly blurs the distinction between party and union functions, as does the statement by Aimé Halbeher enumerating the activities of the PCF Renault workplace branches:

In the last months of 1975, thanks to the action of a [PCF] cell, a worker in the press-shop who had been fired was reemployed. In another section the communists and their cell supported action for the maintenance and extension of machine tool production, which had been under threat. On the production line, the PCF cell is alone in fighting against the phasing out of temporary labour. In an unskilled section, the PCF cell has intervened and undertaken activities in order to have a disciplinary measure lifted . . . . (Halbeher, 1976, p. 268)

This represents another full catalogue of industrial activities, but Halbeher claimed in the same article that, 'some may think that this provides competition with the trade union. It does no such thing.[26] Clearly, though, in this particular case, the PCF workplace branch was acting as a surrogate trade union and engaging in the regulation of employment. This blurring of functions within the workplace was reinforced by personnel overlap, a feature which will be considered in greater detail below. In this particular case (Renault). Aimé Halbeher had been a full-time CGT official responsible for the automobile industry within the national CGT Metalworkers Union, before becoming in November 1974 the coordinator of CGT unions within the Renault group, and then secretary of the PCF section in the Boulogne–Billancourt plant.[27] This potential confusion also existed within the PS. Cayrol's study shows that a high percentage of PS workplace branches had trade union representatives among their members, as follows: in 46 per cent of workplace branches, some members held office within the CGT, in 67 per cent some held office within the CFDT (and in only 24 per cent of cases were they members of the FO).[28]

It might be expected that trade unions would respond unfavorably to this incursion into the industrial sphere by the political parties. However, according to Henri Jourdain, the PCF had not received any adverse reaction from the trade unions relating to workplace branches[29]; given the 'priviledged relationship' between the PCF and the CGT, this is hardly surprising. For the CFDT, Edmond Maire claimed that it was necessary for political parties to be present in the workplace to ensure that they would not be cut off from the daily reality of workers' lives.[30] Six months earlier, he explained that trade unions should nevertheless remain in control of industrial demands and that there was still a need for differentiation between the party and the union at the workplace level.[31] He warned that, if any political organisations became mixed up in strikes they would automatically become associated with a minority of workers.[32] For the CGT, trade unions would not at all be discomfited if a political party called on workers to act for the objectives that the CGT supported, according to Henri Krasucki (deputy leader of the CGT and member of the PCF Political Bureau): 'As trade unionists, we do not have an exclusive right to defend industrial demands. It is a convention in the French workers' movement that trade unions are responsible for the conduct of industrial activities. There are specific responsibilities for parties and for unions but no particular restrictions.[33] Could this be any party? In theory, yes, according to Georges Séguy, although 'we reserve the right to point out which parties contribute effectively to the defence of workers' interests and which parties actually jeopardise them'.[34] In a previous television interview however, he had explained the relative advantages of the parties of the Left: 'There are those who defend class-based positions and those, for example, left-wing extremists who want to betray workers in the workplace. There are also reformists. Our opinion is founded on a class-based analysis'.[35] Clearly this statement would leave little choice and is a clear nod in the direction of the PCF. The CFDT also made its position clear, but at a later date. In 1979 it complained that the PCF had wanted to be omnipresent in the workplace and active in those spheres which even by the PCF's own reckoning formed a part of trade union activity: 'CFDT branches have reported many examples of PCF activists attempting to substitute themselves for trade union branches ... intervening in strikes or criticising CFDT activities or the lack of its activities'.[36] After its 22nd conference in 1976 the PCF intervened more directly in industrial activities, 'in certain cases calling strikes ... or formulating proposals in terms of industrial demands',[37] a point admitted on occasions by PCF members themselves.[38] Michel Charzat, one of the original organisers of workplace branches in the PS at the beginning of the 1970s, explained that the CFDT had, however, never complained about PS workplace activities, unless it felt threatened.[39] This is the key factor. The CFDT did not feel particularly threatened by the PS workplace branches, and justifiably so. In a large chemical plant in Pierre-Bénite (in the Lyons suburbs), the PS workplace branch in only had 10 members, many of whom had other responsibilities within the party and were thus unable to take an active part in the activities of the workplace branch.[40] PS workplace branches were not in a position to threaten the activities of the trade unions. In a survey carried out with delegates to the 1977 PS conference in Nantes, only 19 per cent claimed that they were active in workplace branches.[41] On the other hand, the PCF had a more significant workplace presence which was capable of providing a threat to trade union activity. However, it would ill behove both trade union confederations to deny political parties access to the industrial sphere, when the former were also claiming the right to participate in the political sphere.

Personnel linkages

Personnel linkages constitute a useful variable for the investigation of party-union relations, as has been shown in Great Britain and in the Federal Republic of Germany (Minkin, 1978, p. 458–83), Breum, et al 1981, p. 249–53). However, no systematic French study exists. This section will evaluate the extent to which personnel linkages caused informal patterns of influence to develop in trade unions and political parties. This in turn will influence the issue of functional differentiation. The different structural levels of trade union confederations and political parties will be investigated here, so it may be useful for the reader to consult the organisational charts to be found in the Appendix.

French Communist Party

Despite the academic attention lavished on the PCF, few sociological studies of its membership exist, and in these the issue of trade union membership has seldom been addressed. It could be expected that all members of the PCF would also be members of a trade union. Although trade union membership is not a precondition for membership of the PCF, as it is in principle with the British Labour Party, it is the responsibility of each member 'to be active in a trade union', (article ten of the PCF statutes). According to Jean Colpin however, communists considered it their duty to join a trade union and many of them considered it their duty to become active members.[42] However, survey data does not completely support this contention, and it has been shown that, in the Bordeaux area, a quarter of PCF members were not members of any trade union at all (Lagroye, *et al*, 1976, p. 144). In the same speech, Jean Colpin heaped praise on the CGT, thus leaving communists in little doubt as to which union to choose. It has been claimed that all communists were in the CGT (Buffin & Gerbaud, 1981, p. 56), but this is an exaggeration, since they were also members of the teaching unions, the FEN and the SNESUP. As the Lagroye study has shown, an overwhelming majority of PCF members were nevertheless also members of the CGT (78.1 per cent), – 7.3 per cent were members of FEN and 9.6 per cent members of other unions. According to this survey, no PCF members were members of the CFDT (nor of FO, which is hardly surprising, given that it was originally set up as a reaction to the increasing communist influence within the CGT). The statement made by Georges Marchais that members of other trade unions (other than the CGT) were joining the PCF must be taken with a pinch of salt.[43]

The PCF conducted one national survey, not of ordinary members, but of conference delegates, which sheds some light on personnel overlap. Of the 1,236 delegates to the 20th Conference held in December 1972 at St-Ouen, 64 per cent were not merely members, but office holders within the CGT.[43] At the level of the Central Committee eleven permanent members (out of 95 elected at the 19th conference in 1970) were CGT office holders; after the 20th Conference there were ten (out of 90); after the 22nd Conference there were nine (out of 95).[44] At the level of the Political Bureau, four were full-time CGT office holders after the 19th Conference (out of 17), four after the 20th Conference (out of 16) and two after the 22nd Conference (out of 18). However, during this period no member of the Party's Secretariat, 'the executive of the party', was a CGT office holder. Within the PCF the CGT was by far the best represented trade union confederation, and the CFDT had no presence at all. At higher levels within the PCF, the CGT was the only trade union confederation represented, but it is significant that at the party's highest levels CGT officials were very much in a minority and formed only one of a series of groups vying for influence. In a party attached to the notion of democratic centralism but wedded in practice to the centralisation of power, members of the CGT were clearly in a subordinate position.

Socialist Party

Research on the sociology of the Socialist Party is less patchy, although in the same way the issue of trade union membership has usually been treated incidentally (Hardouin, 1978, Bacot, 1979. Although it might also be expected that all members of the PS would belong to a trade union (in line with article 12 of its statutes), this is not the case, as can be seen from two regional surveys. As the 1970s progressed, however the percentage of PS trade union members increased, perhaps as a result of exhortations similar to the one made by Pierre Joxe, calling on socialists to become members of trade unions.[45]

Table 1.6 Trade union membership among PS members in the Bas-Rhin (%)

	1973 March	1975 April
Non members	40	29.2
CFDT	17	25.3
CGT	10	9.2
FO	10	5.3
FEN	14	24.6
Others	9	6.1

Source: Ferretti, 1976, p.8.

Table 1.6 shows that in the Bas-Rhin a variety of trade union confederations were represented within the PS. In 1973 the CFDT was marginally ahead of the others. The figures reflect the traditional image of the non-communist Left, with a high representation coming from the teachers' union, the FEN. By 1975 the percentage of trade unionists had risen significantly, as had the number of CFDT and FEN members. CGT membership remained more or less static (FO membership declined quite markedly). The Lagroye survey of the Bordeaux area also demonstrates that an appreciable number of PS members were not members of a trade union, as can be seen from Table 1.7. The CGT and the CFDT had equal representation. The major difference between this survey and the previous one lies in the fact that a large number of PS members were also members of FO. It is clear that in certain geographical areas the PS could not afford to neglect the interests of FO members.

Table 1.7 Trade union membership among PS members in the Bordeaux area (%)

union members	62.2
non-members	35.8
no reply	2.0
CGT	12.4
CFDT	12.4
FO	28.8
FEN	17.6
Others	22.9
Non specified	5.9

Source: Lagroye, *et al.*, 1976, p. 144.

Cayrol has shown that at the National Conference held in June 1973 in Grenoble many delegates were not members of a trade union confederation, as can be seen from Table 1.8. FEN was well represented, as was the CFDT. The CGT on the other hand had few representatives at this level of party organisation, and this can be explained in part by the fact that, according to Pierre Carassus (one of the leading CGT officials in the PS), the presence of CGT members within the PS was not always welcome.[46]

Table 1.8 Trade union membership among PS conference delegates (1973) (%)

Non members	32.1
CGT	7.0
CFDT	18.3
FO	9.6
FEN	23.8
Others	9.2

Source: Cayrol, 1974, p. 937.

22 Party–union relations

Although no survey was conducted for the Pau Conference in February 1975, Cayrol noted in a further article that there had been an influx of CFDT members into the Socialist Party, subsequent to the *Assises du Socialisme* in October 1974, which led to a major realignment of forces on the non-communist Left (Cayrol, 1975, p. 45–51). By the time of the Nantes Conference in 1977, there had been important developments in PS sociology, as Table 1.9 shows. While there was a small reduction in the number of trade unionists amongst PS delegates, the number of delegates who were members of the CFDI increased significantly, giving further credence to the claim that the *Assises du Socialisme* constituted a watershed for PS–CFDT alignment. Moreover CFDT members were the youngest, (FO was a dying force).

Table 1.9 Trade union membership among PS conference delegates (1977) with age variables (%)

	All	−35	35–44	45+
Non members	16	15	12	21
CGT	10	12	10	7
CFDT	27	35	27	17
FO	11	5	8	22
FEN	28	27	37	21
CGC	1	0	1	2
Others	7	6	5	10

Source: Sondage, 2/3 1978, p. 103.

As for the upper echelons of the party, there is little data for any serious evaluation of a concerted trade union presence. Commenting on the PS post-Pau *comité directeur* (which administers and controls the party between conferences – article 32 of PS statutes), Harmel noted that seven members were full-time office holders; four from the CFDT, Jeanson, Acquier, Gouyet and Coffineau; one from FEN, Marangé; two from the CGT Germon and Carassus (and none from FO). Only one member, André Acquier, was on the executive bureau (which administers the leadership of the Party – article 40) (Harmel, 1975, p. 82). In his eagerness to show the linkages between the PS and the trade union confederations. Harmel omitted to mention the size of these bodies – 131 and 27 respectively, which amounted to a very limited trade union presence within the higher echelons of the party.

One final point is worth making. Trade union membership helped to reinforce factionalism within the PS. In Ferretti's 1975 sample members were asked to name the faction within the PS with which they identified. The sample is small, but, as can be seen from Table 1.10, a considerable proportion of Mitterrand supporters were not members of a trade union at all, while a relatively large number of CERES supporters were also members of the CFDT. This has been explained by Michel Charzat thus: CFDT members were attracted to the CERES because it did not have a tainted history of sympathy for the French colonisation policy in Algeria, as did other sections of the party.[47] Pierre Héritier and many others from the CFDT joined the CERES, in spite of certain differences over policies and political style, because 'it was the most left-wing of the groupings within the PS and the most committed to the strategy of the Union of the Left'.[48]

Table 1.10 Trade union and PS faction membership among PS members in the Bas-Rhin 1975 (%)

	1975 Motion I (Mitterrand)	1975 Motion II (CERES)
Non members	34.6	24
CFDT	18.6	36
CGT	12	6
FO	5.3	2
FEN	24.0	24
Others	5.3	8

Source: Ferretti, 1976, p.10.

A considerable number of PS members were not members of trade unions and thus were less likely to be sympathetic to trade union concerns. Nevertheless, there was a significant trade union presence amongst activists. At the higher echelons of the Socialist Party, evidence suggests that trade unions were not well represented and indeed less so than was the case with the French Communist Party. There is certainly no evidence of a 'transmission belt in reverse', with the CFDT controlling the PS, apparently a serious concern for some of the acolytes of François Mitterrand and Jean-Pierre Chevènement (Hamon & Rotman, 1982, p. 336). Trade unionists were too few in number, from different confederations and members of differing factions within the PS. This pluralism had its advantages. It gave the PS a potential opportunity to establish informal patterns of influence within all the major trade union confederations. It gave the PS access to a wider spectrum of trade union opinion and also to a broader reservoir of potential electoral support.

Equally, there were disadvantages. The PS was unlikely to achieve a consensus in its ranks on issues relating to the industrial sphere, and this helps to explain its relative paralysis and silence on such issues. The PS could not identify with one particular trade union confederation, as did the PCF, which would clearly simplify the choices to be made in the industrial sphere. Moreover this trade union pluralism helped to reinforce the factionalism that already existed within the party.

Confédération Générale du Travail

Georges Séguy estimated the number of PCF members within the CGT at 300 000 (out of a claimed membership of 2,300,000 at the time), around 13 per cent, 'however the overwhelming majority were not members of any political organisation' (Séguy, 1975, p. 254). Henri Krasucki estimated the number of PCF members at 200,000.[49] Adam put the figure a little higher, 17 per cent, whilst Ranger put the figure at 10 per cent, and Barjonet, 12–15 per cent (Adam, 1968, p. 524–41, Ranger, 1969, p. 182–86. Barjonet, 1968, p. 124). There is however a consensus – there was a relatively low percentage of PCF members in the CGT overall. Debate has centred on the extent to which CGT officials and office holders were also members or officials of one single political party, namely the PCF. At an intermediate stage within the organisation of the CGT, the level of workplace representatives, Georges Séguy was at pains to point out that the number of communists is lower than the number of trade unionists who were not members of any political party (Séguy, 1975, p. 254). However, from then upwards within the structures of the CGT, the picture changes quite dramatically. Every single secretary of all the CGT organisations *Unions Départementales* (UD) was a member of the PCF (even the secretary of the UD of Monaco!).[50] As for leaders of national unions, *fédérations*, 24 (out of 35) were members of the PCF (Harmel & Tandler, 1982, p. 19–20).[51] Within the Executive Commission, which is responsible for the organisation and the administration of the CGT and hence plays an important role in its decision-making process, there was a dominant communist presence. After the Vitry Conference in 1969, 38 of its members (out of 75) were also members of the PCF (Harmel, 1970, p. 18–23). After the Le Bourget Conference in 1975, there were 57 PCF members (out of 93), with just four PS members.[52] After the Grenoble Conference in 1978, there were 48 PCF members with seven socialists, (out of 93) – a small but inconsequential increase for the PS as a result of Georges Séguy's policy of *ouverture*.

At the highest level of CGT organisation there stands the Confederal

Bureau, in which traditionally there has been parity between PCF members and non-PCF members. After the Vitry Conference in 1969, there was even a brief period when non-Communists were in a majority. This lasted until Jean-Louis Moynot joined the PCF a short time later. After the Nîmes conference in 1972, there were nine communists and one socialist (out of 15), and subsequent to the Le Bourget conference in 1975, there were eight communists and one socialist, Jean-Claude Laroze (out of 16)[53] A second PS member Gerard Gaumé,[54] was added at Grenoble, whilst the full complement of PCF members was retained. This PCF predominance at the higher levels of the CGT organisation has been explained in different ways. According to Georges Séguy, 'it is for the most part because, many officials, particularly young ones, feel the need to extend or complement their union activity with political activity, normally with the Communist Party' (Séguy, 1975, p. 250). According to André Berteloot, a non-communist national secretary of the CGT, 'this situation has come about simply because communists are activists who are available, well-informed, dedicated and extremely hardworking'. He continued revealingly; 'if trade union membership was extended and if other members took on these responsibilities, the class-based spirit . . . which they [communists] support might diminish, which in turn would weaken the CGT.[55] Georges Séguy added that, if there were many members of the Communist Party with important responsibilities within the CGT, this could not be explained by any ulterior motive. However, an ulterior motive does spring to mind; namely, the PCF's attempts to control the activities of the CGT. It is customary in these circumstances to quote Lenin's remarks on the need for a trade union to act as a 'transmission belt' between the communist party and the mass of workers and the need for communists to take over the organisation of the trade union structure, thus ensuring that in spite of certain functional differences between the party and the union, the latter acts even within the industrial sphere in tune with the former's political objectives (Hammond, 1957). Clearly PCF members occupied the most strategic decision-making positions within the confederation, and the statement by Georges Séguy, a communist himself, that this did not compromise the independence of the CGT, is unconvincing (Séguy, 1975, p. 26–7).

The central question remains. Did this then mean that the PCF was able to control the activities of the CGT? According to Barjonet, writing at the end of the 1960s, the relations between the CGT and the PCF 'cannot be reduced to a simple issue of domination and subordination' (Barjonet, 1968, p. 122). He advanced three sets of reasons to support his claim. Firstly, there were many non-communists within the CGT.

However, as has been demonstrated, the whole organisation of the CGT was dominated by PCF members. Moreover communist members short-circuited non-communist members in positions of authority.[56] Secondly, not all CGT leaders were communists. However, non-communists did depend on communist votes for their election, and this left them in a vulnerable position. Some were not always as non-communist as they claimed, since, on occasions, some of them identified closely with communist positions (Landier, 1981, p. 177). It has also been argued that the socialists on the Confederal Bureau further legitimised the fictional independence of the CGT (Lavau, 1981, p. 127). Thirdly, Barjonet notes that some communist leaders of the CGT, (Benoît Frachon and Gaston Monmousseau for example), were not mere party apparatchiks, but trade unionists with a strong personality who had a clear sense of the importance of the industrial sphere. However, a recently published biography of Benoît Frachon provides no evidence to suggest that he neglected the political objectives of the PCF (Girault, 1989). The issue of functional differentiation was also significant during the period of the Union of the Left. It has been claimed that certain members of the CGT were on occasions not always prepared to put the political objectives of the party before the industrial interests of the union. Indeed Georges Séguy has been described as a trade unionist and not a party apparatchik.[57] Moreover, the fact that Georges Séguy appeared at a Communist Party rally at the time of the 1978 legislative elections tends to undermine this interpretation. Whilst it may be the case that on occasions communist trade unionists acted in response to the constraints of the industrial sphere and not in response to the political needs of the party (a point confirmed by Jean-Marie Mick, the communist mayor of Pierre-Bénite[58]), their prime loyalty lay nevertheless, with the Communist Party.

There is one further point which Barjonet did not raise: factionalism, which as will be seen, was a major issue within the PCF during the 1970s (Hayward, 1981). Internal party debates centred on the response to Eurocommunism which, according to Elleinstein, was represented by three criteria: 'first, a radically new concept of the relationship between democracy and socialism; secondly, the absolute independence of communist parties in the West vis-a-vis the CPSU; and thirdly, a major democratisation of the internal functioning of these communist parties' (Kindersley, 1981, p. 66–79). Given the state of flux within the PCF, it would have been difficult, even for a loyal party apparatchik, to know on occasions which message to relay within the CGT. The 'transmission belt' had already ceased to function. To take up Ross's terminology, the PCF had not allowed the CGT to become relatively autonomous.

Communists were firmly in charge of the structures of the CGT, but they did not all share the same opinions on many issues, not least the internal functioning of the party and party-union relations. It was not until after the break-up of the Union of the Left and the establishment of a firm sectarian line within the PCF that the latter was able to control the activities of the CGT more comprehensively.

Confédération Française Démocratique du Travail

Personnel linkages between the CFDT and political parties were quite different from those just studied. There has been no major survey of CFDT membership during the period in question. However, Edmond Maire noted in 1977 that 80 per cent of CFDT members were not members of a political party at all, which means that 20 per cent were.[59] At another level of union organisation, that of conference delegates to individual national unions, numerous surveys were undertaken by Andrieux and Lignon. At the 17th conference of the Chemical Workers' Union (FIC–CFDT) held in November 1970, 26.6 per cent of the delegates were members of a political party; 18.8 per cent of the delegates to the 35th Conference of the Metalworkers' Union (FGM–CFDT) held in May 1971; and 27.2 per cent of the delegates to the 2nd conference of the white collar union UCC–CFDT held in March 1972 (Andrieux & Lignon, 1973, p. 292–317). At the confederal level, the CFDT undertook a number of surveys. At the Conferences of Nantes in May–June 1973, Annecy in May 1976 and Brest in May 1979, 27.4 per cent, 41 per cent and 35.5 per cent of delegates were members of a political party respectively.[60] This increase from 1973 to 1976 may have occurred as a response to the exhortation made by Edmond Maire to join a political party.[61] The small reduction from 1976 to 1979 could be explained by a disaffection with the political sphere, consequent on the break-up of the Union of the Left in September 1977.

Table 1.11 Party membership of CFDT conference delegates (1973–79)

	Nantes 1973		Annecy 1976		Brest 1979	
PS	117	10.0%	336	23.2%	269	19.7%
PSU	114	9.7%	154	10.6%	88	6.4%
Extreme-left	9	0.8%	89	6.2%	53	3.9%
PCF	3	0.3%	10	0.7%	15	1.1%
Others	–		3	0.3%	33	2.4%
Total	243	20.8%	592	41.0%	458	33.5%

Source: See note 60 at the end of this chapter.

As Table 1.11 shows, there was a significant evolution in the pattern of party membership. At the beginning of the period, a considerable number of CFDT delegates were also members of the *Parti Solialiste Unifié* (PSU), as well as the PS. However after the *Assises du Socialisme* a large proportion of PSU members, including its leader Michel Rocard, decided to join the PS, it is not surprising that there were fewer PSU members and more PS members. Roger Bonnevialle, the general secretary of the *Union Régionale* of the Loire, explained that he joined the PS straight after the *Assises du Socialisme*, along with 450 other members of the CFDT.[62] It is also worth noting that between 1973 to 1976 there was a smaller but nevertheless significant influx of extreme-left delegates, who were to become a focus for factionalist politics. The ensuing decline in the number of CFDT delegates who were members of the PS may be explained by disaffection with political activities in general, but it also may be explained by the fact that some CFDT activists felt ill at ease in PS circles since the political cultures were quite different.[63] As for the PCF, it had very few supporters amongst CFDT members at this level. No study has been made of the political affiliations of the secretaries of *Unions Départementales*, nor of the national unions or the National Council. At the highest level of the CFDT's organisational structure stands the National Bureau, which, in 1973, contained eight or nine members of the PSU and two (or perhaps four or eight) members of the PS, out of a total of 30 .[64] However, this pattern certainly did not prevail. It is known that Edmond Maire left the PSU at the time of the *Assises du Socialisme* to join the PS.[65] This does not mean that CFDT members assumed positions within the upper echelons of the PS, in the way that Georges Séguy and Henri Krasucki had within the PCF. There is no evidence to show that, during the period of the Union of the Left, members of the CFDT National Bureau were also office holders in the upper echelons of political parties. Evidence suggests that a dynamic mutually reinforcing process was taking place within the PS and CFDT. Although on a small scale, the PS was becoming significantly better represented within the CFDT, and, as it became a national political force, it became more attractive as a conduit for CFDT members' political activities at least until the election year 1978. This contributed in turn to the process of making the PS a national force. As the PSU fragmented and many of its members joined the PS, it became less significant within the CFDT in personnel terms. As for the PCF, its personnel links with the CFDT were non-existent.

The consequences of this personnel overlap are clear. The PS was not so well represented within the CFDT as was the PCF within the CGT. There has never been a suggestion that the CFDT provided the PS with a transmission belt for the latter's political objectives. Any other descriptions of CGT-PCF relations are also inappropriate for CFDT-PS relations. The CFDT was not relatively autonomous of the PS, it was indeed autonomous. The PS and the CFDT were quite separate organisations. However, during the period of the Union of the Left, CFDT members became increasingly more exposed to the political preoccupations of the PS, either by becoming members of the PS themselves or by having members of the PS in their ranks too. This relationship has been described as one of 'committed autonomy' (Groux & Mouriaux, 1989, p. 201): the CFDT and the PS were autonomous but committed to a similar perspective of political change, which during the mid 1970s was most likely to come about as a result of the advances made by the latter.

Conclusions

During the period of the Union of the Left a complex set of relations developed between the trade union confederations and the political parties. Trade unions and political parties insisted upon their functional distinctiveness, at a national and local level, but on occasions these claims were difficult to justify in practice. Trade union confederations insisted on their right to participate in the political sphere, and both political parties attempted to increase their influence in the industrial sphere. During the 1970s both the PCF and the PS made a special effort to gain a foothold in the workplace and they both greatly increased their tally of workplace branches. In certain plants some workplace branches, and particularly those set up by the PCF, attempted to engage in the regulation of employment, and thus played a significant role in the industrial sphere. However, it can be assumed that in the majority of firms workplace branches did not impinge on industrial activities. The trade unions were for the most part relatively sanguine about this incursion by the political parties into the industrial sphere, although on a few occasions the CFDT did complain about the activities of certain PCF workplace branches. Functional differentiation was further blurred, both at national and local level, by personnel overlap. Although most grass roots trade union members were not members of a political party, many trade union activists were also activists within a political party and vice versa.

Nationally, a clear pattern of party-union alignment emerges. The CGT and the PCF had a 'privileged' relationship which worked to the advantage of the latter. The CGT was not relatively autonomous, but partially autonomous by default. The PCF had a large number of members in critical positions within the decision-making structures of the CGT. However, the PCF was prey to factionalism during the mid 1970s and, as a result, lost control temporarily over the CGT. At the end of the 1970s, after the break-up of the Union of the Left, the PCF leadership adopted a more authoritarian line within the party and thus was able to re-establish a greater level of control over the structures of the CGT. On the non-communist Left, relations were quantitatively and qualitatively different. The CFDT and the PS were linked within a framework of committed autonomy. Most PS members were members of a trade union and, although they belonged to different trade union confederations, the CFDT was the most popular. Trade union pluralism within the PS provided it with greater access to different trade union confederations but also helped to reinforce factionalism within the party.

The political links of CFDT members underwent significant change during the period of the Union of the Left. At the beginning of the 1970s few of its members and activists had been members of a political party. If they were, it was the PSU which was the most popular, closely followed by the PS. Once the PSU began to fade as a political force, the PS moved into the ascendant, and at the same time the PS became increasingly better represented within the CFDT. The relationship between the PS and the CFDT was one of 'committed autonomy' within a loose and varied framework of party-union relations. By the end of the decade, however, the intensity of their relationship had waned, and their commitment to working together within the political sphere had been lost.

Notes

1. *Nouvelle Revue Socialiste*, no. 27, 1977, p. 9.
2. *Cahiers du Communisme*. January–February 1973, p. 316. This was not repeated at the 21st and 22nd Conferences.
3. *Cahiers du Communisme*, December 1971, p. 168.
4. *CFDT Syndicalisme*, 15 March 1973, p. 92–93.
5. *Le Peuple*, 16–30 November 1973, p. 3. *Le Monde*, 16 December 1975.
6. *L'Humanité*, 10 July 1972, *Le Monde*, 9 May 1972, *Le Peuple*, 1–15 June 1972, p. 9.
7. *Le Peuple*, 15–31 January 1978, p. 3–4, *CFDT Syndicalisme*, 17 November 1977, p. 11, *L'Humanité*, 8 October 1977, *Le Monde*, 16 November, 1977, *L'Humanité*, 8 October 1977.
8. *Syndicalisme et Politique*, Paris, Parti Socialiste, 1975, p. 33, 43.
9. *Vie Ouvrière*, 21–27 November 1977, p. 38.
10. *CFDT Syndicalisme*, 26 December 1974, p. 10–11.

11. *CFDT Syndicalisme*, 22 June 1972, p. 7.
12. *CFDT Aujourd'hui*, March–April 1975, p. 8–10.
13. *Le Monde*, 8 January 1977.
14. *Cahiers du Communisme*, November 1974, p. 57. *Cahiers du Communisme*, December 1971, p. 12–13.
15. Different figures were provided by Colpin. In his book *Communistes à l'entreprise*, Paris, Editions Sociales, 1979, he quotes 6,572 for 1974, (p. 188). His figure for 1976 was 8,072, *Cahiers du Communisme*, February–March 1976, p. 250.
16. Jourdain, H. 'Rapport présenté le 28.6.1973 à la première réunion de la Commission Nationale pour les activités politiques idéologiques et d'organisation du Parti dans les grandes entreprises' (personal archives).
17. *Motion nationale d'orientation. Le Poing et la Rose*, no. 38, 1975. This priority was not always respected according to the Paris Federation contribution to the following conference at Nantes (1977), *Le Poing et la Rose*, April 1977, p. 16.
18. Interview, Anne Trégouet 21 December 1986.
19. 'Entreprises', *Frontière*, June 1973, p. 16–18.
20. In 1979 he was replaced by Claude Germon, a member of the CGT's Executive Commission, and a prominent socialist dissident within the CGT.
21. He was subsequently replaced by Michel Coffineau (a member of the CFDT) and Anne Trégouet (a member of the CGT).
22. *L'Humanité*, 22 November 1971.
23. *Combat Socialiste*, December 1978, p. 15,17.
24. Jourdain, H. 'Rapport présenté le 28.6.1973 à la première réunion de la Commission Nationale pour les activités politiques idéologiques et d'organisation du Parti dans les grandes entreprises'. (personal archives).
25. *Combat Socialiste*, December 1978, p. 12.
26. Halbeher, A. 'Tout dépendre de l'activité du parti à l'entreprise'. *Cahiers du Communisme*, February–March 1976, p. 268–70.
27. *Nouvel Observateur*, 27 July 1975, p. 21.
28. The total comes to more than 100, because within the same workplace branch different trade union confederations may have been represented, Cayrol, R. 'Les socialistes à l'entreprise'. *Revue Française de Science Politique*, April 1978, p. 300.
29. Personal correspondance (dated 2 October 1983).
30. *Le Monde*, 5 November 1975.
31. *CFDT Syndicalisme*, 29 May 1975, p. 10.
32. *CFDT Syndicalisme*, 4 January 1973, p. 7–8.
33. *L'Humanité*, 28 October 1975.
34. *Le Monde*, 26 October 1976.
35. *L'Humanité*, 3 June 1976.
36. *CFDT Syndicalisme*, 13 November 1979, p. 9.
37. 'La CFDT et l'action des partis politiques', *CFDT Aujourd'hui*, March–April 1976 p. 8–10 p. 14–26. At a later date the CFDT became more critical of the PCF, see *CFDT Syndicalisme*, 15 November 1979, p. 7–10.
38. 'PC entreprises, PC syndicats, PC entreprises, Cinq communistes en discutent', *France Nouvelle*, 1 December 1975, p. 12–14.
39. Interview, Michel Charzat 25 February 1985.
40. Interview, André Servanin 11 May 1987.

41. *Sondage*, 2/3 1978, p. 105.
42. *Cahiers du Communisme*, February–March 1978, p. 248.
43. *Cahiers du Communisme*, November 1974, p. 57.
44. Zaidner, M., 'Quelques données statistiques'. *Cahiers du Communisme*, January–February 1973, p. 278. For the 20th Conference (1970) no statistics were made available. For the 21st Conference (1974) there were statistics, but no trade union membership variable. For the 22nd Conference (1976) there were no statistics, although an article 'Contribution à la sociologie du CF' by J-P, Molinari, appeared in *Cahiers du Communisme*, January 1976, p. 39–49. There was no trade union membership variable. G. Séguy, the General Secretary: H. Krasucki, a member of the Confederal Bureau: 3 secretaries of national unions, G. Frischmann, G. Lanoue and R. Le Guen; and P. Gensous, secretary of the World Federation of Trade Unions (1969–78).
45. *Le Quotidien de Paris*, 26 June 1974.
46. 'Interview avec Pierre Carassus' *Repères*, February 1976, p. 64.
47. Interview, Michel Charzat 25 February 1985.
48. Interview, Pierre Héritier 21 February 1985.
49. In an interview in Harris, A. & de Sedouy, A., *Voyage à l'interieur du parti communiste*, Paris, Seuil, 1974, p. 240.
50. *La mainmise ou comment le PCF dirige la CGT*, Numéro spécial, May 1978, p. 21–25. This trend was confirmed by another study, appertaining to the CGT after its 40th Conference (1980), in which it is shown that 100 per cent of all UDs have a Communist Secretary. Harmel, C. & Tandler, N., *Comment le parti communiste contrôle la CGT*. Paris, Bibliothèque d'Histoire Sociale, 1982, p. 87–90.
51. Roy estimated that 80% of all secretaries of UDs and national unions were members of the PCF. *Le Monde*, 2 December 1978.
52. *La mainmise ou comment le PCF dirige la CGT, op cit.* p. 8–17.
53. *Le Monde*, 28 June 1975. He subsequently left the PS in 1979. Interview, 26 February 1985.
54. *Le Monde*, 1 December 1978.
55. *L'Humanité de Dimanche*, 15–21 October 1975.
56. Interview, Pierre Jourdain February 1985.
57. According to Louis Gélin, *Le Matin*, 8 January 1982.
58. Interview, Jean-Marie Mick 11 May 1987.
59. *L'Humanité*, 10 October 1977.
60. *CFDT Syndicalisme*, 7 June 1973, p. 2. 'Les délégués au 37e Congrès Confédéral de la CFDT', *CFDT Aujourd'hui*, November–December 1976, p. 48–49. 'Les délégués au 38e Congrès Confédéral de la CFDT'. *CFDT Aujourd'hui*, January–February 1980, p. 29.
61. *Nouvel Observateur*, 3 June, 1974, p. 35.
62. See interviews with R. Bonnevialle and M. Coffineau in *Que faire aujourd'hui*, no. 5 p. 48–49 and 50–51 respectively.
63. See interviews with A. Jeanson and J. Ducos in *Que faire aujourd'hui*, no. 5. p. 47–48 and p. 52 respectively. This point was also made by Pierre Héritier, interview 21 February 1985.
64. *Le Monde*, 5 June 1973.
65. Interview, Pierre Héritier 21 February 1985.

Chapter 2
Trade Union Confederations and the Common Programme of Government

The Union of the Left drew its importance from the manifesto that the two major political parties had signed the Common Programme of Government, which provided the cement for their political unity. Party manifestos are in themselves significant because they provide the only clear statements of party policy available to voters. They define political objectives and the means by which they may be attained and, as such, are central to the *raison d'être* of a party. They also provide a recognisable identity for a political party, a focus for aggregating differing interests and a centralising force, around which, amongst others, a party can be mobilised. 'One has to take them [manifestos] seriously because they are the background for any mass media discussion of party policy, they are discussed and represented by the speeches of party leaders and they are . . . the basic source for the campaigns of the constituency candidates' (Robertson, 1976, p. 76). These remarks hold true in spite of the discrepancy that may arise between the claims of opposition and the deeds of government. Indeed it is interesting to note that the French Socialist government in the 1980s was so anxious to prove its commitment to its manifesto that three years after acceding to power it published the '110 Propositions' of François Mitterrand – its pre-election manifesto – complete with a detailed list of the way in which these proposals had been implemented.[1]

Remarks referring to a single political party also hold true for an alliance between political parties. The Common Programme of Government provided the only direct and clear statement of the policy proposals of the Union of the Left and was central to its very existence. The Common Programme of Government assumed further significance because it provided an instrument for measuring the strategies of the separate political parties within the Union of the Left. The state of the relationships between the PCF and the PS was reflected in the debate surrounding the Common Programme of Government. It was of prime symbolic importance: not only confirming the Socialist Party's Epinay strategy, but also capping the myth of Left unity, recalling 1936 and the Popular Front, and implying to the more myopic, a reversal of the historical schism of 1920 (Bell & Criddle, 1984, p. 74). The status of the Common Programme of Government was also enhanced by its very success. It was the first time during the Fifth Republic that the parties of the Left had succeeded in putting together such a wide-ranging and detailed joint manifesto. After years of negotiation between the parties of the Left, the Common Programme of Government 'opened up a new phase. The Union of the Left was no longer a project for the future; the election of a united Left became a real prospect. The Union of the Left was no longer a simple mechanism for winning and exchanging votes, as in 1967, it now had a political content' (Sur, 1977, p. 377). Moreover, the Common Programme of Government served as a point of reference for the Right and its own manifestos, the 'Programme de Provins' and later the 'Programme de Blois'. In short it was central to French political life in the 1970s.

Clearly no study of the relationship between the trade union confederations and the Union of the Left can neglect the Common Programme of Government. It gave a blueprint for future policies which would have a direct impact on trade unions and on the economic and political lives of their members and supporters. Moreover the reaction of the trade union confederations would affect its success. Finally the response of the trade union confederations to the Common Programme of Government would provide a clear indication of the nature of the relations between them and the political parties of the Union of the Left. In the first section of the chapter we propose to examine the background to the negotiations leading to the signing of the Common Programme of Government and study the document's contents. This will be followed by an analysis of the way in which the CGT and the CFDT responded. The Common Programme of Government was only supposed to last the lifetime of one Parliament. It was unsuccessfully renegotiated in 1977 before the legislative elections of the following year, and the second section examines this process of renegotiation and the ensuing response of the trade union confederations.

The Common Programme of Government

On 27 June 1972, the text of the Common Programme of Government was agreed upon at a special meeting between the leaders of the PCF and of the PS. It was then ratified by the central committee of the PCF, the *comité directeur* of the PS, then the national conferences of the PCF and of the PS, before yet another meeting was arranged, this time including a delegation from the *Mouvement des Radicaux de Gauche* to give it the final imprimatur. This was not a spontaneous outburst of left-wing fraternity. The Union of the Left formed the culmination of a strategy that the PCF had been pursuing since the 1950s. Indeed during the 1960s the French Communist Party campaigned actively for the unity of the Left, which would be sealed by signing of some form of joint manifesto.[2] In this way the PCF hoped to tie the PS into a more radical set of policy initiatives than the latter wanted, with the result that the sirens of social democracy could be safely ignored, at least for the time being. At that particular time the non-communist Left was less than enthusiastic – during the campaign before the 1965 presidential elections, François Mitterrand turned down an offer of PCF support conditional on the signing of a common programme (Giesbert, 1977, p. 210) – because any such union would undoubtedly have been dominated by the PCF.

However, the logic of the Fifth Republic's electoral system and the consequent need for electoral coalitions overcame non-communist reticence. A joint manifesto would add credibility to the Left's claim to be a Union. It would also encourage vote switching from one party to the other at the second round of the elections, an important tactic for maximising the number of seats to be won. After a series of meetings in 1966 a pact was signed on 20 December with the provision that, at the second round of the elections in those constituencies where the Left could hope to win, both political formations would call on their voters to vote for the best placed candidate of the Left. However, until remaining points of divergence had been resolved the confederation of the non-communist Left at that time, the *Fédération de la Gauche Démocrate et Socialiste* (FGDS) was still unwilling to sign a common manifesto. In February 1968 the FGDS and the PCF signed a joint declaration which enumerated a long list of points of convergence, and a series of points of divergence under three different headings – institutions and the defence of liberties, economic and social problems, and foreign affairs.[3] There were still major obstacles to unity, which were indeed exacerbated by the differing responses to the Events of May. However as Jean Poperen explained – the experience of May 1968 transported the Union of the Left to a higher strategic level, beyond that of a simple electoral coalition. From then onwards it was not just a question of harrassing the government, of opposing it, but of replacing it: as such a tactical agreement was insufficient, a political alliance was needed; one-off 'rapprochements' were inadequate, a programmatic agreement was indispensable (Poperen, 1976, p. 363). The results of the 1969 presidential election demonstrated to the socialists that a third force strategy reminiscent of the Fourth Republic was doomed to failure. Gaston Defferre, the socialist candidate, performed disastrously; a coalition with the French Communist Party was perceived to be essential, and a new Socialist Party was set up at a conference held in July 1969 at Issy-les-Moulineaux. Its new First Secretary, Alain Savary, was in favour of immediately engaging in dialogue with the PCF and four joint working parties were set up to discuss points of difference. At its conference held in June 1971 at Epinay the new Socialist Party committed itself to a closer relationship with the French Communist Party. Its new leader, François Mitterrand, was a clear supporter of a Union of the Left strategy.

Both the PCF and the PS initially chose to develop their own manifestos, but within the perspective of a Union of the Left strategy. The PCF produced its programme 'Changer de Cap', which was approved at a meeting of the central committee held on 7 October 1971.[4] The PS produced its own 'Changer la Vie', which was approved at an extraordinary national conference held in March 1972 at Suresnes.[5] Immediately afterwards contacts between the two parties resumed and the working parties were reconvened. Considerable progress was made in spite of an unsuccessful attempt by the President of the Republic, Georges Pompidou, to exacerbate differences between the PCF and the PS over foreign policy, by calling a referendum in April on the first enlargement of the European Community. Important points of divergence continued to exist, particularly on the issues of nationalisation and defence, but within the space of four months, a detailed joint manifesto, the Common Programme of Government, was finally agreed upon. The electoral logic of the Fifth Republic had finally triumphed. This show of unity should not disguise the fact that intense rivalry still existed between the two major parties of the Left. At a meeting of the central committee just after the signing of the Common Programme of Government. Georges Marchais explained that it would be dangerous to be under any illusion as to the sincerity or steadfastness of the Socialist Party:

we most certainly do not intend to exchange our programme for the Common Programme. On the contrary, we consider the latter as a step in the right direction, which will make it possible to create the most favourable conditions to mobilise the masses around *our* ideas, *our* solutions, *our* objectives'.[6]

Speaking on the same day, to the Congress of the Socialist International in Vienna, François Mitterrand defined the French Socialists' fundamental objective: it was to recreate a great Socialist Party in the space occupied by the PCF itself, so as to demonstrate that of the five million communist voters, three million of them could vote socialist.[7]

The Common Programme of Government contained the following proposals. According to Georges Marchais, in the same speech to the Central Committee, the Common Programme of Government 'defined a policy which if properly implemented would establish an advanced democracy opening up the way to socialism'.[8] This claim was exaggerated, since the Common Programme represented a classic example of the democratic management of the existing capitalist system. The first section proposed a number of socio-economic changes – improvements in wages, working conditions, employment, health, town planning, housing, education, research, sport, leisure, culture, women's rights, the family, young people and so on. The minimum legal wage (SMIC) was to be fixed at 1,000 Francs per month. A limit on wage differentials was proposed, although not defined. The second section covered aspects of the political economy for the most part – improvements in workers' rights, nationalism, economic planning, regional development, industrial policy, small businesses, fiscal policy, prices and inflation, foreign trade and monetary policy. In terms of the long march towards socialism, this section can be described as the most radical, and considerable attention was paid to the extension and democratisation of the public sector. Various sectors of the economy were to be completely nationalised, banking and insurance and the mining, armaments and aeronautical industries. The state was to take a majority holding in the electronics and chemical industries. The state would acquire shares – possibly a majority holding – in the steel and oil industries, air and maritime transport companies, telecommunications and motorway companies. Nine major companies would be nationalised: Dassault, Roussel-Uclaf, Rhône-Poulenc, ITT-France, Thomson-Brandt, Honeywell-Bull, Péchiney-Ugine-Kuhlmann, Saint Gobain-Pont à Mousson, and Compagnie Générale d'Electricité. The state would also acquire shares – possibly a majority holding – in Usinor-Vallourec, Wendel-Sidélor, Schneider, Compagnie Française des Pétroles-CFR-Total. Workers' rights, both in the private and public sectors, were to be strengthened, although there was a difference of opinion, the only overtly stated one in the document, between the two major parties as to the way in which this should take place, whether by means of 'democratic management' advocated by the PCF or 'workers' control' advocated by the PS. The Common Programme of Government presented both these proposals. The third section was concerned with civil liberties, political institutions, decentralisation, the Civil Service and the media and advocated a number of reforms of a liberalising nature. The final section dealt with France's foreign, defence and aid policies. The two major parties managed to submerge their differences over attitudes to the European Community and to Eastern Europe.

The political parties offered the trade unions a number of opportunities to increase their influence, either directly, or vicariously, as a result of the increased influence of employees in general. In this way the distinction between the political and the industrial spheres would be further blurred – the trade unions were being drawn into the policy-making process, a clear aspect of the political sphere. Trade unions were to have representatives on various quangos, the Sports Council and the National Youth Council, and on the management committees of local transport systems, education committees, bodies responsible for news broadcasting and nationalised industries. They were to assume an important role in stabilising prices, although there was no explanation of the way in which this would be done; they were to be consulted on the measures needed to improve the health service; they were to be associated in defining the objectives for town planning initiatives; they were to be consulted on all aspects of education policy and they were to be asked to help organise vocational training. They were to be consulted on new employee rights in nationalised industries, and to participate in economic planning, although there was no mention of the role of trade unions in any future wage-bargaining agreements, whether in the public or the private sector. In the industrial sphere, the powers of workers' representatives were to be increased. Labour inspectors were to be chosen from lists provided by trade unions. Trade unionists were to be granted the right to meet and to put up notices within the workplace, and employees were to elect health and safety committees with increased powers.[9] With this manifesto the political parties of the Union of the Left provided the trade unions with a significant opportunity to increase their influence in the policy-making process in the political sphere, and also to reinforce their position in the industrial sphere. No concessions were demanded of the trade unions. How then did they respond?

The trade union response to the Common Programme of Government

Confédération Générale du Travail

The response of the CGT left no doubt as to its position. Its Confederal Bureau met on 27 June 1972 and warmly congratulated the parties on the signing of the Common Programme of Government, describing it as one of the most important events that the French workers' movement had ever known.[10] An extraordinary meeting of the Executive Commission was called for 10 July to examine the consequences of the agreement. In its final declaration, it considered that the content of the Common Programme corresponded to the majority of the CGT's own concerns and to the objectives of the confederation's own programme. Apparently, all the industrial demands of the workers in the trade union organisations had been taken into consideration. The economic and political means for their achievement had been clearly laid out. The programme was resolutely directed against the domination of the capitalist monopolies, and the anticipated nationalisation measures would be extensive enough to permit society to control the economy. Moreover, according to the CGT statement, the programme defined the methods of 'democratic management' which would insure the real participation of the workers – a surprising conclusion given that the only point of explicit divergence within the document referred specifically to this issue. Finally, the Common Programme of Government would strengthen the position of the working class in its constant fight for the defence of its immediate demands, in the face of the reactionary attitudes of the employers and the government.[11]

It came as no surprise that the CGT was so effusive. According to Benoît Frachon, the general secretary of the CGT until 1967, the great weakness of the parties of the Left lay in the fact that they had not managed to agree on a joint manifesto.[12] In this respect he was repeating the views put forward by the French Communist Party. At the time of the Events of May 1968, both Benoît Frachon and Georges Séguy advocated a Union of the Left based on a common programme.[13] The Executive Commission met on 31 March 1971 and adopted a major policy document, 'Thèmes de reflexion sur les perspectives du socialisme pour la France', which called for an alliance of political parties on the basis of a 'common programme of social progress, of economic and political democracy, of independence and of peace'.[14] Speaking at the 38th conference of the CGT held in April 1972 (just prior to the signing of the Common Programme of Government), Georges Séguy tried to push the political parties together and, in doing so, helped to blur further the distinction between the political and industrial sphere. Should the parties of the Left decide to draw up a common programme, the CGT would be prepared to take part in this process.[15] Indeed, the Executive Commission statement quoted above claimed that the CGT had actually contributed to the drawing of the Common Programme of Government. The CGT had taken the opportunity of using its meetings with the parties of the Left to put its views across.[16] The CGT did not however actually participate in the working groups which were set up to define a common position, according to Henri Jourdain, one of the PCF's leading negotiators. Yet, as he explained, 'this did not mean that in these negotiations we did not consider, *inter alia*, the positions and the demands of the CGT'.[17] The CGT would of course have been able to put its views at all levels of the organisation of the PCF, as a result of the personnel linkages which existed between the two organisations. Indeed, after one meeting with the PCF, a spokesperson for the CGT announced that its principal objectives had been taken into account and that all the forces on the Left, trade unions and parties, should meet to establish a common programme.[18] In addition, it was claimed that the Common Programme of Government would provide an essential complement to trade union activity in the industrial sphere. According to Georges Séguy, 'the Common Programme of Government corresponds for the most part to what we expected and takes into consideration what we proposed. For years and particularly in May 1968, we bitterly regretted the lack of such a manifesto and we had to acknowledge the limits of trade union activities'.[19] The CGT was clearly acting in concert with the PCF.

The CGT did not confine its support to mere statements of good intent, it also used its organisation for campaigning purposes. Just after the Common Programme of Government was signed, *Vie Ouvrière*, the CGT's magazine with the widest circulation, devoted a number of issues to an exposition of its benefits.[20] This campaign culminated in a special edition *La CGT et le Programme Commun*,[21] which had a print-run of 1,100,000 copies, instead of the normal 250,000.[22] This issue gave a detailed description of the Common Programme of Government, comparing it to the policies of the CGT, in terms of the following – purchasing power, pensions, working hours, labour law, employment, women, young people, health, housing, transport, education, leisure, nationalisations, democratic management, workers, rights, fiscal policy, foreign policy and political institutions, and the means by which these policy objectives would be attained. This was followed by a simulated question and answer session with the leaders of the CGT, a historical overview of the CGT's calls for a Common Programme of Government, and a discussion with workers from one of the companies proposed for nationalisation, the chemical company Roussel-Uclaf. The crowning glory was provided by contributions from Georges Marchais, François Mitterrand (and even Robert Fabre, the leader of the MRG), with a final statement by Georges Séguy. There was no statement of the possible deficiencies of the Common Programme of Government, as expressed later, for example, at the National Confederal Council meetings held in November 1972 and after the following year's legislative elections in March 1973.[23] As for the nationalisations, a key subject for debate, the CGT chose not to print a list of the industrial sectors it would nationalise, saying simply that 'the essential ones were in the Common Programme of Government'. Yet, the CGT had previously proposed the nationalisation of the steel, oil and maritime transport companies, as well as the automobile industry, which were not included in the final version of the Programme.[24] However, nothing should be allowed to detract from the qualities of the Common Programme of Government. Other CGT organisations provided fulsome support for it – national unions[25] local organisations and UDs,[26] some of which organised rallies, (the UD-CGT Seine-Saint-Denis.[27]) or day schools (UD-CGT Loire[28]).

Did this position on the Common Programme of Government and the campaign in support of it compromise the autonomy of the CGT? Not surprisingly Georges Séguy claimed that this was not the case, since 'the CGT offered its support to the Common Programme of Government and not to the parties',[29] a point echoed at a National Confederal Council meeting in November 1972 by Marcel Caille, who, in a tortuous keynote speech, claimed that support for the Common Programme of Government would not bring trade union independence into question.[30] However, it is disingenuous to suggest that support for a manifesto can be separated from support for the political parties that have produced it. Moreover, as will be seen in greater detail in the following chapter, CGT support for the Common Programme of Government was extended in the following year to support for the Union of the Left at the legislative elections. The Executive Commission issued a statement calling on all CGT organisations to take an active part in the victory of the united Left and its Common Programme of Government.[31] Just prior to the elections the issue of the CGT journal *Le Peuple* had the banner headline, 'Programme Commun convaincra' across its front page.[32] Other CGT organisations, national unions,[33] and *Unions Départementales*,[34] followed suit. After the result of the legislative elections had become known, the CGT intensified its support for the Common Programme of Government. At the National Confederal Council meeting held in March 1973, Georges Séguy claimed that the Common Programme of Government was the *only* serious rallying point, and the *only* serious basis for unity and joint action for the working class and progressive forces, when faced with the domination of big business.[35] The CGT's commitment to the Common Programme of Government was total and unequivocal.

Confédération Française Démocratique du Travail

The CFDT reacted quite differently to the signing of the Common Programme of Government. It did not respond immediately. It later claimed that it had been caught unawares,[36] but it seems more likely that it did not know what position to take. At a meeting of the Executive Commission held some ten days after the publication of the Common Programme of Government, it was decided that the various structures of the confederation would be consulted before any public statement was made.[37] In this way it would be able to gain more time. The CFDT National Bureau was to meet on 14–15 September 1972. In the interim, the CGT attempted to push the CFDT into supporting the Common Programme of Government. A few days before, Georges Séguy made a speech in which he reminded other trade unions of the need to support the Programme.[38] The National Bureau chose however not to heed Séguy's comments. It passed a resolution underlining the functional differences between trade unions and political parties, and claiming 'it was not in the nature of trade unionism to decide on a programme of government nor to exercise power in the political sphere'.[39] The PCF joined the fray, bringing into question the CFDT's real motives for not supporting the Common Programme of Government. It noted that in the CFDT statement there were many ideas which were reminiscent of those of the PSU, a non-signatory of the Common Programme.[40] This point was obliquely conceded by Albert Detraz, one of the national secretaries of the CFDT, who complained that the Common Programme of Government was relevant only to a part of the Left,[41] (that is, not the PSU of which he was a member at that time).

According to a somewhat disingenuous National Bureau statement the signing of the Common Programme of Government constituted an important event, but, as it only pertained to one parliamentary period, it could not be considered as a project for the creation of a socialist society. Nevertheless the Common Programme of Government included a number of policy initiatives which the CFDT supported; an increase in the minimum legal wage (SMIC), improvements in health and welfare services, the reduction in the length of the working week, the increase in pensions, the improvements in employment chances and in terms of individual and collective rights.[42] However, it claimed that the Common Programme of Government would not lead to a major improvement in quality of life since the demands of profitability and 'productivism' were still dominant within the document. Finally, the CFDT claimed that the parties had omitted a certain number of safeguards needed to resist the drift towards 'state centralism'. This final statement was not surprising given that only two years earlier at its 35th Conference, the CFDT had redefined its objectives whose emphasis on the decentralisation of political and economic decision-making was contrary to the approach inherent in the Common Programme of Government. The Programme had expressly stated that nationalisation was not meant to lead to increased state control but belief in such a commitment was clearly not widespread. The PS had actually advocated a decentralised form of workers' control in the Common Programme of Government, in the face of opposition from the PCF. Either the CFDT did not believe that the PS shared the same definition of workers' control, or that the party as a whole was absolutely committed to it – a realistic interpretation in fact. At that time it was also thought that the PCF would be the dominant partner within the Union of the Left, and so would sacrifice workers' control on the altar of democratic management. This too was a realistic interpretation, since Georges Marchais had previously described workers' control as 'anarchy' and 'reactionary'.[43] Indeed the CFDT was very conscious of the fact that the influence of the CGT, and by extension the PCF, would be increased. Jacques Moreau, one of the confederal secretaries of the CFDT, explained the risks – 'if Rhône Poulenc is nationalised, who will control the enterprise committee there? The CGT . . . The PCF has understood how it could use these institutions, how it could move its pawns forward, how it could run everything'.[44] The National Bureau statement also made it clear that the CFDT would not participate in committees in support of the Common Programme of Government, neither would it associate itself with any declarations of support. However, the impact of this position was softened somewhat by a remark made at the ensuing press conference by Albert Detraz who explained that individual members of the CFDT could support the Common Programme of Government, but they should not make public their links with the CFDT.[45] The confederal position was echoed by other organisations within the CFDT, national unions such as the

Chemical Workers' Union,[46] and *Union Départementales*, such as UD-CFDT Val de Marne.[47]

In the previous chapter the position of the CFDT was unequivocal: it defended its right to become involved in the political sphere, and yet, in this section the CFDT used the issue of functional differentiation to disassociate itself from the political sphere and from the debate surrounding the Common Programme of Government. The CFDT was prepared to pass judgment on the Common Programme of Government but at this stage was not going to support it. Finally, it is worth drawing attention to one clairvoyant remark made at that time by Albert Detraz. He warned of the risks of being too closely identified with the Common Programme of Government and consequently of being dragged into any internal conflict.[48] Should the Union of the Left founder, 'the CFDT would get locked into the logic of the politics of the Common Programme'.[49]

The renegotiation of the Common Programme of Government

The Common Programme of Government was signed at a moment of convergence between the two major political parties of the Left, with the proviso that it would last for the lifetime of one Parliament and that it would be renegotiated before the next legislative elections which were to be held in March 1978. However, the economic and political environment was to change quite dramatically in the intervening period, not least because of the repercussions of the oil crisis. The latent rivalry between the two parties was rekindled and convergence gave way to conflict. Moreover, as has already been shown, the two leaders of the PS and the PCF saw the signing of the Common Programme of Government as an opportunity to advance their own particular objectives at the expense of the other. Within twelve months of signing the Common Programme of Government, both political parties had held conferences at which differing positions became manifest. At the beginning of January 1974 it was mooted that working parties should be set up to clarify and bring up to date certain aspects of the Common Programme of Government. However, these moves were overtaken by events (Verdier, 1976, p. 282). Georges Pompidou had been ill for some time and in April he died. The parties of the Left had no time for discussion of manifestos during the run-up to the presidential elections, and yet they put on a remarkable show of unity by backing one single candidate, François Mitterrand. He ran his campaign on his own manifesto, with no specific mention of the Common Programme of Government

(Colliard, 1979, p. 120), much to the chagrin of Georges Marchais who complained in a Central Committee meeting in April 1974 that 'we have not been able to obtain any clear commitment from François Mitterrand that he would fight the campaign on the Common Programme' (Hinker, 1981, p. 122–23).

Relations between the PCF and the PS became increasingly strained and, at the former's 21st conference held in October 1974, 'a brutal hardening of attitudes vis-a-vis the PS' was noted (Evin & Cayrol, 1978, p. 69). What explained this change in strategy? Firstly, the resurgence of the Left was primarily of benefit to the PS and not the PCF, contrary to what may have been expected at the beginning of the decade. Moreover it was generally thought that the signing of the Common Programme of Government had in fact been more beneficial to the PS than to the PCF. Secondly, the PCF's suspicions of the rightward drift of the PS were being revived. In October 1974, 1,500 members of the non-Communist Left met at Paris for the *Assises du Socialisme* and in the report of its proceedings there was no mention made of the Common Programme of Government. As was explained in the previous chapter, this key development in the evolution of the relations between the PS and the CFDT led to a large number of CFDT and PSU activists joining the PS, not least Edmond Maire and Michel Rocard, the two leaders. Indeed the latter actually criticised the Common Programme of Government in his speech to the *Assises du Socialisme*.[50] This rightward drift was consummated within the structures of the PS at its next conference held in January 1975 in Pau, when the pro-communist faction, CERES, was ousted from the leadership. Thirdly, the leader of the PCF, Georges Marchais, suffered a heart attack and during his period of convalescence, the more orthodox faction within the PCF was able to reassert itself, amongst other ways, by gaining the editorship of *L'Humanité* for one of its supporters, Roland Leroy, who then proceeded to use this vantage point to attack the PS (Johnson, 1981, p. 69). Finally, as was seen in the previous chapter, the PS had been relatively successful at setting up workplace branches and this posed a threat to the PCF which had been previously dominant in this area.

The municipal elections of 1977 proved to be a watershed. The Union of the Left demonstrated its electoral value and won 155 of the 221 large towns (with more than 30,000 inhabitants), with both the PS and the PCF making gains, the former more than the latter however. At the Central Committee of the PCF held to analyse the results, a further call for the renegotiation of the Common Programme of Government was made. A committee was to be set up, with representatives of the PCF, the PS and the MRG and it was scheduled to meet on 17 May.[51] A television debate between the Prime Minister Raymond Barre and François Mitterrand was to take place on 12 May. On 10 May *L'Humanité* published a costing of its latest version of the Common Programme of Government, which assumed a growth rate of 6 per cent – clearly an unattainable figure, as France was starting to drift into recession as a result of the oil crisis. This prognosis was published at that particular moment to cause François Mitterrand maximum embarrassment before the television debate. To judge by François Mitterrand's performance, the ploy was definitely successful.

On 17 May François Mitterrand, Georges Marchais and Robert Fabre met and decided to set up a working party to renegotiate the Common Programme of Government. The following month, the PS held its conference at Nantes, one of the recent conquests of the Union of the Left, and François Mitterrand made it clear that the renegotiations regarding the Common Programme of Government should be concluded quickly. Differences between the PCF and the PS centred on the minimum legal wage (SMIC) and on the nationalisation programme. The PCF proposed a minimum legal wage of 2,400 francs (for April 1978), whilst the PS insisted on a figure of 2,200 francs, so as to reduce the risk of potentially inflationary pressures building up within the economy. There was also disagreement over wage differentials – the PCF had moved to a position where it wanted to reduce the ratio to 1:5 (that is, between the lowest and highest paid) whereas the PS were unwilling to put a figure on this. In addition the latter wanted to keep the same number of companies to be nationalised whilst the PCF wanted to increase the number to fifteen, with the addition of four major steel companies, the oil company CFP-Total and the automobile group Peugeot-Citroën. This echoed parts of the PCF's previous manifesto, 'Changer de Cap' and also parts of the CGT's original proposals. There was also an acrimonious debate over subsidiaries – the PS was only interested in nationalising subsidiaries which were wholly owned (100 per cent) by the holding companies, whereas the PCF wanted to nationalise all subsidiaries where the holding companies had a majority share (51 per cent). For the PCF, this came to a total of 1,450 firms in all.[53] The three political leaders met at the PS headquarters on 14 September and although a number of small compromises were made, the major differences remained.[54] The leaders met a week later and although the PCF dropped its demand for the nationalisation of CFP-Total and Peugeot-Citroën and also reduced the number of subsidiaries to be nationalised, it maintained its other demands and no agreement was reached. The meeting broke up in confusion and no date for a further meeting was fixed.

The Common Programme of Government had not been renogotiated, and the Union of the Left was in complete disarray. The PCF had decided to torpedo the negotiations earlier, in the spring of 1977. It thought the Left would probably win the legislative elections, but the PCF would not reap the fruits of victory. Moreover, it would see its own audience with an increasingly militant working class threatened (Kergoat, 1983, p. 242). The PS had not wanted to compromise. It did not want to be accused by the centre and right-wing parties of being 'soft on communism', nor did it want to arrive in government with a series of election promises which it could not or would not honour.

The most dramatic and surprising negotiating gambit came afterwards from the PS. Its prime consideration was electoral victory and Left-wing unity was a prerequisite for this. Any policy differences could be sorted out afterwards.[55] The PS decided on a number of significant compromises. Previously it had stipulated that the minimum legal wage should only increase to 2,200 francs; now it was suggesting 2,400 francs, which brought it into line with the PCF, the CGT, and the CFDT. It was also prepared to increase the number of firms to be nationalised,[56] but this did not lead to a conciliatory response from the PCF. On the contrary, the latter hardened its position.[57] A month later the PS gave a costing of its own up-dated Common Programme of Government, based on a more modest estimate of France's potential economic growth (4.9 per cent in 1978 and 5.6 per cent in 1979),[58] and this too was heavily criticised by the PCF which described it as 'crisis and austerity management'.[59] Consequently the political parties of the Left went into the 1978 legislative elections with two similar but separate manifestos. After the first round of the elections the leaders of the three parties met, the first time for six months, to conclude an electoral agreement whereby the candidates of the Left with the lowest score at the first round withdrew in favour of more popular candidates of the Left. They agreed to meet on the day after the second round of the elections to renegotiate the Common Programme of Government once more. In the event they did not bother. The election defeat underlined and compounded their disunity.

The trade union response to the renegotiation of the Common Programme of Government

Confédération Générale du Travail

During the period between the initial negotiations about the Common Programme of Government and the subsequent renegotiations in 1977, the CGT held its 39th conference in June 1975 at Le Bourget and defined its major strategic guidelines for the future. Speaking on behalf of the Confederal Bureau, Georges Séguy put the CGT position:

the reinforcement of the Union of the Left and the joint activities to gain power and implement the Common Programme of Government remain the *only* realistic and accessible perspective for all those who really want to beat the Right and substitute democratic and progressive policies for the present policy. We most definitely form a part of that group.[60]

Indeed the slogan declaimed at all CGT demonstrations during the mid-1970s was 'union, action, programme commun'.

At the time when the political parties were beginning to commence the renegotiation of the Common Programme of Government, the CGT brought out its own manifesto, 'Les Solutions et les Propositions de la CGT', whose publication coincided with the PS conference held at Nantes. The CGT demanded that the minimum legal wage should be increased to 2,200 francs per month (for April 1977), a figure which was favoured by the PCF but not at that time by the PS. At that time the CGT made no specific proposals regarding wage differentials, but the CGT maintained a maximalist position on the nationalisations issue. It proposed the nationalisation of the banks, insurance companies, the atomic energy industry, the major groups within the electronics, chemical and pharmaceutical, aeronautical, aerospace and armaments industries, and in addition the steel, oil and car industries and the major maritime transport companies.[61] This list corresponded to the CGT's original 1972 demands. As previously noted, the PCF proposed the nationalisation of the four major steel companies, CFP-Total, and Peugeot-Citroën, although it was prepared to drop the nationalisation of the latter two companies in order to reach some form of compromise with the PS. On these two major issues, the minimum legal wage and the nationalisation programme, the CGT and the PCF were in close agreement.

At a major speech in September 1977 two days after a meeting between the CGT and the PCF, and six days before a crucial meeting between the leaders of the political parties, Georges Séguy turned to the question of wage differentials, and although, as previously indicated, no particular figure was expressed in the 'Les Solutions et les Propositions de la CGT', he suggested that a ratio of 1:5 or 1:6 (between the lowest and the highest paid) would be reasonable. This brought the CGT into line with the CFDT on this particular issue. He followed this up with an attack on those who were 'prudent and moderate' in economic affairs and with a denunciation of the Swedish and Portuguese socialist experiences,[62] which had recently been praised by François Mitterrand at the PS conference in Nantes. Georges Séguy was attempting to drive a wedge between the PS on the hand, and the CGT, PCF and CFDT on the other. On 14 September, the day on which talks between the political parties were actually to break down, a number of CGT national unions contacted their CFDT counterparts, urging them to put pressure on the PS to sign the renegotiated Common Programme of Government.[63] Hundreds of CGT branches apparently sent telegrams (Fabre, 1978, p. 94). Later during the month of September, the Confederal Bureau of the CGT met and called on the political parties to come to an agreement. It skirted round certain contentious matters, such as wage levels, but joined in the debate on the nationalisation of subsidiary companies. It maintained that the nationalisation programme had no sense unless the subsidiaries were included and that it would never have supported a manifesto which had not taken them into account.[64] This was recognised for what it was – open support for the PCF.[65] At the same time a special issue of *Vie Ouvrière* was published, stressing *inter alia* the need for the nationalisation of the subsidiaries.[66] At an extraordinary meeting of the Executive Commission it was decided to step up the CGT's campaign with the publication of a pamphlet *il faut que vive le Programme Commun*,[67] which was to have an enormous print run of six million copies, and which was to be distributed by national unions,[68] and *Unions Départementales*.[69]

The CGT slowly became sensitive to the charge of political partiality. At the last meeting of its National Confederal Council before the legislative elections, a resolution was passed stressing the functional distinctiveness of trade union confederations and political parties,[70] but in the circumstances this claim rang hollow. At the end of the 1977 the CGT had met the political parties of the Left, an occasion it used to demonstrate convergence with the position of the PCF and dissatisfaction with the position of the PS. The CGT claimed that there were no major disagreements with the PCF. With the PS however, there were differences over wages, the means for reducing unemployment, the nationalisation of the subsidiaries and of the oil, steel and autombile industries.[71] Moreover, according to Georges Séguy, the PS did not take the CGT delegation seriously.[72] When the PS costed its own up-dated version of the Common Programme of Government, the CGT intervened in the debate, and Georges Séguy listed a dozen policies which would be jeopardised as a result of PS spending estimates.[73]

At the time of the renegotiation of the Common Programme of Government and the break up of the Union of the Left, the CGT demonstrated a clear willingness to participate in the political sphere. By taking part in the political debate surrounding the renegotiation of the

Common Programme of Government, the CGT participated indirectly in the election process and aligned itself with one of the actors, the PCF. Interestingly, later at the CGT's 40th conference held at the end of 1978 in Grenoble, Georges Séguy admitted that, during this period, the CGT had referred more and more to the Common Programme of Government and less and less to the CGT's own programme, which in itself had led to a certain confusion between the two.[74]

Confédération Française Démocratique du Travail

A considerable number of CFDT activists had rallied to the PS, and it seemed likely that this would have an influence on the CFDT's position regarding the Common Programme of Government. This was only partly the case. At the 37th conference of the CFDT held in Annecy in May 1976 there was criticism of the restrictive nature of the Common Programme of Government.[75] This was interpreted in different ways. Quite remarkably, the CERES journal *Repères* gave the impression that the CFDT was becoming less critical of the Common Programme of Government.[76] The headline in *L'Humanité* read, 'Edmond Maire confirms his distance from the Common Programme',[77] whilst in the right-wing newspaper *Le Figaro* the headline was 'Edmond Maire: we won't be responsible for implementing the Common Programme'.[78] If the leadership of the CFDT had wanted to dissimulate its position, it could not have been more successful. The CFDT also produced its own policy document at the time when the political parties were beginning to commence renegotiations of the Common Programme of Government in mid 1977, *Texte de la Plate-forme de Revendications et Objectifs Immédiats*.[79]

On the issue of wages, the CFDT advocated a minimum legal wage of 2,200 francs (as of April 1977), the same as the CGT and the PCF, although not the PS. The CFDT showed greater interest in the question of wage differentials and put forward a ratio of 1:6 (between the lowest and highest paid). In an interview with *Le Figaro* a short time before, Edmond Maire claimed that the CGT and the PCF were coming round to the CFDT position on wage differentials.[80] Indeed it has been shown in this chapter that the PCF, and then later the CGT, were prepared to provide a more specific commitment to the reduction of wage differentials. They wanted to diminish the individuality of the CFDT and to isolate the PS. On the nationalisation issue, the CFDT stressed the importance of avoiding state control and the need to set up workers' control structures. The document gave no indication of the companies or industries which should be nationalised. However, at the press conference called to launch the document, Edmond Maire stated somewhat unexpectedly that the dominant economic groups in banking, the media and education should be brought into public ownership. The CFDT also launched a major campaign to put its position across, with a print run of 100,000 copies for *CFDT Syndicalisme* and a special issue of the more attractive *CFDT Magazine* devoted to this subect scheduled for the autumn.

After the renegotiations broke down, the CFDT Executive Commission statement expressed surprise at the fact that this had happened as a result of the inability of the PCF and the PS to agree on the shape of the nationalisation programme.[81] Interestingly for a trade union confederation which had distanced itself from the Common Programme of Government, it was curious to see that in this issue of *CFDT Syndicalisme,* the front page headline should read 'recreate the conditions of unity'. In spite of its previous references to the inadequacies of the Common Programme of Government, the CFDT had become aware of its strategic importance in electoral terms, and it attempted to bring the parties of the Union of the Left together. Its Executive Commission stated unexpectedly that it had no objections in principle to the number of nationalisations originally suggested in the 1972 version of the Common Programme of Government, the crucial point being the way in which these companies were to be democratised. It criticised the PCF for being inflexible about the number of subsidiaries to be nationalised and for neglecting the central issue of the position of the workers within these nationalised companies. It also questioned the PCF's costing of its new version of the Common Programme of Government and asked whether the PCF had not changed its overall political strategy. Its criticism of the PS was more muted. It claimed that the PS was not sufficiently attentive to the demands of the workers and not specific enough in its proposals for works councils. The CFDT also met the different political parties of the Left, an occasion which was interpreted by Pfister in *Le Monde,* as an attempt by the CFDT to encourage the PCF and the PS to resume their talks.[82] A report of the meetings was provided by Jacques Moreau one of the CFDT's confederal secretaries. According to him, the views of the PS were insufficiently clear, but he made no further significant criticism. He claimed that the explanation of the PCF for the breakdown of the renegotiation talks was unconvincing and that the PCF should not ignore the differences that existed between it and the CFDT.[83] In this unconvincing attempt to be evenhanded, the CFDT was nevertheless able to demonstrate its own political predilections.

It is ironic that the CFDT was casting doubt on the constancy of the PCF's strategy at the very moment it was changing its own. Whilst the Moreau Report, which was approved by the National Council in January 1978, made no explicit reference to the Common Programme of Government,[84] the inference was unmistakable. The emphasis of CFDT activity would in future lie with the industrial sphere and trade union activities in the workplace. In his speech to the National Council, Moreau implied that participation in the political sphere had led the confederation to neglect its activities in the industrial sphere. Hamon and Rotman quoted Moreau as saying that his report was aimed at liberating the confederal strategy from the vicissitudes of the political sphere, which they interpreted elsewhere in their book as a 'poke in the eye for the defunct Common Programme – 'pan sur le bec du défunt programme commun' (Hamon & Rotman, 1982, p. 229–98). Was the change in strategy a direct consequence of the disenchantment felt in the CFDT following the break-up of the Union of the Left? Jacques Moreau insisted that it would have taken place anyway and that it was a way of 'infusing trade unionism with life'.[85] The break-up of the Union of the Left nevertheless strengthened the resolve of the CFDT leadership to pursue this new strategy.

In spite of the announcement of the new strategy, the CFDT did not immediately abstract itself from the political sphere, nor from the debate surrounding the Common Programme of Government. In the new year the CFDT published a report on economic planning and the nationalisation programme, which 'would help to extricate the political Left from its divisions by putting forward unifying proposals.[86] The most important of these referred to the number and the type of nationalisations. The CFDT proposed the nationalisation of the banks and the nine companies which had been originally proposed in the Common Programme of Government, and in addition, the nationalisation of the steel and energy industries. The CFDT's own previous candidates for nationalisation, the media and education, were not even mentioned. Moreover it proposed the nationalisation of all the subsidiaries, 66 per cent of whose capital was owned by the parent company and therefore not the 51 per cent of the PCF, or the 100 per cent of the PS), which amounted to 450 firms (not the 227 of the PS, or the 729 of the PCF). In spite of the new strategy inherent in the Moreau Report, the CFDT was still present in the political sphere and attempting to mediate between the political parties of the defunct Union of the Left. A slightly mischievous article a few weeks later noted that 'it would be somewhat comical to imagine the Common Programme renegotiated by those who previously had been its critics.[87]

After the failure of the Left to win a majority in the legislative elections, which clearly signalled the failure of a political approach based on the Common Programme of Government and after the change in CFDT strategy marked by the publication of the Moreau Report, Edmond Maire could safely claim, 'we had gradually realised that this programme was not really common, that it did not respond to a large number of workers' aspirations and that it had little chance of succeeding because the PCF would not accept being overtaken by the PS'. He also explained rather disingenuously that the CFDT had not become involved in the debate over the costing of the Common Programme of Government because qualitative expectations could not be reduced to quantitative data.[88] Indeed the CFDT's collective memory was beginning to play tricks, because by the time of its 38th conference held in May 1979 in Brest, it claimed that during the election period 'the CFDT had spoken its mind. From August 1977 onwards, it had criticised the inadequacy of the parties' manifestos, particularly as regards employment'[89] – an issue which was hardly mentioned at all during this period. At the end of 1977 the CFDT became increasingly involved in the political debate surrounding the renegotiation of the Common Programme of Government and even attempted to act as an arbiter between the political parties of the Union of the Left. In this way it became a direct and unequivocal participant in the political sphere, a fact which was highlighted by the ostentatious change of strategy inherent in the Moreau Report.

Conclusions

The Common Programme of Government sealed the Union of the Left between the PCF and PS and was to lie at the heart of the politics of the Left and indeed of the whole French political system for a major part of the 1970s. The trade union confederations responded to it in different ways, particularly in the initial stages. The CGT, which had been campaigning for some time for this type of political initiative, gave wholehearted support to the Common Programme of Government, even though in certain areas, such as the nationalisation programme, its own proposals were more extensive. The CGT was aware of the strategic significance of the signing of the Common Programme of Government for the French Left and moreover was prepared to undertake an extensive campaign in support of it. The CFDT, on the other hand, was less enthusiastic and justified its position in part at least by its unwillingness to become caught up in the political sphere. Although aware of the positive aspects of parts of the Common Programme of Government, the CFDT was dissatisfied with the document's overall ideological thrust.

By the time of the renegotiation of the Common Programme of Government the political environment had changed markedly. Support for the PS was increasing, whereas support for the PCF was waning. The PCF was left with two options. It could either try to tie the PS into a more radical version of the Common Programme of Government which would have strengthened the PCF's position within the Union of the Left and made the PS less attractive electorally, or it could sabotage the renegotiations of the Common Programme of Government and put the blame on the PS. This would harm the electoral chances of the entire Left, but in this way the PS would be denied its preponderant position and the PCF could hope to regroup its forces at a later date. In the event when it was unable to achieve the first option, it switched to the second. The response of the trade union confederations was instructive. They did not attempt to restrict themselves to the industrial sphere. They became increasingly engaged in the political debate surrounding the renegotiations. The CGT continued to support the Common Programme of Government and indeed admitted at a later date doing so at the expense of its own programme. When negotiations broke down, its proposals for a renegotiated Common Programme of Government reflected those of the French Communist Party, and in the process it became increasingly critical of the Socialist Party. More surprisingly, the CFDT became directly involved in the political debate surrounding the renegotiation of the Common Programme of Government and even attempted to act as a go-between. Furthermore with its overt criticism of the role played by the French Communist Party in the breakdown of the renegotiation talks it became increasingly partisan. Given the constellation of political forces at that time, this partisanship was tantamount to providing support for the Socialist Party – an uncomfortable position, considering the latter's differing position on certain policy issues, notably the minimum legal wage and wage differentials. Once the CFDT realised that a renegotiated Common Programme of Government was indeed a lost cause, it reverted to a new strategy where the emphasis lay quite definitely within the industrial sphere. Even then, it could not resist the temptation to participate in the debate surrounding the possible resurrection of the Common Programme of Government.

Notes

1. *La Lettre de Matignon*, 22 May 1984.
2. According to Georges Marchais in Fajon, E. *L'Union est un combat*, Paris. Editions Sociales, 1975, p. 76.
3. *La Revue Socialiste*, March, 1968.
4. *Changer de cap*. Paris. Editions Sociales. 1972.
5. *Changer la vie*. Paris. Flammarion. 1972.
6. His emphasis, in Fajon, E. *L'Union est un combat, op cit*, p. 88–89, 93.
7. *Le Monde*, 30 June 1972.
8. See Georges Marchais in Fajon, E. *L'Union est un combat, op cit*, p. 112.
9. *Programme commun de gouvernement*, Paris, Editions Sociales, 1972.
10. *Le Peuple*, 1–15 July, 1972, p. 2.
11. *Le Peuple*, 16–31 July, 1972, p. 2.
12. Quoted in Branciard, M., *Syndicats et partis*, Paris, Syros, 1982, Vol II, p. 178.
13. Quoted in Hamon, H. & Rotman, P., *La deuxième gauche*, Paris, Ramsay, 1982, p. 203–204.
14. Published as an appendix in Krasucki, H., *Syndicats et socialisme*, Paris, Editions Sociales, 1972, p. 10–23.
15. *Le Peuple*, 1–31 May, 1972, p. 13.
16. *Le Peuple*, 16–31 July, 1972, p. 2.
17. Private correspondance dated 2 October, 1983.
18. *Le Peuple*, 1–15 June, 1972, p. 6–7.
19. *L'Humanité*, 8 September, 1972.
20. *Vie Ouvrière*, 5 July, 1972. 12 July, 1972. 26 July, 1972. 9 August, 1972.
21. *Vie Ouvrière*, 18 October, 1972.
22. *Le Monde*, 18 October, 1972.
23. *Le Peuple*, 1–15 December, 1973, p. 21. *Le Peuple*, 1–15 April, 1973, p. 16–19.
24. *Le Peuple*, 1–15 March, 1972, p. 45.
25. *La voix des industries chimiques*, CGT–Chimie, September 1972, p. 4.
26. *UD–CGT Haute Garonne*, UD–CGT Haute Garonne, no date.
27. *L'Humanité*, 26 January, 1973.
28. *Courrier*, UD–CGT Loire, no. 26, 27 October, 1972.
29. Quoted in *Le Monde*, 18 October, 1972.
30. *Le Peuple*, 1–15 December, 1972, p. 11.
31. *Le Peuple*, 16–31 January, 1973, p. 2.
32. *Le Peuple*, 1–15 March, 1973, p. 1.
33. *Le Travailleur de l'Etat*, CGT–Travailleurs de l'Etat, February 1973.
34. *Travailleur du Pas de Calais*, UD–CGT Pas de Calais, February 1973.
35. My emphasis, *L'Humanité*, 27 March, 1973.
36. *CFDT Syndicalisme*, 4 March, 1976, p. 54.
37. *Le Monde*, 10 July, 1972.
38. *Le Monde*, 9 September, 1972.
39. *CFDT Syndicalisme*, 21 September, 1972, p. 1–2.
40. *L'Humanité*, 18 September, 1972.
41. *L'Unité*, 22 September, 1972, p. 9.
42. *CFDT Syndicalisme*, 16 November, 1972, p. 7–9.
43. Quoted in Poperen, J., *L'Unité de la gauche*, Paris, Fayard, 1976, p. 419.

44. *Frontière*, December 1972, p. 13.
45. *CFDT Syndicalisme*, 21 September, 1972, p. 2.
46. 'La CFDT et le Programme Commun', *Chimie-militants*, November 1972, p. 7–12.
47. *Le Courier de l'UD*, UD–CFDT Val de Marne, December 1972.
48. *Frontière*, December 1972, p. 10.
49. Interview, Albert Detraz 12 July, 1983.
50. *Pour le socialisme*, Paris, Stock, 1974, p. 60.
51. *L'Unité*, 246/1977, p. 8–9.
52. *Nouvel Observateur*, 5 September, 1977, p. 26–27, 19 September, 1977, p. 44.
53. For a detailed list of the nationalisations, see *Le Monde*, 21 September, 1977.
54. *Nouvel Observateur*, 19 September, 1977, p. 39–43.
55. According to Claude Alphandéry, Hamon, H. & Rotman, P. *L'Effet Rocard*, Paris, Stock, 1980, p. 172.
56. *Le Monde*, 6 January, 1978.
57. *Cahiers du Communisme*, February–March 1978, p. 123–35.
58. *Le Monde*, 15 February, 1978, 18 February, 1978.
59. *L'Humanité*, 15 February, 1978, 17 February, 1978.
60. His emphasis *Le Peuple*, 1–31 July, 1975, p. 13.
61. *Le Peuple*, 15–30 June, 1977.
62. *Le Peuple*, 1–15 September, 1977, p. 3–12.
63. *CFDT Syndicalisme*, 29 September, 1977, p. 2.
64. *Le Peuple*, 1–15 October, 1977, p. 2.
65. *Le Monde*, 20 October, 1977.
66. *Vie Ouvriére*, 3–9 October, 1977.
67. *Le Peuple*, 1–15 November, 1977, p. 4–5.
68. The CGT–Metallurgie sent out model tracts. *Courier fédéral*, 20 January, 1978.
69. The UD–CGT Alpes-Maritimes printed 80,000 copies of '*il faut que vive le Programme Commun*', (personal correspondance, dated 17 March, 1982). The UD–CGT of the Dordogne printed 25,000 copies, according to the minutes of a meeting held on 18 November, 1977. A member of the Bureau of the UD–CGT. Antoinette Santoyo, explained that there had *never* been any difference between the position of the *Union Départementale* and the confederation, (my emphasis), (personal correspondance dated 19 March, 1982).
70. *Le Monde*, 18 November, 1977.
71. *Le Peuple*, 15–31 January, 1978, p. 2–5. Some local CGT organisations met with local parties. The UD–CGT Seine-Maritime complained of differences of opinion with the local PS and MRG, (personal correspondance dated 6 April, 1982).
72. *Le Monde*, 22 December, 1977.
73. *Vie Ouvriére*, 20–26 February, 1978, p. 7.
74. *Le Peuple*, 1–31 December, 1978, p. 9.
75. *CFDT Syndicalisme*, 4 March, 1976, p. 54–58.
76. Leroi, 'Les syndicats après et avant les élections', *Repères*, April 1978, p. 54.
77. *L'Humanité*, 26 May, 1976.
78. *Le Figaro*, 26 May, 1976.

79. *CFDT Syndicalisme,* 16 June, 1977.
80. *Le Figaro,* 3 June, 1977.
81. *CFDT Syndicalisme,* 29 September, 1977, p. 2.
82. *Le Monde,* 9 October, 1977.
83. *CFDT Syndicalisme,* 17 November, 1977, p. 11.
84. *CFDT Syndicalisme,* 2 February, 1978, p. 2–3.
85. Interview, Jacques Moreau 4 April, 1986.
86. *Le Monde,* 7 February, 1978.
87. *Libération,* 1 March, 1978.
88. *Nouvel Observateur,* 10 April, 1978, p. 36–37.
89. *CFDT Syndicalisme,* special number, December 1978, p. 16.

Chapter 3
Trade Union Confederations and Elections

Elections provide the ultimate, if imperfect, yardstick for measuring the popularity of a party, the acceptability of its manifesto and the credibility of its leadership. They are the means by which political parties attain power and govern. In short, elections lie at the heart of the political sphere and contesting elections is one of the prime functions of political parties. Trade unions do not contest political elections as such. Unlike their counterparts in Great Britain, French trade unions do not have an opportunity to choose candidates for political elections. Nor do they have the dubious advantage of helping to pay for the expenses of such elections. They are however by no means indifferent to this process, since the outcome of elections may have a significant impact on their activities and objectives as trade unions, and on the lives and aspirations of their own members and supporters. Moreover, their members are voters and may exercise an influence on the result of the elections. Trade unions provide a framework of political socialisation which helps to shape voter preference. Indeed, trade unions capable of delivering a labour vote can play a significant role in the political process.

Political parties need the support of trade unions and the votes of their members, and there is a link between trade unions and the political process at election times, which has been overlooked by the major studies on elections or on voting behaviour in France. This link, interesting in its own right, is doubly so in the context of this particular book. It sheds further light on the issue of functional differentiation, and provides another means of investigating the ways in which French trade unions participate in the political sphere. Through the medium of the electoral process it is possible to study in greater detail the relations between trade union confederations and the political parties of the Union of the Left. Since the Union of the Left ran from June 1972 to September 1977, our analysis will focus on the legislative elections of 1973 and the Presidential election of 1974. Although the legislative elections of 1978 fall outside this time-span, they too will be analysed, since the breakdown in the talks to renegotiate the Common Programme of Government clearly occurred within the perspective of the 1978 legislative elections. The chapter is divided into two sections. The first investigates the ways in which the trade union confederations participated in the electoral process and provided support for the political parties of the Union of the Left. The second aims to identify the impact of trade union participation on electoral behaviour.

Trade union confederations and elections

The legislative elections 1973

The Left went into the legislative elections in 1973 in a spirit of unblemished harmony. Although the two major parties of the Left fielded their own candidates at the first round, the electoral pact worked smoothly, leaving the best placed candidate with the support of the whole of the Union of the Left in opposition to the candidate of the Right. The electoral pact was more systematic and more compelling than had been the case at the time of the legislative elections in 1967. At the first round of the elections, the PCF obtained 21.4 per cent of the votes cast, and the *Union de la Gauche Socialiste et Démocratique*, made up of the PS and the MRG, obtained 20.8 per cent: this combined vote amounted to 42.2 per cent, a significant improvement on the results of the 1968 elections (36.5 per cent). In all, the PCF won 73 seats and the UGSD 100, an increase of 39 and 51 respectively over the results of the 1968 elections.

Just as the trade union confederations had responded quite differently to the signing of the Common Programme of Government, so their reaction to the 1973 legislative elections was different. The CGT expressed unreserved support for the political parties of the Union of the Left, whereas the CFDT was more guarded in its response. The Executive Commission of the CGT met at the beginning of 1973 and issued a statement underlining the importance of these elections 'for the most immediate interests of the workers, and for their future'. Moreover, 'employees have the possibility of extending their activities in the industrial sphere, by voting effectively'. After attacking the record of the government and extolling the virtues of the Common Programme of Government, the Executive Commission statement noted that an effective vote was one for the united Left,[1] that is the parties that had signed the Common Programme of Government, thus excluding the *Parti Socialiste Unifié* and other sections of the extreme-left. After the first round of the elections Georges Séguy stated that the CGT would do all it could to beat the representatives of the Right and to ensure that the candidates of the Left were elected.[2] Support had centred on popularising the contents of the Common Programme of Government, through the trade union press nationally,[3] and locally,[4] through meetings organised by the national unions and the *Unions Départementales*.[5] Posters were put up in workplaces, proclaiming, 'Vote for the candidate of the Common Programme and complement trade union action'. In spite of the fact that it had not supported the Common Programme of Government, Edmond Maire made it clear in October 1972 that the CFDT wanted to see the Left triumph at the first and second round of the elections.[6] However, he refused to align the CFDT totally with the PCF and the PS, and reiterated the CFDT's reservations about the Common Programme of Government, calling on trade union members to do everything for the victory of 'popular forces',[7] which would include all the political parties on the Left, not just the PCF and the PS, but also the extreme-left and the PSU. A significant theme of CFDT strategy at that time was that electoral activities were insufficient on their own. Winning the elections would only lead to significant advances in terms of the transition to socialism, if controlled by the workers themselves.[8] Although the CFDT was hazy about the means by which workers would control the actions of governing parties, it claimed that political change could not be left to the political parties alone. Nevertheless, between the two rounds of the elections, the CFDT became less reticent about its support for the victory of the Left, which was seen as providing new opportunities and hope for meaningful changes in society.[9]

The Presidential election 1974

At the beginning of the month of April 1974, delegations from the PCF, PS and MRG met to decide on a common candidate for the Presidential elections, and François Mitterrand was chosen. The PCF had decided not to put up its own candidate for the elections. There was a doubt hanging over the PCF's readiness to participate in any government and, its leader, Georges Marchais, would not have made a popular candidate at that time (Salomon, 1980, p. 195). Not surprisingly, Georges Marchais had a different view – in a speech to the Central Committee, he explained that a PCF candidate would only encourage the Right to think that the Left was split.[10] However, as this had not stopped the PCF from fielding candidates on other occasions, it can be assumed that it considered that the election of François Mitterrand would consolidate its own position. As he was tied into a series of manifesto commitments consequent on the signing the Common Programme of Government, he would be dependent for political support on the PCF, the senior and more influential partner in the coalition. Given the unity of the Left and the disarray on the Right, it is not surprising that François Mitterrand led after the first ballot. After a closely fought second round, he obtained 12,971,604 votes, 49.2 per cent of votes cast, and was narrowly beaten by Valéry Giscard d'Estaing.

Both trade union confederations rallied to François Mitterrand. Even before his candidacy was announced, the Confederal Bureau of the CGT was calling for a single candidate of the Left who would defend the principles of the Common Programme of Government.[11] Once his candidacy was announced, the Executive Commission of the CGT published a statement, calling on all workers to vote for him.[12] For the CGT, there were no doubts. In a special presidential edition of *Vie Ouvrière* Georges Séguy explained unequivocally – 'the choice is simple, on the one hand there are eleven Right-wing or inconsequential candidates, on the other, there is François Mitterrand, the joint candidate of the Left'.[13] The Executive Commission called on its organisations, members and supporters to campaign actively to beat Giscard d'Estaing, 'the representative of the forces of the old conservative reactionary Right'.[14] The CGT produced posters, with the slogan, 'The CGT votes for François Mitterrand for the Common Programme of the Left'.[15] The officials of the Metalworkers Union of the CGT, its largest national union, were called on, 'to use everything available: posters, tracts etc. to organise the maximum number of meetings with members and other workers, and to organise discussions in the workplace'.[16] The Metalworkers Union sent out model tracts to its activists,[17] and it insisted on the fact that its members should join local support committees for the common candidate of the Left, 'charged with the task of implementing the Common Programme of Government'.[18] This message was passed on at *département* and local level; in the Loire-Atlantique and St-Nazaire for example, tracts and broadsheets were produced, all in support of François Mitterrand.[19] The CGT supported François Mitterrand wholeheartedly, whilst trying to ensure that he did not escape from his commitments to the Common Programme of Government.

The CFDT's support was wholehearted too. It could however have been faced with an embarrassing conflict of loyalties. Charles Piaget, the leader of the long and famous strike in the Lip watch factory and one of the CFDT's own trade union representatives, planned to stand as a candidate for the Presidential election. However, his candidacy was undermined from within the CFDT itself.[20] Edmond Maire explained that the CFDT would not support this candidacy because there was a risk of confusion between trade union and political functions.[21] Trade unionists should not contest elections. However, behind a cover of functional differentiation, the CFDT was also ensuring that the Left's vote was not split. In the same trade union journal, it was explained that the CFDT was opposed to any candidate who wanted a platform for any minority organisation and who was not interested in some form of unity. This referred to the candidates of the extreme-left. Arlette Laguiller of *Lutte Ouvrière* and Alain Krivine of the *Ligue Communiste Révolutionnaire* as well as to potential candidates like Charles Piaget. The leaders of the CFDT had clearly decided to support François Mitterrand. Commenting on a meeting of the National Bureau held in April 1974. Edmond Maire stated that the CFDT intended to remain outside the process to choose a candidate, since this was a function of political parties; however the CFDT hoped that the political parties of the Left would choose a candidate who would win. Edmond Maire added, 'if the parties were to choose François Mitterrand, and if he represented all the forces of the Left, and not just those associated with the Common Programme of Government, then the CFDT would support him enthusiastically'. It is true that the CFDT did not participate in the decision to choose the candidate, but it obviously made an effort to be part of the wider political debate surrounding the choice of candidate. In this respect, the CFDT was clearly straying into the political sphere, in spite of its former statements to the contrary. The National Council of the CFDT met the following week and voted overwhelmingly to support the candidate of the Left,[22] claiming that he was the candidate which represented the entire Left, the supporters of workers' control and of the Common Programme of Government. Whilst the CGT was anxious to attempt to tie François Mitterrand into a commitment to the Common Programme of Government, the CFDT was anxious to tie him into a commitment to its own definition of workers' control. After the first round, the Executive Commission published a statement, congratulating François Mitterrand, criticising the Right and calling on those voters who had voted for him at the first round to do so at the second.[23]

As for campaigning, Albert Detraz claimed that the CFDT did very little, since it had been caught unawares by the sudden death of Georges Pompidou.[24] However, available evidence does not corroborate this statement. The National Council of the CFDT called on different CFDT organisations to show that they were committed to the success of the Left. It put out a special issue of *CFDT Syndicalisme* and other forms of propaganda.[25] In its internal newsletter, the Metalworkers Union of the CFDT called on its organisations to step up the campaign for the victory of François Mitterrand. Furthermore, the 34th conference of the CFDT-Metalworkers Union was postponed from April to November 1974 because it was expected that activists would have been busy during the election campaign.[26] In an article in *CFDT Syndicalisme* after the election, it was stated that there had been a 'clear and massive commitment' by CFDT activists to the campaign for the Presidential election.[27] In nearly all the different national unions and regions, a large number of initiatives had been taken. More than a million tracts, leaflets and posters had been distributed. Meetings and press conferences had been organised with the participation of the leaders of the CFDT; on 13 May in Toulouse, Chambéry, Annecy, Creil; on 14 May in Nice, Cannes, Marseille, Clermont-Ferrand, Pau, Bayonne; and on 15 May in Avignon, Bordeaux. In the Pays-de-Loire the regional committee asked the individual unions to write to all their members. In Lyon on 15 May there was a large rally attended by representatives of the CFDT and the other unions the CGT and the FEN, and also the political parties of the Union of the Left, the PCF, PS, MRG, as well as the PSU. According to Edmond Maire, nearly 80 per cent of CFDT members took part in this election campaign.[28]

In 1974 the CGT and the CFDT were themselves on the crest of an 'entente' wave and between the two rounds of the election they made a joint appeal on behalf of François Mitterrand who, it was claimed, would provide an opportunity for 'the negotiation and the satisfaction of the most urgent industrial demands in terms of wages, employment, working conditions, trade union rights and progressive economic reforms'.[29] The desire to beat the Right was so great that the two trade union confederations were prepared to come together and gloss over some of their major ideological and policy differences, concerning democratic management and workers' control, attitudes to the Common Programme of Government, wage differentials and the nationalisation programme. A few days later, the CGT and the CFDT issued another joint statement in support of François Mitterrand, this time in conjunction with the teachers' union FEN, and a third was issued on the eve of the second ballot.[30]

It is interesting to note certain developments in the nature of trade union support from 1973 to 1974. The CGT had become an enthusiastic supporter of the candidate of the Union of the Left, François Mitterrand, the representative of the Socialist Party, even though he had an ambiguous relationship with the centrepiece of the CGT's political strategy, the Common Programme of Government. This mirrored the position taken by the French Communist Party. More remarkable was the way in which the CFDT became a wholehearted supporter of the candidate of the Union of the Left. There were many reasons for this. The presidential elections were more important than the legislative elections – the stakes were that much greater; the prize worth that much more.[31] For the leadership of the CFDT, it was essential at that stage not to be confined to the sidelines of the political sphere. Jacques Moreau, one of the leaders of the CFDT at the time, put it in somewhat different terms:

we were stuck, regardless of our views on the Common Programme of Government. The PSU had lost its vitality and was a drain on us. We had the same objective as Mitterrand: the desire to reduce the influence of the PCF with the working class. We could not remain absent from the fray any longer (Hamon, & Rotman, 1982, p. 272–73).

However, this does not explain the intensity of support provided by the CFDT and its readiness to campaign. The prospect of the candidate of the Left winning spurred on the leaders of the CFDT, as can be seen from the comments made by Edmond Maire in an interview in *Nouvel Observateur:* 'another element was also important . . . the chances for winning were greater than ever . . . and as the result was going to be close, we had a particular responsibility . . . our involvement could have been one of the factors ensuring this success'.[32] Any caution was thrown to the wind:

Quickly, that was the key. Quickly, because the power relationship with the Communists had never been so good. Quickly, because François Mitterrand . . . rallying the forces of the Left had not opposed the return of certain prodigal sons. Quickly, because the dynamics of the Presidential election . . . made it possible to brush aside the manifold and contradictory fears of activists who were used to splitting hairs. (Hamon, & Rotman, 1982, p. 274).

The CFDT's enthusiastic electoral support can also be explained by the issue of trade union rivalry. The victory of the candidate of the Left would make the Socialist Party more influential and this would contribute to making the CFDT a more important counterbalance to the CGT (Hincker, 1981, p. 190). Clearly the CFDT was beginning the process of alignment with the Socialist Party which was to culminate later that year with the *Assises du Socialisme*.

The legislative elections 1978

As was seen in the previous chapter, the political environment changed quite dramatically from 1974 to 1978. The unity of the Left was shattered and the political parties of the Left went into the elections with separate sets of policy proposals on certain issues and no agreement on common candidates. Only the PS and the MRG agreed on an electoral alliance, ensuring that they would not both field candidates in the same constituencies at the first round of the elections. According to the figures published by *Le Monde,* the PCF obtained 5,787,436 votes (20.62 per cent), the PS and MRG combined 6,964,449 (24.81 per cent), whereas the government majority obtained 12,970,840 (46.21 per cent). The leaders of the three parties met the day after the first round of the elections and, instead of renegotiating the Common Programme of Government so as to provide a solid programmatic base for the Left's electoral objectives, the parties agreed on a joint declaration advocating withdrawal in each constituency of all but the leading candidate on the Left, so that an overall optimal result could be obtained.[33] At the second round the political parties of the Left won 48.5 per cent of the total votes cast and the political parties of the Right won 51.5 per cent. The contest was less close in terms of seats; the PCF won 86, the PS 104 and the MRG 10, a total of 201, whereas the Right won 290 seats giving them an unassailable majority within the National Assembly.

The elections provided the focus for the rivalry between the political parties of the Left. The response of the trade union confederations to the 1978 legislative elections was conditioned by their position as regards the renegotiation of the Common Programme of Government. As has been seen in the previous chapter, the statements issued by the Confederal Bureau meeting at the end of September 1977,[34] and the Executive Commission meeting at the beginning of October 1977,[35] coupled with the campaign 'long live the Common Programme', underlined the alignment of the CGT to the position taken by the PCF. According to Georges Séguy, workers wanted to beat the Right at the elections, but that this should not be done at any cost. The conditions of the Common Programme of Government must be right.[36] The CGT met with the parties of the Left in mid–December 1977. According to the statement issued afterwards, the meeting with the PCF demonstrated that the two organisations had convergent proposals, but the meeting with the PS underlined serious divergences in certain key areas.[37] However, in terms of official and direct participation in the electoral process, the CGT remained uncharacteristically coy. The Confederal Bureau stated that it did not intend to give any recommendations regarding which political party to vote for, though it did give an indirect recommendation. Workers were to vote in terms of their class interests,[38] which was another clear nod in the direction of the Communist Party. Equally a statement from the Executive Commission indicated a choice, if only by association, by criticising the Socialist Party's position on the Common Programme of Government.[39] This approach was replicated by national unions, for example the Metalworkers Union.[40]

Just before the first round of the elections, Georges Séguy criticised the PS yet again but gave no further recommendation as to voting preference. He did however insist on the need to participate in the elections.[41] The electoral pact agreed upon by the political parties of the Left after the first round of the elections was warmly greeted by the CGT,[42] which was an indication of the latter's desperation, since only a few months earlier Georges Séguy had stated, 'if the Union of the Left was to be reduced to a simple electoral pact, we would not campaign for it in the way we have campaigned for the Common Programme of Government'.[43] However the electoral pact and the semblance of unity on the Left was sufficient for the Confederal Bureau to issue a statement on 14 March calling on workers to vote for the joint candidates of the Left,[44] meaning the candidates of the Socialist Party as well as those of the French Communist Party. In its analysis of the results of the 1978 legislative elections, the Executive Commission of the CGT claimed that it would have been better if the political parties of the Left had agreed on a joint manifesto containing ambitious social objectives and reforms of economic and democratic structures.[45] In his opening speech to a meeting of the National Confederal Committee just after the elections, Georges Séguy bemoaned the disunity of the Left, but placed the blame for this on the Socialist Party: 'those politicians on the Left who thought they could obtain some electoral advantage by flattering reformist illusions as a result of extracting the class-based aspects of the Common Programme of Government committed a grave error'.[46]

In terms of campaigning, the CGT's strategy changed quite markedly from that adopted in the previous elections. As a confederation, it did not formally campaign at all. However, as was seen in the previous chapter, its campaigning activities centred on its version of the Common Programme of Government, which in turn provided vicarious support for the PCF. Communists in the CGT, Georges Frischmann, André Sainjon, Michel Warcholak, Georges Lanoue and René Le Guen, did of course campaign for the PCF.[47] The most spectacular example of CGT involvement in the campaign was provided by Georges Séguy, who took the platform at a PCF meeting in Gentilly on 7 February 1978, along with Georges Marchais. The former explained that, 'the only way open to workers to exert a real impact on major decisions is to vote on 12 March for the candidates of the French Communist Party'.[48] Although Georges Séguy claimed to be intervening as an individual member of the PCF, this claim was disingenuous since he could not be disassociated from his position as General Secretary of the CGT.

Despite its new official stance of aloofness, the CFDT became involved in the election campaign. At the time when the CFDT was advocating a change of strategy and a return to an emphasis on the industrial sphere, the headline on the front page of *CFDT Syndicalisme* was proclaiming, 'Yes, a left-wing alternative is still possible'.[49] Speaking over a year later at the CFDT's 38th conference in Brest, Edmond Maire explained that 'all of us were counting on the legislative elections to solve our problems in the industrial sphere'.[50] In an unconvincing attempt to distance itself from the now defunct Union of the Left the National Council resurrected the notion of the 'Union of Popular Forces'. It stated that CFDT organisations, activists and members would do everything they could, both at the first and the second rounds, for the victory of the 'Union of Popular Forces'.[51] In real terms, this amounted to the parties of the Union of the Left, since, according to a statement made by the National Bureau two weeks later, this 'Union' did not include the candidates of the extreme-left or of the ecologist and regionalist groups who were not prepared to withdraw at the second round of the elections and give up their places to the candidate of the Left in the best position to beat the candidate of the Right.[52] The week before the elections, the headline on the front page of *CFDT Syndicalisme* exclaimed, '12th March – Make victory possible'. For the CFDT, this victory would mean better wages, better working conditions, new rights and new powers; this was the indispensable step on the way to workers' control.[53] After the first round of the elections, the CFDT urged its members to, 'assure the victory of the Left' and called on all its members to campaign to secure this victory. However the CFDT never actually explained what this campaign would entail. The message was relayed in part at least throughout the structures of the CFDT: some *départements*, such as Loire-Atlantique,[54] and some branches,[55] called on their members to vote for the candidate of the Left. At the second round the CFDT called on its members to overcome their reticence and vote for the candidates of the Left.[56] This would include the candidates of the PCF, which had been recently criticised by the CFDT. After the second round, the National Bureau met on 21 March to analyse the election results and to decide confederal strategy for the future. Both political parties were criticised. Extra criticism was reserved for the PCF which was considered responsible for breaking up the Union of the Left. The PCF had not hesitated 'to assassinate the hope' of victory.[57] In its report to the next National Council meeting, the National Bureau recommended that the CFDT should have nothing to do with the 1981 presidential elections.[58]

The two major trade union confederations, the CGT and CFDT, were put into a difficult position by the inability or the unwillingness of the political parties to agree on a common front in September 1977. They had been drawn into the political debate surrounding the Common Programme of Government and the elections, which posed no major problem until the political parties started to disagree. Both confederations were more reticent in supporting the candidates of the parties of the Left at these 1978 legislative elections than they had been in 1974, when harmony on the Left reigned. In 1978 the trade union confederations found themselves taking opposing sides in this particular debate, the CGT on the side of the PCF and the CFDT on the side of the PS, thus compromising their claims to trade union autonomy and also undermining the foundations of trade union unity. Unlike their British counterparts, French trade unions were less enthusiastic about providing political parties with practical support at election times. Nevertheless, there was a fluctuating level of support, which was itself conditioned by a number of features. Firstly, practical support was only given once the confederations had already committed themselves to a certain level of declaratory support; hence the relative ambivalence of the CFDT's campaign at the time of the 1973 legislative elections. Secondly, practical support was at its greatest level when the political parties of the Left were united on their choice of candidate. In 1974 it was possible to support the Left in general, without overtly and explicitly favouring one party or another. When the Union of the Left split in 1977, the trade union confederations were faced wih a considerable dilemma. Both resolved the problem by ritualistically calling for the victory of the Left, but for a Left which no longer existed, so campaigning was more or less neglected. For the most part the trade confederations did not campaign overtly for individual political parties, but they nevertheless made their preferences known obliquely.

Trade unions and voting behaviour

Both major trade union confederations participated in the electoral process during the 1970s, but it remains to be seen whether their activities had any impact on voting behaviour? Trade union membership is only one of the factors of political socialisation that may shape voting behaviour, and political socialisation is only one of the factors which may condition voter preference. Thus any attempt to establish a direct relationship between trade union membership and voting behaviour must be undertaken carefully. Commenting on the British situation. Butler and Stokes indicated the problem of isolating this one particular variable. Nevertheless, they warned of the need 'not to attribute to the union's persuasiveness political allegiances which are actually formed from perceptions of the norms and interests of a class' (Butler, & Stokes, 1971, p. 190). They claim however that there was a clear correlation between trade union membership and voting for the Labour Party, even if this link is becoming increasingly tenuous.[59] Writing more recently, Franklin has claimed that union membership is one of the variables accounting for class voting. However, with the switch to issue voting, 'supportive variables which used to reinforce the central influences are now essentially propping up a structure that has lost its backbone' (Franklin, 1985, p. 125). Few French electoral surveys have considered trade union membership as a variable conditioning voting behaviour. This could be explained by the fact that union membership density is relatively low in France, so penetration into the working population is not highly developed. Moreover trade union pluralism makes it difficult to arrive at a representative sample. In order to attempt to establish a link between trade union membership and voting behaviour in France during the period of the Union of the Left, it is proposed to make use of available political geography material and opinion poll data.

Political geography has occupied pride of place in the development of political science in France, partly as a result of the pioneering work of André Siegfried and partly because of its mathematical potential for 'scientific' exactitude. In the literature, three major surveys have attempted to establish a geographical correlation between trade union membership and voter preference. They have all referred to periods earlier than the 1970s and have all encountered major methodological problems. In his study of trade unionism at the time of the Popular Front, Prost attempts to assess the level of support for the different trade unions on the basis of the number of conference delegates per geographical area. This then can be readily compared with support for the different political parties on the basis of election results. However, on his own admission, this approach is fraught with difficulties, and his conclusions are notoriously difficult to interpret (Prost, 1964, pp. 23, 163–74). A second study defined trade union support in terms of the results of 'social' elections – elections to health service boards. These results were then compared with those of legislative elections. This study was carried out at the beginning of the 1950s, and one obvious weakness immediately springs to mind. FO had only just been established, in 1947–48, and so had been slow to organise officially, which helps to explain its poor showing. The author noted other methodological problems. Abstentions for 'social' elections were far greater than for the legislative elections of 1946 and 1951, thus impeding comparability. There was also no data on the campaigns for 'social' elections (Goguel, 1953, p. 246–71). The third survey was carried out by Adam, who also attempted to compare the results of 'social' and legislative elections. He concluded that his study only provided an approximate explanation of the correlation between support for trade unions and for political parties. Aggregate figures based on the *département* masked the substantial differences that may have existed at the local level. Workplaces, where 'social' elections took place, did not always coincide with constituencies, the basis for the legislative elections, particularly in urban areas. Although he found considerable areas of convergence between the level of representation of the PCF and the CGT, there were also areas of major divergence. What is more, it was not possible to establish a meaningful level of convergence between other trade union confederations and political parties (Adam, 1964, pp. 165–71).

Table 3.1 Results of the 1st round of the 1973 and 1978 legislative elections in St-Pierre des Corps

	1973			1978	
Longuet	(PCF)	45.2%	Vigier	(PCF)	46.3%
Lussault	(PS)	18.9%	Lussault	(PS)	21.7%
Royer	(ind)	28.3%	Royer	(UDF)	24.5%
Others		7.6%	Others		7.5%
Total		100.0%			100.0%

Source: Mairie de St-Pierre des Corps

No survey relating to the period of the Union of the Left has been undertaken. Reliable local union membership figures were not available and in the 1970s there were no 'social' elections like the ones used previously and subsequently. The new version of health board elections did not reappear until the 1980s and the elections to industrial tribunals did not start until 1979. Mindful of the recommendation made by Prost and Goguel that local monographs were needed for a clearer interpretation of more global data, the author undertook a survey of St-Pierre des Corps, a small town adjacent to Tours.[60] Its attraction for this methodological approach lies in the fact that it was a one-industry town (the major employer was the railways), and so the SNCF workplace elections would provide a relatively faithful representation of trade union support. Moreover there was a greater chance that the same individuals would be participating in both 'social' and legislative elections. As Table 3.1 shows, support for the PCF was constantly high in the 1973 and 1978 legislative elections, in spite of the fact that there was a change of candidate. Equally, as can be seen from Table 3.2, the CGT consistently obtained a high poll in the elections for the SNCF equivalent of the works committee, the *comité mixte*.

Table 3.2 Results of the 1973 and 1978 elections for the works committee *(comite mixte)* of the SNCF Depot in St-Pierre des Corps (%)

	1972	1978
CGT	51.0	49.8
CFDT	29.5	33.5
FO	8.4	8.2
CFTC	0.8	–
FGAAC[61]	10.3	8.5
Total	100.0	

Source: Confédération Générale du Travail, Tours

These results are certainly not coincidental, and this is something which could have been intuitively expected. There is a correlation between voting for the CGT in 'social' elections and for the PCF in legislative elections, but it is not possible to determine a causal relationship between the two. St-Pierre-des-Corps is a working class town, and it is clear that class played a determining role in voter preference. However, it is not possible to disentangle these different variables. Moreover, it is not clear how these particular figures can be interpreted to provide information about the PS and the CFDT. The similar increase in support for the PS and the CFDT during this period does not permit us to establish a causal relationship on the basis of this figures. Political geography provides some interesting pointers, but the methodological weakness inherent in this approach makes it impossible to come up with any conclusive evidence as to the impact of trade union membership upon voting behaviour.

Opinion polls provided more useful data. However, although many opinion polls were conducted during the 1970s on the question of voter preference, most of them failed to consider trade union membership as a variable in voting behaviour, an omission which would be inconceivable in Britain. There are five notable exceptions.[62] When interpreting them, care must be taken, since they were carried out by different organisations with different sampling and compensation techniques: the three which appeared in the *Nouvel Observateur* were conducted by Sofres and were post-election surveys. The other two surveys investigated voters' intentions and were conducted by IFOP and Louis-Harris.

As can be seen from Table 3.3, union members are more likely to vote for the political parties of the Left than are non-union members. A very high proportion of CGT members (88 per cent) voted for the Left at the first round of the 1973 legislative elections, as did approximately two thirds of CFDT members. Over half of CGT members (58 per cent) voted for the PCF and just under a third of CFDT (30 per cent) voted for the PS. There are some further interesting points. Nearly a third of CGT members (29 per cent) voted for the PS. 11 per cent of CFDT members voted for the extreme-left. Just over a quarter of CFDT members (27 per cent) voted for the government majority and a surprisingly large number (21 per cent) voted for the PCF. As a parenthesis it is worth noting the difference in voting behaviour between CFDT members and activists. A straw poll taken at the 36th conference after the 1973 legislative elections showed that of the 1,170 delegates who responded, 587 (50 per cent) voted for the PS – a considerable increase on ordinary members, while only 16 voted for the PCF – a sizeable reduction. A total of 147 (12.5 per cent) voted for the PSU, a figure which would correspond quite well to this particular opinion poll sample.[63] The final interesting point to emanate from Table 3.3 is that at this time more members of the 'reformist' FO voted for the Left than did CFDT members. More voted for the PS, and, in spite of official emnity directed towards the communists, 20 per cent of them voted for the PCF.

Table 3.4 demonstrates the high level of potential support for François Mitterrand from CGT members (82 per cent) (and also from the FEN) at the time of the 1974 Presidential elections. Here again support from CFDT members was less pronounced, with just over half of them (54 per cent) intending to vote for François Mitterrand. This nevertheless represented a significant change in relative terms – this was more than the proportion of FO members who intended to vote for the candidate of the Left (48 per cent). The number of CFDT members who were prepared to vote for the candidates of the extreme-left was very low (4 per cent) which can be explained by the fact that the PSU did not put up a candidate on this particular occasion, and by the fact that the

Table 3.3 Voting preference according to trade union membership 1st round, 1973 legislative elections (%)

	CGT	CFDT	FO	Other	Non-union members	Total members
Socialist Party	29	30	43	23	20	24
Communist Party	58	21	20	21	23	30
Extreme Left	1	11	3	4	4	4
Centre	3	6	5	16	14	11
Gov. Majority	6	27	23	31	36	28
Other Right	3	5	6	5	3	3
Total	100	100	100	100	100	100
Total Left	88	62	66	48	47	58

Source: *Nouvel Observateur*, 28 May, 1973, p. 51.

Table 3.4 Voting intentions according to trade union membership 1st round, 1974 Presidential election (%)

	CGT	CFDT	FO	FEN	CGC	Total union members	Total electorate
MITTERRAND	82	54	48	75	20	58	41
Extreme Left	3	4	1	2	–	2	1.5
GISCARD	4	23	26	14	50	19	26
CHABAN	7	13	19	2	23	14	23
ROYER	1	2	3	4	2	4	6
Others	3	4	3	3	4	3	2.5
Total	100	100	100	100	99	100	100
Total Left	85	58	49	77	20	60	42.5

Source: *Le Point*, 29 April, 1974, p. 64.

leadership of the CFDT campaigned actively if discreetly against extreme-left candidates. It is interesting to note that, in spite of recommendations from the CFDT leadership, over a third of CFDT members were still prepared to vote for the candidates of the Right. Table 3.5 underlines the high level of support for François Mitterrand at the second round of the Presidential elections amongst CGT members (90 per cent). It demonstrates a higher level of support for the candidate of the Left amongst CFDT members (73 per cent). The CFDT's election campaign of wholehearted support for François Mitterrand had paid off.

A part of the CFDT membership had responded to the exhortations of its leadership and voted for the Left: nevertheless a significant if declining minority still remained impervious to these overtures.

Table 3.5 Voting preference according to trade union membership 2nd round, 1974 presidential election (%)

	CGT	CFDT	FO	Others	Non-union members	Total employees
MITTERRAND	90	73	52	64	53	61
GISCARD	10	27	48	36	47	39
Total	100	100	100	100	100	100

Source: *Nouvel Observateur*, 10–16 June, 1974, p. 56.

Why did such a large proportion of CFDT members refuse to heed the call of their leaders to vote for the candidate of the Left? This can be explained by the instrumentalism of some CFDT members and their relative distance from the mainstream of trade union activities. It has been shown that only a minority of members were likely to read the confederal publications, the weekly *CFDT Syndicalisme* and the monthly *CFDT Magazine*, although more would read the broadsheets published by various national unions (Verdier, *et al*, 1981, p. 14, 23–25). Writing at the end of the 1960s, Adam *et al* showed that 88 per cent of CFDT members had never put up posters, 58 per cent had never collected union subscriptions, 53 per cent had never been on a picket-line, and 58 per cent had never participated in any delegation to see the employer. The overwhelming majority had not held office, 77 per cent of CFDT members had however, participated in discussions with workmates about the contents of tracts, yet 36 per cent of CFDT members had not been to a trade union meeting for six months or more (Adam, *et al*, 1970, pp. 137–39). In addition, wider political forces were also at work. Adam *et al* also showed that at the end of the 1960s only a minority of CFDT members placed themselves on the Left on a left-centre-right spectrum. Indeed it was only at the 35th conference held in 1970 that the CFDT espoused the notion of workers' control and even then with differing levels of enthusiasm. It would have taken some time for this major change in CFDT ideology to percolate down into the whole of the organisation. Another factor was almost certainly significant for CFDT members' political socialisation, the influence of religion. Adam *et al* have shown that a majority of members were regular church-goers, in spite of the fact that the CFDT had become formally 'deconfessionalised' in 1964. It has also been shown that there was no better variable than religion for distinguishing the Left from the Right. According to Michelat and Simon, 'our data lead us to recognise that catholicism has played a key historical role in the organisation and consolidation of a system of images, perceptions and sentiments which lead to the exclusion of the Left (and in particular the Communist Left) from the universe of legitimate political options' (Michelat & Simon, 1977, p. 171). The CFDT's Catholic heritage tended to militate against any close and total identification of all its members with the political Left.

Table 3.6 Voting intentions according to trade union membership 1st round, 1978 legislative elections (%)

	CGT	CFDT
Socialist Party	31	54
Communist Party	47	6
PSU/Extreme-left	4	6
MRG	3	3
Ecologists	2	7
CDS	–	3
PR	3	11
RPR	2	1
No reply	8	9
Total	100	100
Total left	85	69

Source: Le Matin, 27–28 October, 1977.

Table 3.6 demonstrates the relatively high level of potential support amongst both CGT and CFDT members for the parties of the Left in the run-up to the 1978 legislative elections. The CGT figure is consistently high overall. A high proportion of CGT members intended to vote for the PCF, but it is interesting to note that at this time the Socialist Party was becoming more popular with CGT members. The large number of CFDT members (54 per cent) who were prepared to vote for the PS is especially worth noting, and this would suggest that the CFDT rank and file were beginning to respond to the clear pro-Socialist alignment of their leaders.

Voting intentions changed markedly. As Table 3.7 shows, support for the PCF amongst CGT members revived sharply, whilst support for the PS remained more or less constant. Although support amongst CFDT

Table 3.7 Voting preference according to trade union membership 1st round, 1978 legislative elections (%)

	CGT	CFDT
Socialist Party	28	36
Communist Party	63	19
Other left	–	15
Total Right	9	26
Total	100	96(?)

Source: *Nouvel Observateur*, 23–30 April, 1978, p. 61.

members for the PS was marginally up on 1973, it had nevertheless fallen considerably over the previous six months. How can these changes in electoral support from October 1977 to April 1978 be explained? Firstly, the survey in Table 3.6 was undertaken early in the campaign before firm decisions about voting intentions had been taken, and so its results need to be interpreted with care. There was ample time for interviewees to change their minds. Secondly, the intervention of Georges Séguy at Gentilly and the oblique campaign in favour of the PCF encouraged CGT members to rally to the French Communist Party. Finally, the minimalist position of the PS on issues such as the nationalisation programme would have lost it support with CGT members. Indeed the PS may have lost support amongst all trade union members because of its initial unwillingness to agree to a number of employment-related issues, (for example, the minimum legal wage).

During the period of the Union of the Left it is clear that trade union members were more likely to vote for the political parties of the Left than other employees: this is especially true for CGT members who were more likely to vote for the Left than other trade unionists. As for CFDT members, their support for the Left in general increased markedly during this period, whilst their support for the PS increased marginally. Members of the trade union confederations thus demonstrated differing patterns of party allegiance. The communist-dominated leadership of the CGT was relatively able to deliver its members' vote. There was fluctuating but overwhelming support amongst CGT members for the PCF. However, just over a quarter of all CGT members favoured the PS, which reflects the broad secular Left-wing traditions of the CGT. The CFDT leaders were less able to deliver the vote of their members. A large number of CFDT members voted for the PS, but it is interesting that many rejected a pattern of CFDT-PS alignment. Many members of the CFDT voted for the PSU in 1973 and groups like the ecologists in 1978, and in spite of the animosity between the CFDT and the PCF, a few of them were still prepared to vote communist. Moreover, a considerable minority voted consistently for the parties of the Right. A causal relationship between membership of a particular trade union and voting for a particular political party is at best difficult to prove. Self selection is clearly a significant phenomenon. As Butler and Stokes have remarked about the British situation, 'the factors which incline people to vote Labour can also incline them to join unions and that this self selection is deeply involved in the greater propensity of union members to vote Labour' (Butler & Stokes, 1971, p. 200). In the French case CGT members had a greater propensity to vote for the PCF, but it could also be argued that workers who voted for the PCF would have tended to join the CGT. Joining the CGT and voting PCF were mutually reinforcing political acts, but not exclusive ones, as the figures in these surveys show. Any correlation between the CFDT and the PS is more difficult to establish, due to the readiness of members of the CFDT to vote for the extreme-left and for the Right, and because the PS received support from members of other confederations (the CGT and FO).

Conclusions

Through a study of national elections in the 1970s it is clear that the CGT and of the CFDT readily became involved in the political sphere. They participated in the electoral process itself, not by putting up their own candidates but by providing support, both declaratory and material, for the political parties of the Union of the Left. Their positions regarding the Common Programme of Government provided further opportunities for vicarious participation in the electoral process. The CGT indicated its clear support for the Left in general, both at the legislative and Presidential elections in 1973 and 1974 respectively. After the breakdown of the renegotiations of the Common Programme of Government in the autumn of 1977, the CGT called for a victory of the Left at one level, but at another demonstrated its disaffection with one element of the erstwhile Union of the Left, the Socialist Party. Implicitly, the CGT supported the PCF, and on occasions this support became quite explicit. The CFDT offered a different perspective. It remained somewhat removed from the legislative elections in 1973, but by the time of the 1974 Presidential election, had become a fervent supporter of the candidacy and campaign of François Mitterrand. By the 1978 elections, it was attempting to extricate itself from the political sphere, but was nevertheless still calling, if less enthusiastically, on its members to vote for the Left, in spite of the latter's disunity. Although less overtly partisan than the CGT, it nevertheless managed to indicate its preferences, mainly by means of a campaign of criticism directed against the PCF.

The final concluding remark relates to the potential impact of the trade union confederations on voting behaviour. The evidence is unfortunately inconclusive. The limited data from political geography material and opinion polls show a correlation between being a member of one trade union confederation and voting for the Left in general. Two patterns of party-union alignment emerge. An absolute majority of CGT members voted for the PCF, and a relative majority of CFDT members voted for the PS. Trade union membership reinforced a tendency to vote for one particular political party, but it has not been possible to isolate this one single variable, trade union membership, and establish with certainty its own individual influence on voting behaviour.

Two further questions need examination. Firstly, why did the CGT side so clearly with the PCF after the break up of the Union of the Left and thus risk being so clearly compromised? Any explanations by the CGT leadership that it was not aligning with the PCF ring hollow. When the Left was united there was no specific need to align openly with one particular party, and claims of trade union autonomy did not need to be put to the test. Moreover, as it was thought at the beginning of the 1970s that the PCF would automatically become the senior partner in the Union of the Left, support for the Left in general would ensure support for the communist cause. When the Left was disunited, it was not possible to avoid taking sides. In addition, a further significant factor came into play. It was thought at this time that the PCF would be eclipsed by the PS in the 1978 legislative elections and, to avoid this, the PCF and its members were prepared to use all the means at their disposal. At an important political watershed such as this, the PCF members within the CGT were prepared to subordinate the industrial interests of their trade union confederation to the political objectives of their party. Even those communists in the CGT who saw themselves primarily as trade unionists first and political activists second were aware of the need to defend the interests of the party at certain crucial times. This was one of those times. It was not in the interests of the PCF members of the CGT to allow the PCF to be eclipsed by the PS, nor to allow the PS, with its potentially ambivalent position on certain aspects of macro-economic and industrial policy, to become the major force on the Left. Although a leading trade unionist, Georges Séguy was an important figure in the PCF and, at times of serious political crisis, was clearly prepared to defend the interests of the PCF and thus openly compromise the self-proclaimed autonomy of the CGT.

Secondly why did the CFDT rally so readily to the support of the Left at the time of the 1974 Presidential elections? Before 1974 the CFDT had been enthusiastic about participating more fully in the political sphere. With the decline of the PSU and the rapid growth of the PS, it became increasingly clear to the leadership of the CFDT that the PS was the most likely to succeed. Moreover this strategy could be attained under the cover of the different interpretations of the unity of the Left and so the CFDT did not have to identify formally with the PS as such. The death of Georges Pompidou merely served to hasten this process. This support for the PS is all the more interesting since, as has been seen in previous chapters, the CFDT did not formally support the Common Programme of Government and did not have in its upper echelons a large number of socialists who could have attempted to influence policy decisions within the confederation. It can only be assumed that the leadership of the CFDT took a conscious decision to use its influence within the political sphere to build up the non-communist left, and more specifically, the Socialist Party.

Notes

1. *Le Peuple*, 16–31 January, 1973, p. 2.
2. *Le Monde*, 6 March, 1973, p. 2.
3. *Vie Ouvrière*, 18 October, 1972.
4. *Le Métallo Nazairien*, February 1973.
5. *Le Peuple*, 16–28 February, 1973, p. 2.
6. *CFDT Syndicalisme*, 26 October, 1972.
7. *CFDT Syndicalisme*, 28 December, 1972, p. 1.
8. *CFDT Syndicalisme*, 1 February, 1973, p. 1.
9. *CFDT Syndicalisme*, 8 March, 1972, p. 1.
10. According to Verdier, R., *PS-PC une lutte pour l'entente*, Paris, Seghers, 1976, p. 283.
11. *L'Humanité*, 6 April, 1974.
12. *Vie Ouvrière*, 17 April, 1974.
13. *Vie Ouvrière*, 1 May, 1974, p. 31.
14. *Le Peuple*, 16–31 May, 1974, p.3.
15. *Vie Ouvrière*, 15 May, 1976, p. 1.
16. *Courrier Fédéral*, 26 April, 1974.
17. *Courrier Fédéral*, 10 May, 1974.
18. *Courrier Fédéral*, 19 April, 1974.
19. *Pour le succès du candidat commun de la gauche*, CGT Loire–Atlantique, *Le métallo nazairien*, April 1974.
20. For the details, see Hamon, H. & Rotman, P. *La deuxième gauche*, Paris, Ramsay, 1982, p. 272.

21. See statement by Edmond Maire, *CFDT Syndicalisme*, 11 April, 1974, p. 4.
22. *CFDT Syndicalisme*, 18 April, 1974, p. 3.
23. *CFDT Syndicalisme*, 9 May, 1974, p. 1.
24. Interview, Albert Detraz 12 July, 1983.
25. *CFDT Syndicalisme*, 18 April, 1974, p. 4.
26. *FGM–CFDT Bulletin du Responsable de Secteur d'Entreprise*, 10 May, 1974, 9/74. p. 1, 6.
27. *CFDT Syndicalisme*, 16 May, 1974, p. 8.
28. *Nouvel Observateur*, 3 June, 1974, p. 8.
29. *Vie Ouvrière*, 15 May, 1974, p. 4.
30. *Le Peuple*, 1–15 June, 1974, p. 28, p. 30.
31. Interview, Albert Detraz, 12 July, 1983.
32. *Nouvel Observateur*, 28 April, 1974, p. 43.
33. *Nouvel Observateur*, no 696b (special number) 16 March, 1978.
34. *Le Peuple*, 1–15 October, 1977, p. 2.
35. *Le Peuple*, 16–30 October, 1977, p.2.
36. *Le Peuple*, 1–15 December, 197, p. 33.
37. *Le Peuple*, 15–31 January, 1978, p. 3–4.
38. *Le Peuple*, 15–30 April, 1978, p. 44.
39. *Le Peuple*, 16–31 March, 1978, p. 2–3.
40. *Courrier Fédéral*, no. 502, 24 February, 1978.
41. *Vie Ouvrière*, 20 March, 1978, p. 13.
42. *L'Humanité*, 6 March, 1978.
43. *Le Peuple*, 15 December, 1977, p. 33. Hence perhaps the retrospective editorial by R. Telliez 'La CGT et l'accord de 13 mars', *Vie Ouvrière*, 3–9 April, 1978, p. 12.
44. *Vie Ouvrière*, 3–9 April, 1978, p. 14.
45. *Le Peuple*, 5–6 April, 1978, p. 2.
46. *Le Peuple*, 15–30 April, 1978, p. 4.
47. *L'Humanité de Dimanche*, 11–17 January, 1978.
48. *Le Monde*, 10 February, 1978, p. 7. In an interview (11 April, 1984). Georges Séguy claimed that this appeared more noticeable because it had not happened before. However he had planned at a previous election to make a similar speech but was unable to do so because of family problems.
49. *CFDT Syndicalisme*, 19 January, 1978, p. 1.
50. *Le Monde*, 11 May, 1979.
51. *CFDT Syndicalisme*, 2 February, 1978, p. 2–3.
52. *CFDT Syndicalisme*, 16 February, 1978, p. 5.
53. *CFDT Syndicalisme*, 9 March, 1978, p. 1.
54. Interview, Bernard Henry 16 March, 1987.
55. Tract, CFDT–Neyrpic–Neyrtec, 16 March, 1978.
56. *CFDT Syndicalisme*, 16 March, 1978, p. 1.
57. *CFDT Syndicalisme*, 23 March, 1978, p. 2.
58. *CFDT Syndicalisme*, 13 April, 1978, p. 9.
59. See article by Ivor Crewe in *The Guardian*, 10 June, 1983. Also Ranney, A. (ed) *Britain at the polls* 1983. Duke University Press, 1985, p. 171. Also Butler, D. & Kavanagh, D., *The British general election of 1987*, London, Macmillan, 1988, p. 275.

60. I am grateful to René Mouriaux for suggesting this particular town.
61. FGAAC = *Fédération Générale Autonome des Agents de Conduite*. For details about the unionisation of the SNCF, see Ribeill, G., *Les cheminots*, Paris, Editions La Découverte, 1984.
62. In *Nouvel Observateur*, 28 May 1973, p. 51. *Le Point*, 29 April 1974, p. 64. *Nouvel Observateur*, 10–16 June 1974, p. 56. *Le Matin*, 27–28 October 1977, *Nouvel Observateur*, 23–30 April 1978, p. 61.
63. *CFDT Syndicalisme*, 7 June 1973, p. 4.

Chapter 4

The Consequences of Party–Union Relations for Inter-Confederal Unity: CGT–CFDT

It has been shown that functional division between trade union confederations and the political parties of the Union of the Left has on occasions been difficult to sustain in practice. Whilst the political parties, and particularly the French Communist Party, have attempted to intervene in the industrial sphere, the trade union confederations have themselves shown little compunction in participating in the political sphere and playing a significant role in the debate over the parties' manifesto, the Common Programme of Government, and in the different election campaigns. There will now be a switch in emphasis, and in the next two chapters it is proposed to examine the politics of French trade unionism in order to investigate the extent to which inter-confederal and intra-confederal relations can be explained in terms of the demands of the political sphere. As Georges Séguy explained in a speech to the 38th conference of the CGT held in April 1972 – 'it is well known that mention of unity in the trade union world cannot, in a country like our own, be separated from the questions of unity in the political world and more specifically from the unity of the Left'.[1]

The study of inter-confederal relations is central to any understanding of French industrial relations. Whilst French trade union confederations are in competition for members and for influence in the industrial sphere they are drawn together in order to maximise their impact: in short, they are locked into a framework of conflictual unity. Throughout French labour history trade union solidarity has waxed, and more often waned, but by the beginning of the 1970s both the CGT and the CFDT were calling for trade union unity of action, which, according to the CGT would make it possible, 'to be successful in defending the industrial claims of the workers and to open up the way for decisive changes',[2] and which, according to the CFDT, would, 'make the working classes more effective as a result'.[3] Unity is strength, as the oft declaimed trade union maxim would have it. In practice in the 1970s this meant CGT–CFDT unity of action (with occasional support from the teachers' union FEN), since neither trade union confederation was able to come to an agreement with *Force Ouvrière*. FO had been set up in 1947–48 as a reaction to the increase in Communist Party influence within the reunited CGT, and subsequent relations between the CGT and FO had been particularly stormy. The CGT claimed to have made some unsuccessful attempts at achieving an agreement (Adam, 1967, p. 588–89), but subsequently treated FO to a torrent of abuse, characterised by this statement from its 1972 conference: 'the leadership of FO continues to reflect a blinkered and sectarian intransigence with regard to the establishing of contacts with the CGT. Its attitude to trade union unity of action is years and years out of date' (a reference to the decision by some non-communists to leave the CGT and set up a new trade union confederation FO).[4] After it formally severed its links in 1964 with its Catholic origins, the CFDT might have achieved some sort of agreement with the strictly secular FO, but this did not occur. Eugène Descamps, the former leader of the CFDT, explained in his memoirs that he had wanted the CFDT to join up with FO and in this way provide a real counterbalance to the CGT (Descamps, 1971, p. 103–4), but this strategy did not meet with success. Moreover, the decision taken by the CFDT at its 35th national conference in 1970 to espouse a class-based analysis of society only served to distance it from the 'reformist' FO and to bring it closer to the CGT. This chapter aims to establish a comprehensive pattern of relations between the two major trade union confederations. The first sections analyses the political and non-political factors which fashioned the relationship between the CGT and the CFDT. This relationship was not static but a fluctuating and dynamic process, and the second section examines the nature of the relationship that developed between the CGT and the CFDT during the period of the Union of the Left.

Factors conditioning CGT–CFDT relations

Rand Smith is one of the few observers, whether in the English– or French–speaking world, to have considered the issue of inter-confederal relations. He noted that two mutually self-reinforcing variables conditioned French trade union unity of action: in the political sphere, the state of relations between the political parties of the Left, the socialists and the communists; in the industrial sphere, labour market demands, and more specifically levels of unemployment. As regards the former, he put forward the idea that 'trade unions are affected directly by political pressures emanating from the Communist and Socialist parties. A kind of bandwagon effect is created, as unity between political parties stimulates cooperation between trade unions' (Rand Smith, 1981, p. 41). It is not however clear how this process would develop. Whilst it is possible to agree with his statement that 'pressures on the CGT, given its ties to the PCF, are evident enough', it is worth reiterating the point that these pressures were not always coherent and effective. He rightly pointed out that the CFDT and the PS came closer together during this period, but he did not explain how this should in itself encourage trade union party of action, since it was known that the CFDT was not in thrall to the PS.

Events in the political sphere had a clear impact on trade union unity of action. Political parties of the Left were not indifferent to the question of trade union unity. Landier has argued that a trade union of unity would benefit the PCF because of the relative strength of the CGT and its 'privileged' relationship with the PCF. (Landier, 1981, p. 215). Equally, it could be argued that the PS would also benefit from the fact that trade union rapprochement would reduce the level of factionalism within its own ranks. Moreover, given that its members were to be found in all confederations it could expect to have an impact on this process of rapprochement. However, in the 1970s the PS was unwilling or unable to play this role. The leaders of the PS were anxious not to alienate their supporters in each confederation and therefore fought shy of any overt interference in trade union affairs. On the occasion of one particular dispute between trade union considerations over industrial strategy, François Mitterrand was careful not to be drawn into the fray.[5] The two confederations disagreed constantly about the impact of events on party–union relations. The CFDT regularly taunted the CGT about its relationship with the PCF. According to Edmond Maire, 'there was a permanent coincidence between the positions taken by the CGT and by the PCF'[6] – a point vigorously denied by Georges Séguy. These charges were a source of irritation for the CGT, and resulted in the counter charge that close links existed between the CFDT and the PS.[7] Trade union unity of action was affected by other political factors, for example the activities of the political parties of the Right, particularly when in government. The introduction of new-style public sector bargaining agreements in the late 1960s and early 1970s met with a varied response from the trade union movement (Dubois, 1974), and the beginning of the 1970s successive governments were more interested in coming to some form of arrangement with the 'reformist' trade union confederations, a strategy which resulted in the CGT and the CFDT being thrust together. Writing in 1974, Roy considered that this form of government action had provided the 'cement' for trade union unity of action.[8] This 'cement' was to harden in 1976 with the introduction by Prime Minister Raymond Barre of an austerity programme which aimed to reduce aggregate demand and to limit wage increases in the public and private sectors.

Trade union unity of action was also affected by the international environment, itself influenced by numerous political factors. Both trade union confederations were and still are in different international union organisations. The CGT was a member of the World Federation of Trade Unions (WFTU), which was normally but not exclusively identified with the countries of Eastern Europe. The CFDT, on the other hand, joined the European Section of the International Confederation of Free Trade Unions (ICFTU), the European Trade Union Confederation (ETUC), in 1974. The CGT has attempted to become a member of the ETUC, but without any success (Mouriaux, 1984, p. 219–23). International events had little direct impact on trade union unity of action during the major part of the 1970s. There was one exception, known as the 'Republica affair': after the revolution in Portugal, a Socialist newspaper was closed down by Communist workers who were opposed to its editorial line. This was a source of disagreement between the PCF and the PS, and also between the CGT and the CFDT, with the CGT supporting the anti-Socialist line taken by the PCF.[9] However, at the end of the 1970s and the beginning of the 1980s, two sets of international events with obvious political overtones were to cause major clashes between the PCF and the PS, and the CGT and the CFDT; the Soviet invasion of Afghanistan and the birth of the Polish trade union Solidarity. Indeed for Moss, it was the disagreement over the Soviet invasion of Afghanistan which led to the formal break-up of trade union unity of action (Kesselman & Groux, 1984, p. 290).

Whilst events in the political sphere had an impact on trade union unity of action, it would be unwise to presume that trade union confederations were idle bystanders. A climate of unity permeated the French Left during the 1970s, and the trade union confederations contributed to its creation. As Georges Séguy explained, 'progress on trade union unity paved the way for the positive evolution of political unity and vice versa'.[10] Moreover this climate did not emanate solely from union headquarters – grass-roots opinion was also favourable to trade union unity of action, according to both Georges Séguy and Eugène Descamps.[11] The CGT and the CFDT underwent an ideological rapprochement. Trade union confederations in France have been established or have split as a result of ideological differences. It was the socialism of the CGT that prompted the creation of the CFTC in 1919, and it was the communism of the CGT that prompted the creation of FO in 1948. However, in the 1960s and 1970s the ideological gap between the CGT and the CFDT narrowed considerably. As previously mentioned, the CFDT (or CFTC as it still was then) formally renounced its Catholic origins in 1964. In 1970 it took another step in the direction of the CGT when it voted to embrace a class-based analysis of society. This decision was received rapturously by the CGT: 'more important than the differences and divergences that exist, this step is the one which is the central element of the CFDT conference. It removes the obstacles on the road to unity and establishes more favourable conditions for industrial demands and the struggle for fundamental change'. This euphoria was not to last. Whilst the CFDT had cleared an important hurdle and had recognised the class struggle as a reality of capitalist society, 'the concepts of the class struggle remain unclear, the means of achieving the transformation of society were not properly thought out and the muddled notion of workers' control was to the fore'.[12] There is no evidence to suggest that the CFDT agreed to these major ideological developments at the behest of the Socialist Party, or as a response to pressure exercised by socialists within its ranks. The trade union confederations were moving to a rapprochement of their own which predated the signing of the Common Programme of Government and which helped to create the climate of unity which permeated the Left at this time.

Rand Smith's other variable conditions trade union of action, change in the industrial sphere, is more debatable. He claimed that working class militancy was inversely related to the level of unemployment and offered the following hypothesis: 'a "favourable" labour market (for worker mobilisation) tends to weaken unity between the CGT and the CFDT', whereas on the other hand an unfavourable labour market tends to strengthen unity. He continued: 'inter-union cooperation is not "needed" for effective worker mobilisation or for "success" in conventional labour market terms (e.g. wage increases)'. On the other hand, 'an "unfavourable" labour market tends to strengthen union unity

Table 4.1 Unemployment in France 1970–80 (% of workforce)

1970	510,000	1.7
1971	569,000	2.1
1972	595,000	2.3
1973	576,000	2.0
1974	615,000	2.3
1975	902,000	4.0
1976	993,000	4.4
1977	1,073,000	4.9
1978	1,183,000	5.2
1979	1,355,000	5.8
1980	1,452,000	6.3

Source: Labour Force Statistics 1968–80, OECD, 1982

for parallel reasons. Working class militancy being low, the two unions will moderate their mutual criticisms in an effort to kindle and build worker support around non-conventional objectives – wages, defence of jobs, etc' (Rand Smith, 1981, p. 40). According to the figures in Table 4.1, labour market conditions measured in terms of unemployment statistics continued to worsen during the 1970s, with the exception of 1973, ironically a period of relatively good relations between the CGT and the CFDT. Trade union unity of action did not improve in proportion to the increase in the level of unemployment. The trade union confederations had already succeeded during the 1960s in engaging in unity of action, and yet there is no evidence to suggest that unemployment or a change in the rate of unemployment were major issues.[13] As will be seen, by the end of the 1970s, when unemployment rates had risen considerably, trade union unity of action lay in tatters.[14] Unity of action was 'needed', in Rand Smith's terms, for effective worker mobilisation but the trade union confederations were not able or willing to act accordingly. Working class militancy may have been low, but this did not automatically mean that trade union confederations would moderate their mutual criticism. It is also worth noting that 'wages, defence of jobs etc', are not as uncontroversial as Rand Smith implies. Because the trade union confederations saw themselves as actors in the political sphere, decisions on these issues were often considered in terms of their political implications. Although the CGT and the CFDT were normally able to agree without much difficulty on the level of the minimum legal wage, they differed on the issue of wage differentials for a long time. Moreover they disagreed on the ways in which wages and jobs should be protected. As will be seen in Chapter 6, there were on occasions differences over the form industrial conflict should take. Whilst it may be argued that certain aspects of the industrial sphere conditioned trade union of action, it is not possible to be as categorical as Rand Smith and to construct a model based solely on one specific feature, unemployment. Other industrial issues, wages and forms of industrial conflict, had a role to play in conditioning trade union unity of action.

In addition, there were other variables which conditioned trade union unity of action, that is institutional and socio-professional factors. Trade union rivalry exists, at all levels of trade union organisation, and this is reinforced and exacerbated by the differing types of workplace elections, for personnel delegates and representatives to entreprise committees. Even at harmonious moments in the 1970s, the CGT and the CFDT were in direct competition at least once every year for votes in the different elections which, by their very nature, would have caused the different trade union confederations to emphasise their specificity in the search for votes. This in turn would have undermined trade union unity of action, even in some geographical areas, Pays-de-Loire,[15] and Rhône-Alpes,[16] and some industrial sectors, metalworking for example,[17] with a long tradition of unity of action. Moreover, establishing and maintaining a distinct identity has been one of the prime goals of trade union education (Bridgford & Stirling, 1985, p. 234–43).

It has already been shown that French trade unionism is divided along ideological and political lines. Whilst the rivalry between different trades in France is not reinforced by organisational structures as in Great Britain, trade union confederations do nevertheless have different constituencies. According to the results of elections to enterprise committees, the CGT was by for the most popular trade union confederation during the 1970s, albeit with declining support, whilst the CFDT had half this level of support. The CGT had the highest level of support in every industrial sector, except for occasions when the CFDT headed the banking and insurance sector (1972, 1977, 1978) the gas, water and electricity industries, the liberal professions (1975), and the fishing and forestry sector (1978).[18] If the results of one particular year are analysed, 1972 for example, the year when the Common Programme was signed, the CFDT was the most popular trade union confederation in only one industry (banking), but it was well represented in the following sectors – petrochemicals, metal production, metal transformation, mechanical engineering, electrical engineering, chemicals, textiles, leather, agricultural and liberal professions. The figures show that the CGT obtained more support from manual workers, whereas the CFDT obtained more support from technical and supervisory staff. There were sound socio-professional reasons for potentially differing views on industrial affairs. The CFDT would be more inclined to defend the interests of technical and supervisory staff whereas the CGT, already more *ouvriériste* would be more inclined to defend the interests of manual workers.

CGT–CFDT unity of action was conditioned by a number of different variables. In the political sphere it was primarily influenced by the state of the relationship between the socialists and the communists, but also by the activities of the political parties of the Right, by aspects of the international environment and by differing ideological traditions. The industrial sphere provided its own set of variables. Whilst it is not clear whether certain developments in the labour market (employment, wages etc) constituted prerequisites for trade union unity of action, it is nevertheless the case that the response to these developments influenced the state of inter-confederal relations, which were also affected by institutional and socio-professional factors. CGT–CFDT relations were not static: they fluctuated considerably, and in the second section of this chapter they will be investigated in terms of three separate moments of the political calendar – before, during and after the period of the Union of the Left.

The dynamics of CGT–CFDT relations

1966–72

The CGT and the CFDT had been engaged in negotiations to establish some form of trade union unity of action for some years before the signing of the Common Programme of Government in 1972. On 10 January 1966 a delegation from the CGT met its CFDT counterpart and signed an agreement proposing certain industrial demands – an increase in the purchasing power of the low paid, families, old people and the handicapped; action to reduce regional disparities in wages: initiatives to encourage bargaining on real wages; measures to defend and extend trade union rights within the workplace. To these were added other demands referring to the political economy at large – a reduction in the level of unproductive expenditure so as to increase public investment in housing, education and health: a guarantee of the right to work assured by the setting up of new publicly owned industries; a reorganisation of the tax system.[19] It is interesting to note that it was reached at a time of considerable ideological disharmony. Although recently secularised, the

CFDT had not yet embraced a class-based analysis of capitalism. It is a measure of the enthusiasm of the trade union confederations to come to some form of agreement that their ideological differences were disregarded at this time. Moreover, this agreement was reached at a time of relatively low unemployment (1.4 per cent in 1965 and 1966), and before a limited precursor of the Common Programme of Government was signed in December of the same year by communists and socialists. According to Gilbert Declercq, at that time CFDT secretary in the Pays-de-Loire, the trade union agreement created an atmosphere which encouraged the political parties to come together, and according to Eugène Descamps, at that time general secretary of the CFDT, the agreement made it possible to dissipate a number of anti-communist prejudices, a significant development within the non-communist political and trade union Left.[20] Contemporary speculation about the future prospects for CGT–CFDT relations threw up the following three scenarios. Firstly, the relationship would break up over questions of ideology or over disagreements as to means of action, and it would be a long time before trade union unity of action was reestablished. Secondly, although there would not be a split between the CGT and the CFDT, the relationship would be 'put into hibernation', and the CGT and the CFDT would agree to a separation by mutual consent with no great damage caused. Thirdly, the relationship would continue, and the CGT and the CFDT would have to make a careful examination of their divergent views on trade union strategy as well as on more fundamental issues. Adam favoured the second scenario (Adam, 1967, p. 589–90). In fact CFDT–CGT relations did improve, if only slowly (Barjionet, 1968, p. 116–20).

Any further speculation on trade union unity of action was brushed aside by the Events of May 1968. This is not the forum for recounting the events themselves, nor for assessing their impact on French industrial relations, but it is clear that the Events of May underlined the fragile state of CGT–CFDT relations (Bridgford, 1989, p. 100–116). According to a note in a CFDT journal, the two confederations had differing views on the significance of the events, their political ramifications and on trade union strategies and attitudes towards collective bargaining.[21] Georges Séguy drew attention to differences over attitudes to the extreme Left and to collective bargaining. However for him, the most crucial differences were political; 'should the two organisations have contributed to setting up a broadly based united front of Left-wing political parties and trade unions – our position – or should they have favoured a 'third force' style political approach which was the position of the CFDT?' (Séguy, 1975, p. 125). The latter option, a throwback to the politics of the Fourth Republic, would have excluded the PCF, which clearly would not have been the policy of the CGT. By the autumn of 1968, the 1966 agreement was null and void.[22] Although the CGT and the CFDT agreed to participate in a joint day of action on 11 March 1969, differences over aspects of the industrial sphere loomed large. Disagreements over attitudes to collective bargaining were further exacerbated with the introduction of the new-style wage agreements in the public sector, which will be investigated further in Chapter 7.

CGT–CFDT relations improved considerably in 1970. At its 35th conference the CFDT changed ideological direction. It adopted a class-based analysis of society and in this way made a major step towards the ideological position of the CGT. Although they differed markedly on their definition of a socialist society this development undoubtedly heralded an improvement in CGT–CFDT relations. Contacts became more frequent. Delegations from the two confederations met ten times during the latter half of 1970 to prepare another agreement on industrial demands which was published in December. It contained the following; the minimum legal wage should be increased to 800 francs per month; purchasing power should be maintained in line with a realistic consumer price index; new salary scales should be introduced; the retirement age should be lowered and pensions should be increased; an hour per month should be made available for all employees for trade union meetings: the working week should be reduced to 40 hours; there should be no redundancies.[23] Contacts increased further. Delegations of the trade union confederations met on fifteen occasions between 1 December 1970 and 21 July 1971,[24] and by the summer Edmond Maire proclaimed that the CFDT's desire to seek unity of action with the CGT was 'irreversible'.[25] There was agreement on a number of campaigns: for retirement at 60, trade union rights and immigrant rights. However, there were still notable divergences over strike action. On the one hand, the CGT favoured large-scale national days of action, whereas the CFDT advocated a form of industrial action which highlighted more specific issues at the local level. Although the level of ideological rapprochement was unprecedented, major differences persisted. 1971 was a year of intense ideological debate, and the confederations published a number of documents, the CGT in April, the CFDT in November and the CGT again in December, purporting to clarify their positions but in fact restating the extent of their ideological divergence.[26] It was nevertheless an indication of the general improvement in CGT–CFDT relations that there was at this time some speculation about the merger of the two trade union confederations. However, Desseigne's claim that 'nothing fundamental now prevents the setting up in the short term of one confederation of French workers belonging to the CGT and the CFDT',[27] was obviously wide of the mark.

The beginning of 1972 augured well for CGT–CFDT relations. At a meeting on 9 February, a common statement on collective bargaining was agreed. Moreover a joint statement was produced on the train drivers' day of action (18 February), and on the metalworkers' week of action (14–22 February). In addition, all national unions were urged to work together.[28] Suddenly, however, events took a turn for the worse. Whilst demonstrating outside a Renault plant, Pierre Overney, a young Maoist, was killed by a security guard, and this event opened up the debate on trade union attitudes to the extreme Left. The CFDT was more prepared to tolerate the activities of extreme leftwingers, whereas the CGT was more critical. According to Roy, 'relations between the CGT and the CFDT were at their worst since 1968',[29] and yet, at that time, the CGT was anxious to play down these differences and to foster harmonious relations with the CFDT. At its 38th conference held in April 1972, the CGT claimed that, 'if unity of action is to develop, it must exclude all preconditions of an ideological nature . . . It is to be achieved on the base of common action. It is unequivocally based on the respect for mutually decided agreements and on reciprocal loyalty'. In the same document, the CGT claimed that, 'the differences and misunderstandings in the trade union movement over major objectives should not hold up the permanent efforts continually developed by the CGT and its organisations to unite workers in their daily struggle to safeguard their immediate interests'.[30] Delegations of both confederations continued to meet regularly and they decided on a joint national day of action for 23 June,[31] which was to provide a unitary prelude on the trade union side to the moves towards unity in the political sphere and the signing of the Common Programme of Government four days later.

In spite of the lack of formal agreement amongst the political parties of the Left and in spite of differences over ideology and also on occasions over approaches to basic aspects of the regulation of employment, delegations from the CGT and the CFDT met on numerous occasions and agreed at the national level on statements, campaigns and strikes, specifically related to trade union activities in the industrial sphere. In this way, the trade confederations helped to form part of the climate of unity which permeated the entire Left.

1972–77

Ironically, as was shown in Chapter 2, the signing of the Common

Programme of Government led to a deterioration in inter-confederal relations. In September 1972 Georges Séguy criticised those confederations that were not prepared to support the Common Programme of Government,[32] and he was particularly critical of the CFDT once it was clear that the latter had decided not to be associated with the Common Programme.[33] In the industrial sphere relations were good however, and the differences over the Common Programme of Government did not stop the confederations meeting the following day and producing a joint list of industrial demands.[34] They followed it up with another meeting advocating a week of industrial action (16–20 October) and a further national day of action in pursuit of these particular demands.[35] In October 1972, the trade union confederations made it known that they had decided to suspend discussions on the Common Programme of Government until a new debate became necessary,[36] and, although they did not always manage to stick to this, (on a number of occasions CGT leaders criticised the position taken by the CFDT[37]) differences over trade union responses to events in the political sphere did not prejudice agreements in the industrial sphere. In the early part of 1973 delegations from the two trade union confederations met. They agreed on demands for an increase in the minimum legal wage to 1,100 francs, a reduction in the retirement age to sixty, an increase in family allowances, a ban on part-time work and short-time contract work, and the protection and extension of trade union rights. They also demanded equal rights for immigrants.[38] According to Roy, 'never, no doubt, had the leaders of the two confederations shown such identical views'.[39] A little later they met on other occasions and agreed statements supporting Renault and Peugeot workers, demanding a minimum wage of 6.32 francs per hour, and putting forward a common platform as regards the social welfare system.[40]

There was an unprecedented level of trade union unity of action in 1974, and it is no coincidence that at this time a spirit of unity pervaded the political Left. At the Presidential election in May the CGT and the CFDT issued a number of joint political statements in favour of the candidate of the Left, François Mitterrand. As Georges Séguy explained in a socialist magazine, the elections drew the trade unions together. The CGT and the CFDT transformed the traditional May day demonstration into a political protest:

so as to provide a contribution to the struggle for the united Left ... we want the 1st May to translate this great explosion of optimism and confidence. This will allow workers to believe that, with the victory of the common candidate of the Left, the month of May 1974 will indeed be the beginning of the new life to which they aspire.[41]

This climate of unity in the political sphere helped to create a climate of unity in the industrial sphere. Immediately after the election, delegations from the CGT and the CFDT met and issued a joint wide-ranging statement which resembled a political manifesto as much as a statement of trade union demands. According to Edmond Maire, this statement was evidence of attempts to go beyond short-term interests. According to Georges Séguy, 'our agreement would improve conditions of trade union action at all levels: it would inspire future struggles and workers' confidence would be reinforced'. Moreover it would also encourage a spirit of tolerance and understanding.[42]

The list of demands was comprehensive: to increase the purchasing power of the low paid more quickly than the rate of inflation; to set up a unified salary scale for each industry; to protect job promotion from the decisions arbitrarily taken by employers; to negotiate real wages and salary scales and make them the subject of collective bargaining agreements; to reinforce the rights of redundant workers; to provide all civil servants and local government employees with permanent contracts; to provide all workers, whether employed or unemployed, with an adequate income; to grant all young people the right to training; to reduce the working week to 40 hours; to increase social benefits; to improve working conditions; to freeze prices; to put a zero VAT rating on basic necessities; to reduce income tax for the lower paid; to link saving schemes to the inflation rate.[43] This was the first time that means and objectives had been defined with such attention to detail (Tincq, 1975, p. 960). Roy maintained that this agreement was not just a catalogue of bits from each trade union platform but that for the first time a joint statement mentioned common points and identical positions.[44] The novelty lay in the fact that it was not merely a list of demands, but it contained a statement on the means to be adopted in order to achieve them. In the joint statement of the previous year the CGT had simply called on their respective organisations to take measures 'in the greatest spirit of unity',[45] without further explanation. In 1974, a strategy for industrial action was agreed, and the logic of a diversified approach was recognised. Industrial action was to be taken at varying levels, in accordance with the needs of each sector. This signalled a readiness on the part of the CGT to agree to the CFDT's decentralised approach. In addition, industrial action was to be channelled through the trade union organisations. This reflected a concern within the CGT (and increasingly within the CFDT) that it was necessary to ensure that the extreme Left on the fringes of the trade unions did not take control of strike activity and use it for its own ends.

Indeed it was admitted that 'joint positions and practices in terms of industrial action were likely to create a climate which would facilitate a favourable outcome to negotiation'.[46] This joint agreement marked the most harmonious period of their relationship. Events in the political sphere obviously provided a positive backdrop for trade union unity of action. Ideological differences still remained but did not jeopardise inter-confederal relations. The climate of unity was such that the two trade union confederations were able to agree on a wide range of industrial demands and also to negotiate a coordinated strategy on industrial action. The CGT and the CFDT continued to issue joint statements on issues in the industrial sphere (the minimum legal wage, the retirement age, the 40-hour week, and the lock-out at the newspaper *le Parisien Libéré*), and also on issues in the political sphere (employment in the public sector, the effects of government policy, the insufficiencies of the Seventh Plan, and the inadequacies of the health service). Following on in the spirit of the 1974 joint agreement, the two confederations called for a nationwide campaign for industrial demands, which would include a national day of action in mid October 1974, lobbying the headquarters of the employers' association, the CNPF, and a host of regional demonstrations[47] – in short a diversified response and not just one national 'catch-all' day of action, traditionally identified with CGT strike activity.

The following year also saw significant examples of trade union unity of action. The CGT and the CFDT published statements on early retirement in January and April and they agreed to launch a common campaign on youth unemployment. They issued further joint statements on industrial demands and agreed to demonstrate together against anti-trade union repression.[48] After the summer holidays the two trade union confederations published another statement calling on their constituent organisations to work together, and a common national day of action was called on 23 September.[49] They also agreed on a number of initiatives which were more overtly political. Joint delegations visited members of the government; the Minister of the Interior (to discuss the rights of immigrants), the Prime Minister (to discuss pensions) and later the Minister of Social Affairs (to discuss pensions again).[50] They decided on another national day of action for the beginning of December. Political unity was further reinforced by a CGT–CFDT rally beneath the Eiffel Tower in July, which was attended by delegations from the PCF and the PS. The CGT and the CFDT joined with the FEN, the PCF, the PS and the MRG in putting out a statement criticising government policy, making a series of demands and calling on their supporters to hold demonstrations throughout Paris.[51]

Events in 1976 showed that the CGT and the CFDT were still prepared to compromise on the issue of industrial action and to combine the national approach of the former with the local approach of the latter. They decided to hold joint union meetings in the workplace on 30 April, to organise a national day of action on 6 May devoted to the question of job security just prior to the parliamentary debate on that subject, and also to a series of locally based strikes for the 13 May.[52] Spurred on by their opposition to the austerity measures introduced by the Prime Minister Raymond Barre, the CGT and the CFDT published a statement on industrial demands and announced the date of the next national day of action (7 October 1976).[53] There was also a series of demonstrations for 23 October 1976 to highlight youth employment.[54] Decisions taken at the beginning of 1977 augured well for trade union unity of action. The two confederations published a statement criticising the government for sanctioning the sacking of trade union activists.[55] This was followed within a week by a statement condemning the government's economic policy and calling on national unions in the public sector to undertake coordinated strike activity at the end of January, and a week later another statement was put out, calling for coordinated demonstrations on a local basis for the latter half of February.[56] A short time afterwards, the trade union confederations issued a long statement of industrial demands specifying the need to maintain and to improve purchasing power, the need for the government to negotiate with the trade unions in the public sector, the need to create more jobs and improve the health service.[57]

This was the most successful period of CGT–CFDT unity of action. In the political sphere the trade union confederations agreed to oppose the government of the Right and to support the representatives of the Union of the Left. In the industrial sphere they agreed on a myriad of joint statements, but more importantly they managed to combine strategies and activities. All this was pursued at a breakneck pace, and the momentum of unity made it possible to ignore the existence of certain unresolved differences. It was of course no coincidence that this high level of interconfederal unity occurred at the time of the Union of the Left.

1977–80

On 14 September 1977 the three political parties failed to agree on the renegotiation of the Common Programme of Government. By 23 September, the break-up of the Union of the Left was complete. Three days later a delegation of the CGT met with its CFDT counterpart.

According to an article in *Le Monde* entitled 'The CGT and the CFDT try to maintain unity', the delegations chose not to hold a press conference after the meeting nor indeed to issue any statement. In this way they hoped to avoid drawing attention to potential differences; 'with the exception of the perceived need to maintain the unity of the Left, their analyses of the situation were quite different'.[58] The momentum of trade union unity of action prevalent in the first part of the year had been checked by events in the political sphere. Georges Séguy explained the CGT position:

if our trade union allies allow themselves to adopt a partisan political stance, trade union unity of action would be affected. We hope that in the interest of the workers, the spirit of unity and the commitment to trade union independence will save all trade unionists from a drift towards partisan political alignment and from the temptation to revert to old-style trade union/political cleavages.[59]

However, as has been seen in previous chapters, Georges Séguy was at the centre of these manifestations of political partisanship. The momentum of trade union unity of action was not however completely lost. The CGT and the CFDT published a joint statement on the insufficiencies of the health service, and delegations from the two confederations met subsequently to arrange a 24-hour strike called for 1 December in protest against government policies.[60] Although in agreement on the level of the minimum legal wage, they chose however not to quote a specific figure, mindful no doubt of the sensitivity of this issue in the political sphere – the PS had not yet agreed to step into line with them and the PCF. In the new year, delegations from the two confederations met and published a joint statement of basic industrial demands, again without stipulating the level of the minimum legal wage. According to an article in *L'Unité*, the PS weekly newspaper, this 'stormy' meeting was dominated by the break-up of the Union of the Left and arguments about who was to blame for it.[61]

At the end of January 1978 the National Council of the CFDT met and agreed on the Moreau Report which signalled a shift in emphasis from the political to the industrial sphere. It was claimed after this meeting that trade union unity of action with the CGT was an essential element of this strategy.[62] However, given that the CGT had not been forewarned and that the Moreau Report involved such a major strategic change in CFDT strategy, it is difficult to understand how trade union unity of action could continue to operate in these circumstances. Speaking at the first CGT meeting after the legislative elections, Georges Séguy asked whether the propensity of the CFDT to move away from trade union unity of action with the CGT was not linked to this strategic reconversion,[63] and a lively exchange ensued between the leaders of the different trade union confederations. According to Kespi in *L'Unité*, the CFDT had previously refused to publish a joint statement on industrial demands before the elections and had also refused to publish a joint statement at the time of the first round of the elections. Moreover it declined to publish a joint statement congratulating the political parties on their subsequent electoral pact. The CFDT would not join with the CGT in this, claiming that the latter was not independent of the PCF.[64] For the first time since 1972 the CGT and the CFDT decided not to organise a joint national May Day demonstration, although interestingly a greater spirit of trade union unity prevailed in the provinces.[65] Representatives from the CGT and the CFDT met in September but were unable to agree on a jointly organised week of action to protest against the high level of unemployment (an issue which previously would not have divided them) and differed over the most suitable form of industrial action to take.[66] They met just before Christmas, only to fail again to agree on tactics for industrial action. The CGT's 40th conference took place at the end of the year, and symbolically the CFDT did not send a message of solidarity, as it had done for the 39th conference.[67] During the conference itself Georges Séguy highlighted ideological differences. With its new industrial strategy the CFDT had revised its analysis of society – it was flirting with the sort of reformism to be found in the other West European trade union confederations.[68]

In 1979 a distinct reduction in the level of trade union unity of action occurred. Contacts were infrequent. In September the CGT launched a week of industrial action on its own.[69] Later the same month delegations from the CGT and the CFDT met but were unable to agree. Two days later however they met again and agreed on a joint statement, which was followed up with a joint week of action centred on industrial demands, low pay, the working week and workers' rights.[70] They met again in January 1980 but were unable to come to any agreement.[71] Trade union unity of action was drawing to an agonising end, but the trade union confederations refused to admit it openly. In addition, they did not want to be blamed for its demise, since, as Robert Bono had said back in 1974, 'disunity would prejudice the interests of the workers, but also of the trade union organisation which refused to continue with trade union unity of action'.[72] As a result, trade union unity of action was only pronounced dead when it was blindingly clear that this was the case. In June 1980 the National Confederal Commission of the CGT met and issued a statement which drew attention to the major ideological differences between the two trade union confederations: the CFDT was criticised for its reformism.[73] After the holiday period Edmond Maire criticised the CGT yet again for showing no interest in trade union unity of action and for being subservient to the PCF.[74] Georges Séguy responded the following day by saying that trade union unity of action at the confederal level was no longer possible.[75]

The break-up of the Union of the Left had dire consequences for trade union unity of action. These consequences were felt immediately, but the unitary momentum in the industrial sphere carried the trade union confederations along and also provided a basis for trade union attempts to rekindle unity of action in the political sphere. Gradually, however, the gap between the CGT and the CFDT began to widen. Ideological differences loomed large, particularly after the CFDT's decision to turn its back on politics and concentrate on the industrial sphere, and other differences, for example over industrial action, were to re-emerge. The unitary will to minimise the impact of such disagreements had been lost.

Conclusions

Unity in the trade union world was linked closely to developments in the political sphere, and the agreement between political parties of the Left had a beneficial impact on trade union unity of action. Given the pattern of trade unionism in France, it would be difficult to imagine the development of trade union unity of action without some form of political unity on the Left, and in this way Rand Smith's hypothesis that political unity is a prerequisite for trade union unity holds true. However to see a direct and automatic correlation between the two spheres is somewhat misleading. Political parties may have wanted to use trade union unity of action for their own political objectives but they were often unable to manage it. As has been shown in Chapter 1, the PCF had the personnel in peace to control the decision-making machinery of the CGT but during the mid 1970s was unable to pass on an unequivocal message. Moreover, the PS was in no position to exercise enough leverage within the CFDT to ensure the latter's compliance. There is no evidence to suggest that the PS used its privileged position within a range of different confederations to encourage trade union unity. In addition, it is important to remember that the trade union confederations did not act as passive bystanders but as participants in a process designed to establish a climate of unity permeating the entire Left. Rand Smith's other hypothesis is less convincing. The link between increasing levels of unemployment and trade union unity of action is difficult to establish. Trade union confederations may have recognised a need for unity of action in labour market terms but on occasions they were notoriously incapable of acting on this. As unemployment increased during the 1970s, trade union unity of action declined. Moreover, in other decades, the 1960s and the 1980s, this hypothesis is even less convincing. Trade union unity of action has shown itself to be a complex and dynamic phenomenon. Ideological perspectives, international considerations, industrial demands, forms of industrial action, workplace rivalry and socio-professional patterns of membership and support have all played a significant, if subsidiary, role. It is a measure of the importance of these other factors that trade union unity of action managed to outlive unity in the political sphere. It is also a measure of the relative inability of the PCF to exercise total control of CGT activities during this period that trade union unity of action did not end more quickly and more abruptly.

Before 1972 the CGT and the CFDT were able to agree on certain industrial demands, even though they had divergent ideological perspectives, and even though the political parties of the Left had not agreed on a common programme. It was no doubt easier for the trade union confederations to engage in some form of unity of action than it was for the political parties to sign a joint manifesto, the Common Programme of Government, and in this way the trade union confederations were able to contribute to the creation of this climate of cooperation. During the period 1972–77, the two trade union confederations enjoyed a particularly high level of unity of action, in spite of the fact that they still had differences, albeit of reduced proportions, on ideological perspectives and on forms of industrial action. Political unity was undoubtedly crucial for the improvement in interconfederal relations. The CGT and the CFDT not only produced a vast number of joint statements on industrial demands, but they overcame their differences over forms of industrial action and established joint means for attaining these demands. Given the French trade union tradition of rivalry and invective, there were also occasions of real disagreement, but they did not threaten the whole climate of unity. With the failure of the renegotiations for the Common Programme of Government, the momentum of trade union unity of action was checked but not stopped completely or immediately. The CGT and the CFDT had differing interpretations of the reasons for the break-up of the Union of the Left, but trade union unity of action continued to operate, albeit at a lower pitch, in the form of joint industrial statements and joint industrial action. After the 1978 legislative elections, political disunity reigned, and trade union unity also began to suffer. Differences over ideology and forms of industrial action were to reassert themselves. Examples of joint agreements and joint industrial action became fewer and fewer, until the trade union confederations actually admitted, three years after the break-up of the Union of the Left, that trade union unity of action was officially over. Events in the political sphere put an intolerable strain on CGT–CFDT relations and dealt French trade unionism a blow from which it has still not recovered.

Notes

1. *Le Peuple*, 1–31 May 1972, p. 12.
2. Document d'Orientation, CGT 37th Conference. Vitry 1969. Confederation proceedings in extenso, p. 464.
3. Résolution générale, CFDT, 35th Conference. Issy les Moulineaux, 1970.
4. *Le Peuple*, 16–31 January 1972, p. 14.
5. *Le Monde*, 23 April 1974.
6. Rapport Général, *CFDT Syndicalisme*, 15 March 1973, p. 82.
7. See the comments made by Henri Krasucki in *Le Monde*, 19 April 1978.
8. *Le Monde*, 24–25 March 1974.
9. Unlike the CGT, the CFDT refused to see this as a simple case of industrial conflict, according to Edmond Maire, *Nouvel Observateur*, 30 June 1974.
10. *Le Peuple*, 1–31 May 1972, p. 12.
11. *Le Peuple*, 16 July–15 August 1974, p. 2. Descamps, E., *Militer*, Paris, Fayard, 1971, p. 247–248.
12. *Le Peuple*, 16–31 January 1972, p. 12.
13. Unemployment in France during the 1960s – Annual averages measured in thousands and % of the working population

1960	1961	1962	1963	1964	1965	1966	1967	1968	1969
233	203	230	273	216	269	280	365	428	337
1.2%	1.1%	1.2%	1.4%	1.1%	1.4%	1.4%	1.8%	2.1%	1.6%

Source: Eurostat Population and Employment, Luxembourg 1977, p. 136–137.

14. Rand Smith's analysis is less apposite for the 1980s. The upward trend in unemployment continued and, from 1981 until 1984, the political parties of the Left were locked, albeit unenthusiastically, in coalition government together. However these circumstances were insufficient to encourage the CGT and the CFDT to act in concert, even when the various government plans threatened to reduce purchasing power. Unity of action may have been 'needed', but the trade union confederations did not act accordingly.
15. Interview, Gilbert Declercq 2 March 1983.
16. Interview, Pierre Héritier 21 February 1985.
17. *Le Monde*, 29 November 1973.
18. For the results, see the following issues of *Revue française des affaires sociales*. (month/year) 4/1972, 1/1974, 1/1975, 4/1976, 1/1978, 1/1979, 2/1979 and 1/1981.

19. Reprinted in *CFDT Aujourd'hui*, January–February 1976, p. 74.
20. *CFDT Aujourd'hui*, January–February 1976, p. 75.
21. *CFDT Aujourd'hui*, January–February 1976, p. 76–77.
22. *CFDT Aujourd'hui*, January–February 1976, p. 78. For Séguy's view, *Lutter*, Paris, Stock, 1975 p. 136.
23. *CFDT Syndicalisme*, 10 December 1970, p. 4.
24. *Le Peuple*, 16–31 January 1972, p. 13–14.
25. Quoted in Hamon, H & Rotman, P., *La deuxième gauche*, Paris, Ramsay, 1982 p. 258.
26. For the text of the first two declarations, see *CFDT Syndicalisme*, 4 November 1971, and for the third see *Revue Politique et Parlementaire*, January 1972, p. 23–26.
27. Desseigne, G. 'Vers un syndicalisme unique?'. *Politique Aujourd'hui*, October 1971, p. 7–8. The CGT dismissed the idea of merger as such and in 1974 Georges Séguy claimed superbly that the CGT would itself be the future unified trade union confederation for French workers. (quoted in *Notes et Documents du BRAEC*, CFDT, June 1981, p. 41.) By 1976, Edmond Maire too implied that merger was no longer on the agenda. (*CFDT Aujourd'hui*, January–February 1976, p. 32–33.)
28. *Le Peuple*, 17–29 February 1972, p. 2.
29. *Le Monde*, 9 March 1972. For further details see *Le Monde*, 16 March 1972, *Le Peuple*, 1–15 March 1972, p. 4. *CFDT Syndicalisme*, 16 March 1972, p. 2.
30. *Le Peuple*, 1–31 May 1972, p. 44.
31. *Le Peuple*, 16–30 June 1972, p. 4.
32. *Le Monde*, 9 September 1972.
33. *Le Monde*, 28 September 1972.
34. For developments, see the chapter by Mouriaux, R. in Kesselman, M. & Groux, G. (eds) *Le mouvement ouvrier français*, Paris, Editions Ouvrières, 1984. p. 93–112.
35. *L'Humanité*, 10 October 1972.
36. *CFDT Syndicalisme*, 15 March 1973, p. 86.
37. Moynot, J-L. 'Et la CFDT?', *Le Peuple*, 16–31 January 1973, p. 7–8. See also the statement by Georges Séguy, *Le Peuple*, 15–30 June 1973, p. 2.
38. *Le Peuple*, 16–30 April 1973, p. 8.
39. *Le Monde*, 6 April 1972, p. 1.
40. *Le Peuple*, 1–15 May 1973, p. 4. *Le Figaro*, 26 April 1973. *CFDT Syndicalisme*, 17 May 1973, p. 1.
41. *L'Unité*, 19–25 April 1974, p. 5, 8.
42. *CFDT Syndicalisme*, 27 June 1974, p. 2. *Le Peuple*, 16 July–15 August 1974, p. 2.
43. *CFDT Syndicalisme*, 6 June 1974, p. 3.
44. *Le Monde*, 28 June 1974.
45. *Le Peuple*, 16–30 April 1973, p. 8.
46. *CFDT Syndicalisme*, 27 June 1974, p. 3–6.
47. *CFDT Syndicalisme*, 5 December 1974, p. 3–4.
48. *CFDT Syndicalisme*, 30 January 1975, p. 20 and 12 April 1975, p. 2. *CFDT Syndicalisme*, 13 February 1975, p. 2. *Le Peuple*, 1–15 June 1975, p. 2. *Le Monde*, 13 July 1975.

49. *Le Peuple*, 1–15 September 1975, p. 2. *CFDT Syndicalisme*, 18 September, p. 3.
50. *CFDT Syndicalisme*, 25 September 1975, p. 20. *Le Monde*, 7 October 1975. *Le Monde*, 18 October 1975.
51. *Le Monde*, 12 July 1975, *CFDT Syndicalisme*, 18 December 1975, p. 10.
52. *Le Monde*, 22 April 1976.
53. *Le Peuple*, 1–15 October 1976, p. 2.
54. *CFDT Syndicalisme*, 15 July 1972, p. 2.
55. *Le Peuple*, 15–31 January 1977, p. 21.
56. *Le Peuple*, 15–31 January 1977, p. 2. *CFDT Syndicalisme*, 6 January 1977, p. 3. 20 January 1977, p. 3. 27 January 1977, p. 3. *Le Peuple*, 1–15 February 1977, p. 3–4.
57. *Le Peuple*, 15–30 April 1977, p. 2.
58. *Le Monde*, 27 September 1977.
59. *Le Monde*, 15 October 1977.
60. *Le Peuple*, 15–30 November 1977, p. 28.
61. *L'Unité*, 20–26 January 1978, p. 15–16.
62. *CFDT Syndicalisme*, 2 March 1978, p. 3.
63. *Le Peuple*, 15–30 April 1978, p. 5–6.
64. *L'Unité*, 14–20 April 1978, p. 8–9.
65. *Le Monde*, 19 April 1978.
66. *Le Monde*, 20 September 1978.
67. *CFDT Syndicalisme*, 16 November 1978, p. 2. *Le Peuple*, 1–31 July 1975, p. 75.
68. *Le Peuple*, 1–31 December 1978, p. 10.
69. *Le Monde*, 9–10 September 1979.
70. *Le Matin*, 15 September 1979. *CFDT Syndicalisme*, 27 September 1979, p. 5. *Libération*, 8 November 1979.
71. *Le Matin*, 8 April 1980.
72. *L'Unité*, 22–28 March 1974, p. 5.
73. *Libération*, 25 June 1980.
74. *Le Monde*, 5 September 1980.
75. *Le Monde*, 6 September 1980.

Chapter 5
The Consequences of Party–Union Relations for Intra-Confederal Factionalism

Previous chapters imply that trade union confederations were monolithic organisations with clear objectives and a coherent set of means to attain them. This was not the case, and confederations were prey to a variety of centripetal pressures. The industrial sphere provided its own tensions, and changes in the labour market – industrial restructuring, differing forms of employment, technological change, new working practices and international competition – provided ample opportunity for divergence over means, if not objectives, within the confederations themselves. However, over the years it is the political sphere which has proved to be the most disruptive, and attempts by political parties to control or influence trade union decisions have put considerable internal strain on trade union confederations. Factionalism has thus been a constant feature of French trade unionism (Mouriaux, 1984, p. 36–39). The 9th of Lenin's 21 conditions for membership of the Communist International advocated communist infiltration of trade unions, and by 1923 communists were in control of the *Confédération Générale du Travail Unitaire* (CGTU), which itself had been set up in 1921 as a result of factional politics. The CGT and the CGTU merged in 1936, and the preamble of the new confederation's statutes formally proscribed factionalism. However factions soon reappeared. In 1947 a minority of members split away from the CGT claiming that it was becoming increasingly dominated by members of the French Communist Party, and in 1948 they set up their own trade union confederation *Force Ouvrière* (FO). In addition a faction within the *Confédération Française des Travailleurs Chrétiens* was established which led in 1964 to the creation of the *Confédération Française Démocratique du Travail*.

A faction has been described as, 'any relatively organised group that exists within the context of some other group and which (as a political faction) competes with other rivals for power advantages within the larger group of which it is part' (Belloni & Beller, 1978, p. 419). This definition, although primarily established for the analysis of factionalism within political parties, also fits other types of organisations, such as pressure groups, and more specifically trade union confederations. In his study of the French Socialist Party, the factionalist party *par excellence*, Hanley also underlined the importance of a subjective element – members of a faction wish to develop a distinct identity within and outside the group at issue (Hanley, 1986, p. 6–7). Factionalism manifests itself in varying levels of intensity. A *courant* is an unorganised grouping whose members share a similar set of views that may be reflected in some form of publication, but they do not threaten to disrupt the whole organisation. A *tendance* takes the fragmentation a stage further. Differences tend to become more systematised and are personified by rivals who contend for control of the whole organisation. Finally, a *fraction* is a structured minority. It has its own distinct doctrine, its own leaders and its own organisation. The prime loyalty of its members is to the *fraction* rather than to the whole organisation, which in turn becomes a fragile coalition of *fractions* (Hayward, 1981, p. 1–2). This chapter will investigate the CGT and the CFDT in turn, in order to discover the extent to which factionalist groups were set up in opposition to the confederal position and the extent to which factionalist politics in the trade union confederations was conditioned by events in the political sphere. At this stage it is worth mentioning the existence of one major methodological problem. Examples of factionalism are difficult to identify. Indeed, as explained by Jean-Louis Moynot, one of the most noteworthy dissidents in the CGT during the late 1970s, individuals do not normally join a trade union to oppose its policies. They spend considerable time ensuring that the trade union's policies are applied; if they do become involved in some form of factional activity, it is only after a considerable period of reflection.[1]

Factionalism in the CGT

At the formal level of CGT there was virtually no opposition at the beginning of the 1970s. At the 38th conference held in Nîmes in 1972, the *document d'action* – the confederal policy statement – was approved with 1,708,133 votes for, no votes against, and 2,620 abstentions. At the 39th conference held in le Bourget in 1975 the *programme d'action* was approved unanimously, bar two abstentions representing 1,445 votes. Finally at the 40th conference held in Grenoble in December 1978, at which, as will be shown later, considerable opposition to the confederal position was expressed, the *programme d'action* was approved with 1,308,721 votes for, 8,550 votes against and 9,643 abstentions.[2] The pressure to conform was intense and at no time did the level of approval drop below 97 per cent. Analysing results of elections to its Executive Commission gives only a hint of possible factionalism. At the 38th and 39th conferences there were the same number of candidates as seats. At the 40th conference there were 121 candidates for 93 seats,[3] which represented a major break with tradition. The results show however that 93 were elected by overwhelming majorities. Claude Germon, the least popular of those elected and, as will be seen, a leading dissident, obtained 89 per cent of the vote, whilst the others obtained derisory scores (less than 0.2 per cent of the vote). Whilst the CGT does not function according to the rules of an organisation like the PCF which is embued with the values of democratic centralism, its electoral ethos is clearly similar.

Conference proceedings show that the 38th conference was a model of harmony, with a level of mutual agreement which would be unimaginable at, for example, the Trades Union Congress. By the time of the next conference, the Common Programme of Government had been signed, the CGT had committed itself to supporting the candidates of the Union of the Left at the legislative elections and François Mitterrand at the Presidential election. At the 39th conference, there was no opposition within the CGT to the idea of the CGT giving support to a manifesto formulated by the political parties of the Left. The only criticism of the leadership came from Aimé Pastre, a representative of the prison officers' association, and Hervé de Fouchier, a trade union representative from INSEE, the national statistical agency. Pastre expressed his concern about the definition of trade union liberties and his disapproval of Georges Séguy's analysis of the situation in Portugal (the latter subject being one which had divided the PCF and the PS, as well as the CGT and the CFDT). He also claimed that the Confederal Bureau had not been sufficiently supportive of prison officers who had been engaged in a dispute the previous year. Fouchier considered that the proposals put forward by the confederation were not precise enough, particularly concerning wages, job creation and the response to trade union repression. All in all, criticism was remarkably muted.

By the time of the next conference, the Union of the Left had disintegrated, the Left had failed to win the 1978 legislative elections, and unity of action with the CFDT was becoming more problematical. In comparison with previous conferences, the 40th conference was a revelation and the floodgates of dissent burst open. A number of speakers criticised the leadership of the CGT on a range of policy and strategy issues. Claude Germon, the Socialist mayor of Massy and member of the Executive Commission, expressed implicit criticism of decision-making within the CGT and of strategies relating to outside organisations, ie, political parties. He expressed satisfaction with the proposal that there would be a permanent opportunity for debate in the columns of the confederal press. He asked the conference to mandate the Executive Commission to set up a new method of preparation for conference: the conferences of the constituent national unions should take place beforehand, thus ensuring a more open and democratic policy-making process; the National Confederal Committee should examine the question of unity of action with other trade union confederations and there should be an ensuing debate within the confederation. In the run-up to the European elections the CGT should not be seen to be supporting one particular party. This last point was an oblique reference to the support provided for the PCF by some communist leaders of the CGT at the time of the 1978 legislative elections. The next speaker, Dominique Mantault, an employee of Thomson–CSF, argued that the CGT was too dependent on the French Communist Party: it was not sufficiently prepared to engage in joint activities with other trade unions and the elected representatives of the CGT were too isolated from what was happening at grass-roots level. The following speaker, Roger Barralis criticised the behaviour of the Confederation after the break up of the Union of the Left. He bemoaned the fact that references by the confederation to the Common Programme of Government had eclipsed the CGT's own programme. Barralis demanded that there should be a permanent opportunity for debate through the columns of the confederal press and that amendments to conference resolutions should be made available before conference took place. Finally, a separate point, he demanded that the decision to support nuclear energy should be put off until the next conference which would then leave sufficient time for a thorough debate. According to Jean Corradi, the representative of the *Union Régional des Mineurs de Fer de Lorraine*, the electoral pact agreed by the political parties after the first round of the legislative elections had not been appreciated by the workers and the CGT would have done better to stick to its own programme. He was opposed to the *cumul des mandats*, whereby it was possible to hold office in a trade union and also in a political party, a particularly widespread activity for members of the CGT and the French Communist Party. Another participant, Pierre Feuilly of the *Société Nationale des Journalistes*, drew attention to the fact that the leadership seemed to use two different yardsticks, depending on whether it was dealing with the PCF or the PS. He criticised Georges Séguy for attending the PCF election meeting, and called on the National Confederal Committee to assure that all political factions were represented on the Executive Commission.

These contributions provide only a sample of the speeches made at 40th conference and of course should not give the wrong impression. The vast majority expressed no criticism of the CGT nor of its leadership. They have been described at length however to demonstrate the strength of feeling and variety of opposition that existed within the CGT at this time. They show that many delegates were critical of the way in which the leadership of the CGT had acted. The speakers made no mention of divergent views on the issues relating to the regulation of employment, but instead they concentrated on issues relating specifically to the political sphere. They did not however criticise the CGT leadership for its participation in the political sphere, but for its support of one particular party, the PCF. Nevertheless, the speeches also show that the leadership was criticised for not encouraging more democratic practices within the confederation and for not being sufficiently prepared to engage in united action with other trade union confederations.

Similar examples of dissent had been heard previously at the end of 1977. At the National Confederal Committee (CCN) meeting held in December 1977. Claude Germon proposed that the confederation's publications should be open to all forms of opinion within the CGT. However this idea was turned down, because it 'would lead to the setting up of *tendances*'.[4] Given the fact that communists were in a majority within the CCN, it is ironic that this reason was used to justify the rejection of this proposal, and it was merely a pretext to ensure that other political groupings could not begin to have a position of influence within the confederation. Nothing should disturb the communist domination of the CGT. At the same meeting Claude Germon put an amendment relating to the debate on nationalisations, the major official reason for the break-up of the Union of the Left three months before. He proposed that subsidiaries should be nationalised only if they were 'necessary for the formulation and application of an industrial strategy'. This proposal would have marked a move away from the position of the PCF. It too was rejected: 'the CCN must be clear and frank. There should be no ambiguous phrases creating a false unanimity, which will then make possible campaigns to weaken or deform the position of the CGT'. The CCN should not be used as a springboard for any criticism of PCF policies. The document of the CCN was passed unanimously. However Claude Germon and Pierre Carassus, both members of the Socialist Party, asked for their disagreement on certain points to be registered. Previously at the Executive Commission meeting held at the beginning of October they had both voted against the motion approving the action of the Confederal Bureau in its support of a PCF interpretation of the Common Programme of Government. At a later date Georges Séguy explained that opposition had emanated from some individuals but not from any single trade union,[5] the implication being that opposition was not widespread. Claude Germon complained that the confederal definition of subsidiaries coincided with the definition proposed by the PCF.[6] At the December 1977 National Confederal Committee meeting, he drew attention to the inconsistencies of the CGT position and, in an ironic aside, cast doubt on the economic regeneration potential of companies such as Sheraton Hotels and the perfume house Rochas, both subsidiaries of Itt-France and Roussel-Uclaf respectively and both candidates for nationalisation.[7] Pierre Carassus explained (in *Le Monde* because *Vie Ouvrière* had refused to publish his remarks[8]) that he was in disagreement with the leadership of the confederation on this question of subsidiaries, because in its statement of 26 September 1977 the Confederal Bureau had given a definition of subsidiaries which had not been discussed previously within the structures of the CGT.[9] At a later date it was pointed out by Gérard Alézard, one of the other secretaries of the Paris *Union Départementale* (UD) and a member of the Central Committee of the PCF, that at the general committee meeting of the Paris UD held on 19 October not one single trade union section had contested the approach taken by the confederation.[10] Here again, one of the communist members of the CGT was attempting to minimise the importance of this disaffection. Campaigns were launched outside the formal structures of the confederation in opposition to the line taken by the CGT leadership. Letters of complaint were sent to CGT headquarters, expressing astonishment at the position taken by some of the leaders of the confederation as regards the nationalisations issue, and claiming that the remarks made by Georges Séguy after the meeting between the CGT and the PS corresponded perfectly to the position taken by the PCF.[11] Claiming that the leadership had received few letters of complaint. Georges Séguy tried again to play down the importance of this wave of dissent.[12]

A potentially more significant example of factional politics was provided after the legislative elections in 1978 by two members of the Executive Commission. Claude Germon and Pierre Carassus, and seven other elected representatives of the CGT, all members of the Socialist Party but members of different national unions. They wrote to the Confederal Bureau, expressing their disagreement with the position that the leadership had taken at the time of the legislative elections. They also asked to be received by the Confederal Bureau so that they could collectively put their point of view in person[13] – an option which was denied them.

Did this important wave of opposition amount to a socialist faction? Of the delegates who criticised the CGT leadership at the 40th conference, it is not clear how many of them belonged to the Socialist Party, and one of them, Jean Corradi, had also been critical of the PS in December 1977.[14] The leading figures however, Claude Germon and Pierre Carassus, were both members of the Socialist Party, as were some of the others. The socialists were clearly an identifiable group. The renaissance of the Socialist Party had helped to strengthen the presence of the socialists within the CGT. According to Pierre Carassus, it was principally after the signing of the Common Programme that it was possible to talk about a 'non-negligible' socialist presence within the CGT.[15] This identity was not necessarily clearly defined, and not all socialists were openly hostile to the confederal position. Jean-Claude Laroze, the only socialist member of the Confederal Bureau before the 40th conference was careful not to associate himself with the activities of the other socialists;[16] it was thought that in the event of a disagreement between the CGT and the PS, he would back the former.[17] Moreover, the socialist dissenters were not totally united. They were not impervious to the factional rivalry that existed within their own party; Claude Germon was a *Mitterrandiste* and Pierre Carassus a member of CERES for example.[18] *Rocardiens* were conspicuous by their absence in the CGT – they were to be found in the CFDT. It would be unwise to overestimate the degree of socialist organisation within the CGT. In 1976 some socialists in the CGT (Claude Germon, Pierre Joxe, Jean-Claude Laroze, Louis Mexendeau and Nicole Questiaux amongst others) started to publish their own small publication *Pour L'Union*, but it only lasted about a year and a half.[19] It may have been that the letter writing campaign in the autumn of 1977 was orchestrated – at least that was the impression that Georges Séguy was trying to give.[20] Socialists did meet together on a few occasions,[21] but they were anxious to show that they were not engaged in factional politics. According to Claude Germon, their activities 'did not imply the organisation of *fractions* or *tendances* which were completely alien to our idea of mass class-based trade unionism'.[22] In his reply to the six CGT members' letter from the *département* of the Loire-Atlantique. Georges Séguy criticised the way in which they had acted; 'setting up a group outside the structures of the confederation was not compatible with the rules of trade union democracy prevailing within the CGT whose statutes did not permit organised *tendances* or *fractions*'.[23] When the Confederal Bureau refused to recognise the specific nature of the nine socialist members of the CGT who wrote in June 1978, it was explained that an approach of this nature would constitute 'an organised *tendance* which was contrary to the principles and the statutes of the CGT'.[24] Georges Séguy refused to accede to the request of organised *tendances*, explaining disingenuously that;

this would be tantamount to recognising the right of parties to interfere in trade union affairs. Everything would be determined and decided by means of negotiations between distinct political *tendances*, that is in fact by the respective political parties. When the parties were in agreement, things would work well enough in the trade union movement. When they were not, the trade union would become a battle-ground for sordid partisan conflicts between different clans and fratricidal combats . . . the organisation of *fractions* is the death of the freedom of expression of trade union democracy and independence and the start of division and splits.[25]

The PCF was the only political party permitted to interfere in the internal workings of the CGT. Later in his opening speech to the 40th conference Georges Séguy did admit that the composition of the executive bodies of the confederation did not always faithfully reflect the diversity of the CGT and the *courants* of thought which existed within it. At the 40th conference political representation was improved marginally, and the number of socialist members elected to the Executive Commission rose from three to seven (out of 93) (Harmel, 1982, p. 111),[26] and Gerard Gaumé, an unknown socialist,[27] was elected to the Confederal Bureau. Socialists were still very much in a minority however. Before the 40th conference and also before the legislative elections, the point was made in a letter to *Vie Ouvrière* that there was no place for the socialists in the CGT – a notion contested by René Buhl, one of the non-communist members of the Confederal Bureau.[28] As Claude Germon explained, leaving the CGT would have reinforced the cleavages between the PCF and the CGT on the one hand and the PS and the CFDT (FO, FEN) on the other.[29]

Remarkably, opposition did not disappear at the end of 1978. The 40th conference acted as a watershed. It gave dissenters a chance to realise their own strength and provided them with a rallying point. Afterwards opposition was to enter a fascinating and unprecedented stage in which not only members of the Socialist Party were involved, but also members of the French Communist Party. Opposition crystalised around a number of highly political issues. The first major example was the Soviet invasion of Afghanistan. Georges Marchais, the leader of the PCF, gave a speech in Moscow in which he approved of the Soviet intervention in Afghanistan; the leadership of the CGT produced a text with similar sentiments. At the Executive Commission meeting held in January 1980, five socialists, Dinah Caudron, Janine Parent, Pierre Carassus, Claude Germon and Pierre Feuilly, voted against the text. The surprise lay in the fact that there were eleven absentions. Eight members of the Confederal Bureau abstained – two of them were members of the Communist Party, Christiane Gilles and Jean-Louis Moynot. In addition, another member of the PCF, Robert Jévodan, one of the secretaries of the *Fédération des Finances*, also abstained.[30] Within the upper echelons of the CGT, a significant number of CGT leaders, and not only socialists, were opposed to the decision to align with the PCF on this issue.

The next major battle within the CGT took place within the perspective of the Presidential election of April–May 1981. At the National Confederal Committee meeting held in December 1980, two amendments were put forward. The first asked for the democratic measures implicit in the resolution and the ethos of the 40th conference to be implemented. The second called on the CGT to give a clear sign that at the second round of the forthcoming elections priority would be given to ensure that the candidate of the Right was beaten, which would mean that at the second round of the elections the CGT would be obliged to support the socialist candidate. Both these amendments were considered unacceptable. Following on in the wake of the PCF, the CGT had reverted to a less open, more sectarian phase which discouraged debate within its structures. In addition, after the break up of the Union of the Left, the PCF and communist members of the CGT were unlikely to provide support for the PS or its candidates. Two national unions voted against the confederal position, the *Fédération des Finances* and the *Fédération des Capitaines et des Officiers de Pont de la Marine Marchande*.[31] As a result, it could no longer be said that individuals alone were in disagreement with the confederal position. In addition, opposition was manifest outside formal structures of the confederation, in the Marseille area,[32] and in the le Havre region.[33] During the next two months there was a flurry of activity. At the national level a number of national unions opposed the National Confederal Committee resolution. Non-aligned members of the Confederal Bureau, Jacqueline Lambert, René Buhl and Ernest Deiss, expressed their disagreement with the confederal position. At the grassroots level, petitions circulated.[34] All in all, this represented a wave of opposition which had not been seen since the non-communists split away from the CGT in 1947 to form FO. This was not merely 'a tiny minority'.

At the National Confederal Committee meeting held in October 1981 in preparation for the 41st conference, further opposition to the confederal line was voiced. According to Jean-Louis Moynot there had been disagreements within the Confederal Bureau over the commitments which had been made at the 40th conference and then later ignored; he referred specifically to the issues of unity of action with the CFDT and internal democracy within the CGT. According to Christiane Gilles, women's rights were being ignored in the CGT.[35] Four unions abstained, (*Finances, Marine Marchande, Maritime* and *UD Loire Atlantique*), when the vote took place.[36] It was after this meeting that Jean-Louis Moynot and Christiane Gilles resigned from the Confederal Bureau in protest at the increasingly sectarian position taken by the confederation.[37] Other battles had been fought and were being fought simultaneously within the CGT over the issue of internal democracy and in particular over the role of its own means of communication, *Radio Lorraine Coeur d'Acier*, and *Antoinette*, the CGT's magazine for women. In both cases, opposition to the confederal line was crushed. Finally, further dissent was expressed over the attitude of the CGT to trade unions in Eastern Europe and more specifically to Solidarity in Poland. After the announcement of martial law by General Jarulezski. Georges Séguy explained in a press conference that it was not the role of the CGT to interfere in internal Polish affairs. Gérard Gaumé, the only remaining member of the PS on the Confederal Bureau, and nine members of the Executive Commission, condemned the fact that trade unionists had been arrested and that all trade union activity in Poland had been suspended.[38] They were joined by a large number of national unions. *Unions Départementales* and local trade union branches, (a list of which grew daily and was published in the newspaper *Libération*), and a CGT trade union coordination committee for Poland was set up.[39] The confusion was so great that there were three groups within the CGT, those supporting General Jarulezski, those opposing his regime and those such as the *Fédération de l'Equipement, Fédération des Travailleurs du Livre*, who, whilst not condemning Jarulezski, demanding that civil liberties be reestablished and imprisoned trade unionists be set free.[40]

The significance of the second wave of opposition lay in its duration, and in its variety. There were numerous strands of dissent within the CGT. There were those who disagreed with the leadership's alignment with the PCF on the question of domestic politics and who, without necessarily supporting the PS, wanted the CGT to cease being equivocal in its support for the Left in general. There were those who disagreed with the leadership's alignment with the PCF on international politics, particularly with reference to the events in Poland, because they believed that, in doing so, the CGT was denying a commitment to free trade unionism. There was no suggestion that the CGT should not become involved in the political sphere, only that the CGT should not do it on behalf of the PCF. Another important strand of dissent focused on the anti-democratic nature of the CGT's internal politics and on the way in which its 40th conference commitments had been brushed aside. By the time of the 41st conference however this second wave of opposition had been crushed. Did this second wave of opposition constitute a faction? Opposition was variable and its character was dependent on the varying issues involved.[41] Dissenters appeared within the CGT at different times and for different reasons. Some, such as the members of the Socialist Party were active in the first wave of opposition: others, non-aligned members such as Jacqueline Lambert and René Buhl, and Communist Party members such as Jean-Louis Moynot and Christiane Gilles, only became overtly active in the second wave. Moreover, Jacqueline Lambert and René Buhl were not active for long (they resigned), and so it would not have been possible to build up a nucleus of factional organisation. Some had been on opposing sides on different issues. The socialists had been alone in the first wave of opposition, and, on the issue of nationalisations, Jean-Louis Moynot had been in opposition to them.[42]

In the second wave of opposition, there were numerous issues, which could not be easily or quickly combined to establish a single coherent political force. The CGT trade union coordination committee for Poland could have provided an effective organisational focus, but Jacques Toublet was at pains to point out 'that the activists who come are mandated to speak about the Polish question and nothing else'.[43] According to Pierre Carassus, he saw the likes of Jean-Louis Moynot and Christiane Gilles on occasions,[44] but this meant little in organisational terms. All in all, there was a number of unfocused *courants* in opposition to the confederal line. What made this dissent so remarkable was that there were so many *courants* and so many issues. Socialist opposition to the confederal line can be readily understood, but the opposition of communists was more surprising. This latter phenomenon can be explained by the development of Eurocommunism within the PCF and CGT which meant that there was no clear line for communists to follow. The period of political and trade union unity at the time of the Union of the Left had made it difficult to control the flow of ideas. A movement of dissent within the PCF centred on the Paris federation, and a number of CGT dissenters were also part of this movement. There was no well-defined PCF line which at that time could be passed on to the CGT, because it was only gradually being established or re-established within the PCF itself. Some of those communists who were dissenters in the CGT were also dissenters within the PCF and they hoped (vainly, as it turned out) that they could use the CGT to influence events within the PCF.[45]

Factionalism in the CFDT

Dissent is a more constant feature of the CFDT's political culture. Indeed some exasperated members and observers would doubtless argue that the right to disagree is one of the CFDT's quintessential features. At the formal level of conference politics dissent is rife. At the 36th conference held in Nantes in 1973 the *rapport général* – the document referring to the activities of the National Bureau for the previous three years – was approved with 20,279 votes for (87.62 per cent), but with 2,864 votes against (12.38 per cent). At the 37th conference held in Annecy in 1976, the *rapport général* was approved with 15,833 votes for (66.03 per cent), 5,127 (21.38 per cent) against and 3,018 abstentions (12.58 per cent). Finally at the 38th conference held in Brest in 1979 the *rapport général* was approved with 13,904 votes for (56.73 per cent), 7,605 votes against (31.03 per cent) and 2,996 abstentions (12.22 per cent).[46] Indeed at the 38th conference the leadership came close to being disavowed, an unthinkable event at a CGT conference. In confederal elections, generally accepted examples of democratic practice were more prevalent at the CFDT than at the CGT. The National Bureau, the executive and administrative body of the confederation, was composed of 31 members; ten representatives from among the national unions; ten from among the geographical units *Unions Régionales Interprofessionnelles* (URI) and ten from the outgoing National Bureau: in addition there was one representative from the white collar union, the *Union Confédéral des Cadres*. In 1973 there were more candidates than positions for the representatives of the national unions (13 for 10) and the geographical units (11 for 10), but not for the others. At the 37th conference there were 17 candidates for the 10 positions from among the national unions, although no extra candidates from the URIs. At the 38th conference there were 14 candidates from among the national unions and there were 11 from among the URIs. Real elections took place. The CFDT was prepared to tolerate a higher level of institutionalised rivalry and internal opposition than the CGT.

At the 38th conference Daniel Got (Saclep Paris) criticised the decision by the leadership of the CFDT not to support the Common Programme of Government. At the time of the original National Bureau decision, four members had abstained.[47] One of them, Pierre Héritier, explained that others had concentrated on the content of the Common Programme of Government and had consequently overlooked its significance in political terms – it provided a significant rallying point for opposition to the government of the Right.[48] Further opposition to the political stance of the confederation was expressed in an amendment which was proposed by Roger Toutain, the general secretary of Hacuitex, on behalf of 37 trade unions (*Banques, PTT, Santé, Textile, PTT-Rhône*) and which touched on a fundamental point relating to the issue of party-union relations. According to this amendment, the transition to socialism would require the election of a left-wing government, but in addition it would require campaigns on all fronts, political, economic, social, ideological, educational and cultural – 'we cannot just leave it to the political parties to define the transition [to socialism]'. The CFDT refused to be restricted to the industrial sphere and demanded the right to play an unequivocal part in the process of political change. This amendment was not put to the vote but partially integrated into the main resolution, an indication of the support it commanded, a point which was recognised by Edmond Maire in his closing remarks. It was significant in shaping the position of the confederation with regard to the functions of trade unions. As a result, the CFDT considered that political change could not be left to political parties alone.

The decision to engage in trade union unity of action was criticised by a number of delegates (Joseph Brunier (*Services Centraux EDF-GDF*), Georges Dufaud (*Hacuitex Annonay*), Gilbert Bredel (*Marins de Commerce*) and Louis Incerti (*Michelin Clermond-Ferrand*), who complained that at grassroots level the CGT was sectarian and uncooperative. An amendment emphasising the risks inherent in a strategy of unity of action with the CGT was proposed by Fermaz (*Métaux Annecy*), but overwhelmingly defeated. Concerns about internal democracy were expressed by a number of speakers; Jean-Pierre Varlet (*EDF-Nancy*) and Jean-Luc Laurent (*Bâtiment – Vendée*) stated that the CFDT leadership should avoid the excesses of centralism and the monopolisation of decisions: Roland Vitot (*Métaux – Besançon et Vesoul*) claimed that those who wanted to apply the decisions of the previous conference were described as extreme left-wingers; and Roland Szpirko (*Equipement mécanique – région parisienne nord*) protested against the number of exclusions from the CFDT for political reasons. In addition, some criticism was voiced regarding strike activity or rather the organisation of strike activity. Jean-Pierre Lomber (*Transport aérien privé*) and Alain Ramos (*Chimie-Paris*) defended the principle of strike committees elected by general meetings of strikers both trade union members and non members – and therefore not directly under the control of trade unions. An amendment to this effect was proposed by Michèle Hoiroux (*Assistance Publique*), but defeated by 18,674 votes (85.06 per cent) to 3,281 (14.94 per cent). Guy Robert (*Saviem Caen*) defended the notion that strikes should be started by a minority of workers and then allowed to grow into more widespread movements; an amendment along these lines put by Magaud (*Services*) was also overwhelmingly defeated.

Opposition to the confederal line emanated from two different sources. There was one principal force, the self-styled *Contribution* – a loose grouping of some national unions and regional organisations, 'inspired by a Marxist class-based analysis of society'.[49] They were responsible for the amendment on the transition to socialism which was finally taken on board by the whole confederation. The national unions, *Hacuitex, PTT, Services-Livre* sent round a pamphlet 'Syndicalisme de Classe et de Masse et Transition au Socialisme' to all their branches in the run-up to the conference, the main thrust of which underlined the divergences between their analysis of the transition to socialism and that of the confederal leadership.[50] It noted that the transition to socialism was not a process which could be developed within a capitalist state. Acquiring control over the apparatus of the state was a prerequisite for the transition to socialism and not just one feature amongst others. However, *Contribution* did not make a homogeneous grouping which agreed on every issue. *Hacuitex* was more prepared to engage in unity of action with the CGT than was, for example, *Services*. However, because of the similar working conditions prevailing in their industries, these two national unions were often in agreement and distinct from national public sector union such as PTT (Schifres, 1972, p. 188–89). Another grouping could be identified: members of the *Ligue Communiste Révolutionnaire*, 'Trotsky's children', according to Edmond Maire. Whilst they did not command the same level of support at the national level as did *Contribution*, they were a strong force amongst grass roots delegates and were particularly conspicuous at this conference in the debate on the organisation of strike activity and the role of strike committees. In his opening remarks to conference, Edmond Maire stated that 'we will combat any attempt to infringe the democratic functioning of our organisation', which was an oblique reference to the organisational tactics of the extreme-left.

By the time of the next conference, the CFDT had changed its position considerably. At the beginning of 1974 the National Council approved a text on the 'Union of Popular Forces', which was an initiative aimed at rallying the entire Left not just the PCF, the PS and the MRG. In this way, the CFDT aimed to support the political objectives of the Left in general, whilst avoiding total identification with the Union of the Left. However, as previously seen, it began to switch strategy. It wholeheartedly supported François Mitterrand at the time of the presidential elections, and, through its support for the *Assises du Socialisme*, contributed to the reinforcement of the Socialist Party. In addition, it made a considerable commitment to inter-confederal unity with the signing in June 1974 of the joint CGT–CFDT agreement. At the 37th conference held in 1976, criticism was intense. François Garrigue from the teaching union SGEN asked whether the CFDT and the PS had not embarked on a de facto common strategy. He asked whether the CFDT had not joined the camp of the Common Programme and in this way subordinated trade union action to electoral demands. He claimed that the teachers' union, wanted the 'Union of Popular Forces' to be open to all the forces of the the Left, including the extreme-left. Jean-Pierre Bompart (*Syndicat de la recherche agronomique*) reaffirmed the necessity for trade union autonomy, particularly with regard to the PS. Jean-Noël Kerdraon (*Défense Nationale*) reminded conference delegates of the need to differentiate between political parties and trade unions. Patrick Hembert (*Syndicat national des personnels des caisses d'épargne*) disagreed with the decision to support François Mitterrand, to participate in the *Assises du Socialisme* and also to conclude an agreement with the CGT. Françoise Hennion (*Syndicat des services*) criticised the fact that CFDT trade unions had been mobilised in favour of the PS and François Mitterrand. Claude Migeon (*Syndicat de la metallurgie de Belfort*) drew attention to a potential functional confusion between the PS and the CFDT, since activists in the party's workplace branches were often also CFDT activists. Finally, Dominique Noly (*Syndicat des Métaux de Lyon 7e*) considered the Assises du Socialisme to be a 'PS takeover bid for the CFDT'. The last of these speakers moved an amendment urging that the 'Union of Popular Forces' should be a mass movement in which the working class would form the vanguard. Moreover, it should be distinct from any strategy based on the Common Programme of Government. The amendment was defeated by 15,436 votes (64.83 per cent) to 6,719 (28.22 per cent), but it showed nevertheless the level of opposition to this particular strategy.

When the idea of the 'Union of Popular Forces' was originally mooted in the National Council of the CFDT in January 1974, it met with hostility. The national unions *Services* and *Bâtiment* feared that it smacked of electoralism. Others, the URIs Bretagne and Provence–Côte d'Azur felt this strategy could offend certain CFDT members who were anxious not to become involved in the political sphere. A number of national unions *VRP, Banque, Finances, Santé, Construction*, and URIs, Bretagne, Provence–Côte d'Azur, Nord, asked for the decision to be delayed so that a debate could take place within the CFDT – this proposal was defeated by 559 votes to 474 votes with 258 abstentions. A number of different amendments were put all demonstrating significant internal divisions within the confederation over the issue of party-union relations. The final text was approved, by 715 votes for, 257 against and 264 abstentions.[51] Some were opposed to the idea of the CFDT becoming involved in the political sphere. Others were opposed to the idea of aligning with a specific constellation of left-wing political forces.

The decision to participate in the *Assises du Socialisme* met with considerable support in some parts of the confederation, but equally with significant opposition. After the presidential election in 1974 François Mitterrand launched an appeal to set up 'a party of socialists', which was greeted favourably by a statement from the National Bureau meeting exceptionally two days later. More or less simultaneously an appeal was launched calling for 'participation in the development of a great socialist force'.[52] This appeal was signed by approximately fifty CFDT members, nine of whom were members of the National Bureau, four were confederal secretaries and thirty two held important responsibilities in national unions or in regional organisations.[53] This initiative led to considerable criticism within the structures of the CFDT, and a fierce debate took place in the columns of the *CFDT Syndicalisme*. Critics focussed on two different features; internal democracy and party-union links. It was claimed that the National Bureau had committed the CFDT, without prior discussion taking place within the confederation itself.[54] Secondly, the National Bureau had committed the CFDT to one particular party,[55] the Socialist Party. The National Bureau had in fact made positive remarks about the *Assises du Socialisme*, and was criticised for this at the following National Council meeting. At this meeting the National Bureau stance was only approved by 59.2 per cent of the vote, with 27.3 per cent against and 13.5 per cent abstentions. Another motion put by the URI Basse-Normandie and the national unions *Banque, Construction-Bois, Hacuitex*, criticised the National Bureau for having engaged the CFDT in an operation which was not consistent with any of the resolutions passed at the 35th and 36th conferences and which was an encouragement to join a particular political party. This motion was defeated by 918 votes (61.1 per cent) to 383 (25.5 per cent), with 201 abstentions (13.4 per cent).[56] Nevertheless, a significant body of opinion was opposed to the CFDT's alignment with the Socialist Party.

A further amendment was put at the 1976 conference by Alain Chesnel on the issue of strike committees; this was defeated by 15,957 votes to 7,507. There was an amendment put by François Wellhoff (*Betor-Région parisienne*) advocating a place for all workers in the CFDT whether of the left or of the extreme-left; this was defeated by 16,355 votes to 6,104. These two issues were considered particularly significant by the extreme-left, and it is a measure of its importance that it could still command such a high level of support at this conference. Finally, a few rare instances of opposition to the confederal line focussed on the industrial sphere. An amendment was put by Claude Hue, on behalf of the trade union branch *Institut Géographique National*, criticising the readiness of the leadership to drop the CFDT's commitment to eroding wage differentials. It was defeated by 15,068 votes to 7,684 with 1,226 abstentions. Two other utopian amendments were carried, one put by Camille Bobillier on behalf of *Métallurgie de Sochaux-Peugeot Monthéliard*, calling for the suppression of firms which take on employees with temporary or short-term contracts, and another by François Guntz, on behalf of *Métallurgie du Bas-Rhin*, calling for suppression of all imposed workrates.

According to Edmond Maire, opposition to the confederal line came from two sources:

On the one hand, there is a small minority composed of activists who are fundamentally opposed to the confederal line. It is composed of cuckoos who come to lay their eggs in our nest. On the other, there are those who signed the text of *Contribution* and who do not question the CFDT's conception of trade unionism nor the majority of the confederation's ideas. With the latter we expect to pursue the debate on the differences, even divergences, that exist between us. Having seen the votes and the debates that have taken place, it can be estimated that these activists represent between twelve and twenty per cent of conference participants.

Commenting on the state of factional politics within the CFDT at this conference. Backmann noted that certain *tendances* were established, 'but nothing institutionalised or permanent'. They were better described as *courants* which permeated the organisation, sometimes seeking points of convergence, sometimes opposing the leadership, sometimes, although less often, making common cause with it.[57] There were two groupings; on the one hand, the extreme Left, the cuckoos, according to Edmond

Maire; on the other, Contribution, which was made up of a number of national unions (*Banque, Santé,* PTT, *Construction Bois*) and one geographical unit (Rhône–Alpes). Both of the groupings had no established homogeneity, no organisation unity, no common platform and no strategy for the acquisition of power within the confederation. *Construction-Bois*, often in sympathy with the *Contribution* line, voted at this conference with the confederal leadership on the important votes. These two groups, the extreme-left and *Contribution*, did not often act in concert. As Claude Vernet (*Hacuitex*), a sympathiser with the *Contribution* line, explained, 'We do not identify with the *courants* of anarchists. Trotskyists and Maoists'.[58]

By the time of the CFDT's next conference, considerable changes had taken place. The Union of the Left had broken up, the CFDT had formally approved the Moreau Report which advocated a return to the industrial sphere, the Left had lost the legislative elections in March 1978, the CGT had held its 40th conference and inter-confederal relations were under severe strain. At the 38th conference held in May 1979 in Brest, opposition was widespread. There was a major ideological disagreement at this conference reminiscent of the debate on the transition to socialism which had occurred at the 36th conference. On this occasion Luc Garnier on behalf of the trade union *PTT de la Loire* put an amendment refering to the notion of the break with capitalism. In the original conference document the CFDT leadership claimed that workers' control was a process, not an endpoint. The amendment claimed that a break with capitalism was necessary, before this process could be set in motion. Had this amendment been passed, it would have been a complete disavowal of the policy espoused by the leadership. It was defeated, but only by 11,938 votes to 9,539. In addition, considerable opposition was expressed to the strategy inherent in the Moreau Report. It was considered a major break with the former strategy of the CFDT, according to Daniel Cholley on behalf of 16 trade unions in the Paris region. Speaking on behalf of 12 branches from the Champagne-Ardennes region, Rémy Huet feared that it would correspond to a U-turn in CFDT strategy. It was considered a sign of the CFDT's willingness to manage the economic crisis, according to Jean-Paul Halgand (*Syndicat national du personnel des Caisses d'épargne*). It was reformist, according to Michel Braaksma (*Construction-Bois Rhône-Alpes*). It would leave the political parties on their own in the political sphere and assist in the restructuring of capital, according to Léon Dion, the general secretary of *Hacuitex*. It would lead to the weakening of trade union activities and to disunion, according to Géo Goubier

(Construction-Bois). (Opposition to the Moreau Report had already been expressed in the National Council meeting held in January 1978 by some of the constituent members of *Contribution, Hacuitex, PTT, Rhône-Alpes*, but also by the Auvergne region organisation[59]).

There was also opposition to the role that the CFDT had played before the elections. Claude Sardrais (*syndicats Métallurgie de la région parisienne*) and Dominique Noly (*syndicat des métaux de Lyon Vlle*) expressed regret at the extent of PS influence over the Confederation. As was explained in Chapter 2, the National Bureau voted at the beginning of October 1977 to meet all the political parties of the Union of the Left. This vote was not unanimous – twenty members voted for, but eight abstained.[60] Some members did not want the CFDT to play such a clear role in the political sphere as an arbitrator between the PS and the PCF. Moreover, at the National Council meeting following the talks between the CFDT and the political parties, a motion was put by Rhône-Alpes and Midi-Pyrénées, claiming that the CFDT had not been sufficiently critical of the Socialist Party.[61]

There was also criticism of the confederal strategy regarding trade union unity of action. Jean-Paul Bourne and Jeanne Couderc criticised the CFDT leadership for changing its position on industrial action and for not joining in national days of action with the CGT. According to Jean-Pierre Moussy (*Banque*) and Joseph Saint-Martin (*PTT de la région Aquitaine*), the CFDT should continue to seek an agreement with the CGT (only two conferences previously the CFDT leadership had been criticised by some sections of the confederation for engaging in unity of action with the CGT). There was also concern expressed regarding the internal workings of the confederation. The CFDT leadership had disbanded a number of trade union branches, for example Usinor-Dunkerque which had been run by extreme left-wingers.[62] Georges Dufaud (*Hacuitex*) asked how the CFDT could continue to criticise democratic centralism in other organisations and yet practise it itself. Six months previously the National Bureau had decided not to set up a national committee for the coordination of strike activity, because it would have operated outside the structures of the confederation and could have been used as a parallel organisation by the extreme-left.[63]

Two other resolutions were approved. The first aimed to improve the structures and democratic functioning of the CFDT. With the introduction of quotas, it made access to participation in decision-making within the confederation more open, particularly for women; however on the other hand, it insisted on the mandating of delegates and it tightened up the rules on expulsions. The second concerning the international relations of the CFDT was passed on a show of hands. Opposition was expressed to the confederal line on one aspect of the industrial sphere. The original conference resolution demanded a 35 hour week but left the question of payment up in the air. An amendment on this point was taken and also passed, against the advice of the leadership.

The confederal line met with considerable criticism at every conference during the 1970s. Dissent was a central feature of CFDT life. For the most part opposition concentrated on issues relating to the political sphere, but occasionally it focussed on industrial issues. Opposition emanated from two specific groupings. The smaller one was the extreme-left. It commanded considerable support at the 36th and 37th conferences, but by the time of the 38th conference its influence was beginning to wane. It was not opposed to the idea of links with political parties as such but was opposed to the idea that the CFDT should be aligned to the Union of the Left, and more particularly to the Socialist Party. At the confederal level opposition from the extreme-left often crystalised around the issue of the organisation of strike activity and strike committees, an issue which found little favour with other sections of the confederations. The ability of the extreme-left to engage in factional politics was compromised by the fact it did not control individual national unions and did not represent one homogeneous force. It was made up of the *Ligue Communiste Révolutionnaire* and also the *Parti Communiste Révolutionnaire (Marxiste-Léniniste)*, who were hardly comrades in arms, being Trotskyist and Maoist respectively. Interestingly, at the confederal level, its opposition often crystallised around an issue linked to the industrial sphere, the organisation of strike activity.

The other major force in opposition to the confederal line, *Contribution*, acted as a relatively coherent group at conference, within the National Bureau and also within the National Council on various occasions. However its composition was not stable and disciplined, and it was not identified with one particular political party. Although it published a joint 'Contribution au débat' for the 37th conference, its constituent elements did not always vote together. At the time of the debate within the National Bureau on meetings with political parties in October 1977 – a major feature in the analysis of the separation of the political and industrial spheres – there were in fact eight abstentions. Four members of *Contribution* abstained (*Banques, Construction-Bois, Hacuitex, Rhône-Alpes*). They were not necessarily opposed to the idea of meeting the political parties as such, as Léon Dion, the general secretary of Hacuitex explained.[64] Two other members of the contribution (*PTT, Santé*) actually voted for the motion, whilst the other four abstentionists (Alsace, Centre-Ouest, Pays de la Loire, Région Parisienne) did so, because it was not the function of the CFDT to become involved in a detailed criticism of the positions of political parties.[65] Opposition to the confederal position in the CFDT was extensive on occasions, but diverse and diffuse.

Conclusions

The CGT and CFDT were not monolithic organisations and were unable to act as such at strategic moments during the 1970s. Under the surface of confederal unity, which was more real at the CGT than at the CFDT, a complex game of factional politics was being played out. In the CGT communists held a dominant position within the confederation, and other factional groups were never able to pose a serious threat to this domination. Socialists shared diffuse feelings of affinity, and, as the leadership of the CGT became more overtly aligned with the PCF, so they played a more important role in factional politics. They developed into a *courant*, an unorganised grouping of individual members, sharing a similar set of views. As the CGT followed the PCF into a more sectarian phase, dissident communists also became a *courant*. There is evidence to suggest that they both acted as a focus for dissent amongst other dissatisfied CGT members who had no specific political allegiance. These two groups could not be described as *tendances*. The two leading protagonists amongst the dissenters, Claude Germon, on the one hand, and Jean-Louis Moynot on the other, were not competing for control of the confederation. The two groups were not organised and structured enough to be described as *fractions*. The prime loyalty of both sets of dissenters lay with the confederation, at least until it became quite clear that the rest of the confederation was not going to change. It is nevertheless significant that Claude Germon left to become a socialist member of the National Assembly; Pierre Carassus left to become a full-time activist in the French Socialist Party with responsibility for workplace branches; Jean-Louis Moynot and Christine Gilles left the CGT and after 1981 became advisors to different socialist ministers. On the other hand opposition within the CFDT to the confederal line was more diffuse and more widespread. Opposition groupings could be described as *courants*. They were unorganised groups of CFDT members, sharing diffuse sets of views. Within the extreme-left there were *mini-courants* because they belonged to different political parties, the LCR and PCR-ML. *Contribution* was a rolling *courant*, since membership evolved according to different circumstances. These groups could not be described as *tendances*, as there was no clear leader of the extreme-left grouping or of *Contribution* at a national level and no evidence to suggest that they were seriously attempting to compete for control of the confederation and supplant Edmond Maire. It is possible that one CFDT trade unionist, Frédo Krumnow, the charismatic general secretary of *Hacuitex*, could have emerged as an alternative leader, but he died just after the 36th conference in Nantes, and there was no one else to take on his mantle. These groups did not correspond to the definition of *fractions*. The extreme-left or at least a part of it did try to set up a parallel organisation within the CFDT, particularly within strike committees, but they were outflanked. Neither the extreme-left nor *Contribution* constituted a fully structured group. Admittedly the latter did attempt to define an alternative doctrine and produced some detailed proposals but there was no doubt as to the loyalty to the members of *Contribution* – they were resolute members of the CFDT first and foremost. There was no suggestion that they attempted to split the confederation.

It is interesting that none of these *courants* in the CGT and in the CFDT were set up in response to confederal decisions relating to the industrial sphere. They did not differ greatly with the confederal line over policies on industrial restructuring, differing forms of employment and technological change. In the CGT *courants* did not become prominent because of their dissatisfaction with the potential confusion between trade union and political party functions in general. The socialists were not opposed to the notion of the trade unions being aligned with political parties, but they were opposed to the idea of the CGT being aligned with one particular political party, the French Communist Party. In this process the socialists helped to reinforce the functional confusion between trade unionists and members of a political party. The dissident communist *courant* within the CGT was established, not because of a dissatisfaction with the potential confusion of functions between the CGT and political parties in general, nor because of the potential confusion between the positions taken on occasions by the leadership of the CGT and those of the PCF. This *courant* was established in part at least as a reaction to the decision of the French Communist Party to move into a more sectarian phase, which would have resulted in the CGT becoming more sectarian too and less progressive in terms of trade union development. As for the CFDT, there was little criticism of its decision to remain aloof from the Common Programme of Government and the Union of the Left in the early 1970s. Opposition grew as the decade progressed, and it became clearer that the CFDT was becoming increasingly drawn into the party political sphere, which, given the politics of the French Left, meant that the CFDT was being drawn into a position of support for the Socialist Party. Ironically, when the CFDT chose to change strategy by moving away from the political sphere and by concentrating more exclusively on the industrial sphere, this strategy was heavily criticised too. Events in the political sphere had a major impact on the internal politics of both trade union confederations, putting great strain on the cohesion of both the CGT and the CFDT. In addition, political factionalism took up a considerable amount of time and energy, and thus had a debilitating effect on the ability of the trade union confederations to act effectively in the industrial sphere.

Notes

1. Interview, Jean-Louis Moynot 13 April 1984.
2. *Le Peuple*, 1–31 May 1972. *Le Peuple*, 1–31 July 1975. *Le Peuple*, 1–31 December 1978. All conference references to CGT will be taken from these documents, unless otherwise stated.
3. *Le Monde*, 30 November 1978, 2 December 1978.
4. *Le Peuple*, 1–15 January 1978, p. 42–3.
5. *Le Monde*, 6 October 1977.
6. For details, see interview in *L'Unité*, 30 September 1977.
7. *Le Peuple*, 1–15 January 1978, p. 29.
8. Interview, Pierre Carassus 28 February 1985.
9. *Le Monde*, 12 October 1977.
10. *Vie Ouvrière*, 13–19 February 1978, p. 4.
11. *Le Monde*, 3 November 1977. *L'Unité*, 20–24 January, 1978, p. 16.
12. *Le Monde*, 28 January 1978.
13. *Vie Ouvrière*, 19–25 June 1978, p. 12.
14. *Le Peuple*, 1–15 January 1978, p. 25.
15. *Repères*, February 1976, p. 64–71.
16. *L'Unité*, 11–17 November 1977, p. 14–15. See also his statement in *Vie Ouvrière*, 13–19 February 1978. Jean-Claude Laroze left the PS at the end of 1979 – interview, Jean-Claude Laroze 26 February 1985.
17. *Nouvel Observateur*, 10 October 1977.
18. Interview, Pierre Carassus 28 February 1985.
19. Interview, Jean-Claude Laroze 26 February 1985.
20. *Le Monde*, 28 January 1978.
21. Interview, Pierre Carassus, 28 February 1985.
22. *Faire*, no 7, April 1976, p. 39.
23. *Le Peuple*, 1–15 December 1977, p. 45.
24. *Vie Ouvrière*, 19–25 June 1978, p. 12.
25. *Le Monde*, 28 January 1978. *Le Peuple*, 1–31 December 1978, p. 13, 62.
26. Harmel, C., *La CGT*, Paris, PUF, 1982, p. 111.
27. According to J-F Kahn, *Nouvel Observateur*, 6 December 1978. Gerard Gaumé resigned in August 1986.

28. *Vie Ouvrière*, 13–19 February 1978, p. 9. Ironically, he resigned as a member of the Confederal Bureau at the time of the second wave of opposition.
29. *L'Unité*, 20 April 1978, p. 9. However he gave up all his CGT responsibilities when he became a socialist member of the National Assembly.
30. Harmel, C. & Tandler, N., *Comment le parti communiste contrôle la CGT*. Bibliothèque d'Histoire Social, 1982, Paris, p. 8–9.
31. *Le Peuple*, 1–31 December 1980, p. 60.
32. Tract (no date).
33. Tract (no date).
34. See the collection of statements in Barralis, R. *et al.*, *Le débat ignoré*, Paris, 1981.
35. *Le Peuple*, 1–15 October 1981, p. 41–43, 47–48.
36. *Libération*, 10–11 October 1981.
37. *Le Monde*, 6 October 1981.
38. *Le Matin*, 15 December 1981.
39. For details, see *Libération*, from 19–20 December 1981 to 21 January 1982.
40. *Le Matin*, 21 December 1981.
41. Interview, Jean-Louis Moynot 13 April 1984.
42. *Le Peuple*, 1–15 December 1977, p. 4–7.
43. See interview in *Que faire aujourd'hui*, May 1982, p. 77.
44. Interview, Pierre Carassus 28 February 1985. Another dissident said that they had not met on a regular basis. Interview, Roger Rousselot 21 May 1987.
45. Interview, Roger Rousselot 21 May 1987.
46. *CFDT Syndicalisme*, 7 June 1973. *CFDT Syndicalisme*, 3 June 1976. *CFDT Syndicalisme*, 17 May 1979. All references to CFDT conferences will be taken from these documents, unless otherwise stated.
47. *Le Monde*, 16 September 1972.
48. Interview, Pierre Héritier 21 February 1985.
49. Interview, Léon Dion 7 April 1986.
50. *Syndicalisme de classe et de masse*, CFDT Hacuitex, PTT & Services-Livre, 1974.
51. *CFDT Syndicalisme*, 7 February 1974, p. 14–15.
52. *Le Monde*, 16 June 1974.
53. *CFDT Syndicalisme*, 11 July 1974, p. 11.
54. See for example the statement by CFDT Hacuitex, *CFDT Syndicalisme*, 13 June 1974, p. 9. URI Pays de Loire, *CFDT Syndicalisme*, 11 July 1974, p. 10.
55. See the statement by URI Basse-Normandie, URI Pays de Loire, *CFDT Syndicalisme*, 4 July 1974, p. 10–11.
56. *CFDT Syndicalisme*, 10 October 1974, p. 13, 21.
57. *L'Unité*, 21–27 May 1976, p. 8–11.
58. According to Roy, J., *Le Monde*, 27 July 1976.
59. *CFDT Syndicalisme*, 2 February 1978, p. 2.
60. *CFDT Syndicalisme*, 13 October 1977, p. 10–13.
61. *CFDT Syndicalisme*, 3 November 1977, p. 10.
62. They actually joined the CGT later, *Le Monde*, 3 November 1979. See also *Partis Pris*, January 1979, p. 13–16.

63. *Le Monde*, 27–28 June 1976.
64. *Politique Hebdo*, 30 May–5 June 1977.
65. *Le Monde*, 9 October 1977.

Chapter 6

Strikes, Trade Union Confederations and the Union of the Left

Chapters 2 and 3 have shown that the trade union confederations participated in the political sphere on behalf of the political parties, and Chapters 4 and 5 have demonstrated that French trade union affairs were very much influenced by events in the political sphere. In the next two chapters the emphasis will switch to the industrial sphere and the consequences of party-union relations for French industrial relations, and more specifically, strikes and collective bargaining. In France, as elsewhere, collective bargaining and industrial conflict do not occupy mutually exclusive ends of a spectrum; they clearly form two interconnected features of one single complex system of industrial relations. However, for purposes of clarity, these two features of French industrial relations will be analysed separately within the framework of this book.

In France the right to strike is enshrined in the constitutions of the Fourth and Fifth Republics, but it has been curtailed for some professional groups in the public sector. Political strikes are formally outlawed, but, because of the problems of delineation between political and industrial strikes, this legal nicety has generally been ignored. Within the French context, considerable academic attention has been paid to the political nature of strike activity. In the early days of French trade unionism, the strike was considered by revolutionary syndicalists;

as the most practical expression and as the most vivid symbol of class war. It involved the direct confrontation of the antagonists. This gave it two particular advantages over other forms of direct action. First: the fact that the material interests of the workers were directly involved made it the ideal ground to fight on . . . Second: the strike, whatever its cause, made crystal clear the fundamental conflict between labour and capital . . . increasing the class awareness of the workers, deepening the chasm between them and their opponents, and spurring them on to further action. It thus had a cumulative effect and a revolutionary value. (Ridley, 1970, p. 104–5).

It was thought that the general strike would bring about the overthrow of capitalism and usher in a socialist society. However, as Maitron observed, perhaps with a hint of nostalgia, the general strike ceased to be a major trade union preoccupation just prior to the outbreak of the First World War, although it has occurred in one form or other in 1934, 1936, 1944, 1953, and May–June 1968.[1] The demise of revolutionary syndicalism *per se* did not necessarily mean that strikes lost their political significance. In the only major English language work on strikes in France, Shorter and Tilly described the strike as an instrument of working class political action. 'Workers, when they strike, are merely extending into the streets their normal process of political participation . . . (Shorter, & Tilly, 1974, p. 343–44). Other observers have underlined the importance of economic and industrial factors in explaining strike activity in France. In his retrospective analysis of strikes in France Dubois has condensed the number of approaches and demonstrate the variety of different economic explanations. According to Perrot, prior to 1890 there was a propensity for strike action during periods of economic growth, and workers were more prepared to strike when purchasing power was holding up well. Andréani indicated that, for the period 1890–1914, the number of days lost through strikes increased at times of economic growth and decreased at times of deflation. According to Goetz-Girey, who studied the period 1914–62, it was economic growth which was most significant factor explaining the level of strike activity, not the level of inflation. In a study of the 1950–71 period, Scardigli showed that the level of inflation played no significant role in conditioning strike activity. The change in the rate of economic growth had countervailing repercussions, with the result that, in the words of Dubois, 'the results obtained by Scardigli demonstrate fully that *the influence of economic factors is never the determining factor*' (his italics).[2] This influence is always mediated by the decisions of the actors involved, an issue which will be considered in greater detail later on in the chapter.

Disentangling the political from the economic and industrial is no easy matter. Strikes may have their roots in the industrial sphere but may have important political ramifications. The national day of action called by all the major trade union confederations for the 24 May 1977 in protest against the package of austerity measures introduced by the Prime Minister Raymond Barre was ostensibly about economic and industrial matters. However, given its size, its form and its target, it had immense political impact. The strike called by the CGT and the CFDT on 17 September 1973 to protest about the lack of civil rights in Chile was eminently political in terms of its subject matter, but of less consequence in the domestic political sphere. The events of May 1968, the most significant strike wave ever in France, had their roots in the industrial sphere, but also provided an excellent example of the potential for political impact in the old revolutionary syndicalist tradition. However, on this occasion trade union leaders were conscious of the need to make up for lost ground in the industrial sphere and were also unprepared to lead the mass of strikers into a battle for political objectives. They settled for a conclusion based primarily, but not exclusively, on improvements in industrial demands, increases in wages and a reduction in the length of the working week.[3] Indeed, instead of ensuring political gains for the Left, the strikes actually led directly to massive short-term political gains for the Right. As André Berteloot, one of the confederal secretaries of the CGT, indicated at a later date, 'the fear engendered by TV images of Paris being laid waste led to the June elections and an absolute majority for the UDR (the Gaullist party)'.[4] The link between industrial unrest and electoral defeat was to weigh heavily on the minds of French trade unionists during the 1970s.

This chapter will examine the place of French strike activity in the 1970s in the political and industrial spheres and, in so doing, evaluate the statement made by Dubois that the decline in strike activity during the 1970s can be explained 'without any shadow of a doubt' in terms of the difficulties experienced by the Union of the Left and the ensuing repercussions for CGT–CFDT unity of action.[5] The chapter will be divided into two major sections. The first will investigate national strike statistics in order to see whether a particular pattern of strike activity can be discerned for the period of the Union of the Left and to see whether the politicisation of strike activity occurred. The second will examine the differing strike strategies of the CGT and the CFDT, the PCF and the PS, with the aim of identifying areas of convergence and divergence.

Strikes in the 1970s

When dealing with French strike statistics, it is first worth recalling what they represent. Strike figures are collected by Labour Inspectors from the Ministry of Employment who receive their information from workforce delegates, managerial staff or strike leaders. Labour Inspectors are usually alerted to the existence of a strike in the course of their normal activity as conciliators, but they also obtain information from local newspapers. The employer does not have to inform the Ministry by law, as is the case for example in the Federal Republic of Germany, so the process is relatively haphazard. In addition, strike statistics do not cover every sector. Since 1962 there is no record of disputes in agriculture. There is a doubt hovering over the accuracy of figures referring to some public sector employees, notably teachers and postal and communications workers. Some national days of action may not have been included in the figures. From 1975 onwards however, Ministry statistics have differentiated between *conflits généralisés* and *conflits localisés*: the former comprise national days of action, multi-industry and industry-wide strikes, the latter comprise strikes which are specific to one particular workplace. Obviously, as the Ministry readily points out, it is not always easy to differentiate between these two forms of strike.[6] Data concerning generalised conflicts can however only really be estimates as there is no reliable way of calculating the number of strikers participating in a national day of action. Figures do not include strikes in protest against redundancies (a significant phenomenon in the 1970s as a result of the repercussions of the oil crisis), since redundant workers are regarded as no longer being in employment. Each conflict is considered a discrete element, so if a strike stops for forty eight hours and starts again, it is counted as two separate conflicts. There is also a certain discrepancy as to the figure for the number of workers involved in strikes. Moreover, although the official figures show certain variables, number of strikes, number of enterprises involved, number of strikers and days lost, they give no information about the economic position of the enterprise, the type of workforce, the relative strength of the different trade unions or previous strike records. Finally, it is necessary to point out that the accuracy of official figures has been called into question by the trade union confederations and also by the employers.[7] Strike statistics are imperfect but they provide the only available national indication of the level of strike activity in France. As can be seen from Table 6.1, the global figures show a tendency towards a reduction in strike activity, however measured, as the seventies progressed. In 1972 the number of workplaces affected and the number of strikers were exceptionally high – the long and bitter strikes at Le Joint Français, Nouvelles Galéries and Pennaroya set the tone for the year. In 1974 the figures for the number of workplaces affected was exceptionally low. In 1976 the total number of workplaces affected, strikers and days lost was again exceptionally high, but from then onwards, the overall level of strike activity declined markedly.

Table 6.1 General strike statistics – France 1970–79

Year	Number of strikes	Number of workplaces affected	Number of strikers (000's)	Number of days lost (000's)
1970	2,942	5,944	1,079.8	1,742.2
1971	4,318	–	–	4,387.8
1972	3,464	72,882	2,721.3	3,755.3
1973	3,731	35,995	2,246.0	3,914.6
1974	3,381	14,771	1,563.5	3,380.0
1975	3,888	23,946	1,827.1	3,868.9
1976	4,348	35,534	2,022.5	5,010.7
1977	3,302	20,287	1,919.9	3,665.9
1978	3,206	12,178	704.6	2,200.4
1979	3,104	22,010	967.2	3,636.6

Source: Ministère du Travail.

There is a consensus amongst those researchers who have investigated the reasons why French employees go on strike. The major identifiable reasons lie clearly within the industrial sphere. An analysis of the strike returns for the year 1971 established that employees go on strike to obtain better wages, to protect their trade union rights, to fight for a shorter working week and to improve their working conditions, as can be seen form Table 6.2. Durand and Harff compared their findings with those form a previous study by Baumgartner and noted that there was relatively little change in the order of importance of different types of grievances. Wages were at the top of the list, and in general 'quantitative' demands still were the most prevalent, in spite of claims to the contrary from other researchers (Clerc for instance) that, as a result of strike activity in May–June 1968, there would be an increase in 'qualitative' demands. (Durand & Harff, 1927, p. 356–75). Morel undertook a similar study, based on strike returns collected by the Ministry of Employment for the last quarter of 1974. A similar pattern emerges. Workers go on strike to obtain better wages, to protect their rights and to improve their working conditions. In addition, Morel noted that many strikes were called because of impending economic difficulties within the firm, a factor not identified by Durand and Harff, which clearly reflects a general worsening of the economic climate (Morel, 1975, p. 184).

A further study was based on strike returns from localised conflicts for the whole of 1976. This statistical *tour de force* by Dassa also underlines

Table 6.2 Frequency of strike grievances I (%)

Wages	49.7%
Trade union rights	10.6%
Reduction in the working week/retirement	9.5%
Employment	5.8%
Fringe benefits and 'monthly pay'	5.3%
Working conditions	4.7%
Job classifications/methods of payment	4.1%
Workplace agreements	3.0%
Work organisation	2.1%
Others	4.1%

Source: Durand & Harff, 1977, p. 366.

the importance of the industrial sphere. As Table 6.3 shows, workers go on strike to obtain better wages, to protect their trade union rights, to campaign for a shorter working week, to protect their jobs and to improve their working conditions. Dassa indicated other contributory factors which help to explain the propensity to strike. The size of the workplace was significant. Certain geographical areas were more strike-prone than others, for example the Paris region and the Rhône-Alpes region. Certain industrial sectors were more strike-prone, the steel, chemical, engineering, electrical, automobile, textile, wood-processing and transport industries. The vast majority of strikes were called in the private sector (95.4 per cent), but in terms of days lost, 21.7 per cent were lost in the public sector. The problem with all these studies is that they are based upon data provided by the Ministry of Employment, which has no procedure for eliciting information about the political aspects of strike activity. Strikes are complex phenomena which may not be explained solely in terms of the immediate grievances that led to them being called in the first place. With this in mind, Durand and Dubois undertook an independent survey which aimed to identify latent reasons for strike activity. Workers were asked whether they went on strike for reasons other than those formally expressed. Of those questioned, 32 per cent were unaware of any other reasons. Of the others, 21 per cent quoted the attitude of management, 18 per cent working conditions, 14 per cent work organisation, 5 per cent purchasing power and finally a mere 4 per cent quoted political reasons (Durand, & Dubois, 1975, p. 19–96). This survey helps to reinforce the findings of the previous studies. According to the Ministry of Employment and to the individual workers themselves, strikes are firmly based within the industrial sphere and are not called for political reasons.

Table 6.3 Frequency of strike grievances II (%)

	Frequency of conflicts	Frequency of grievances
Wages	89.0	53.1
Negotiations/trade union rights	17.4	10.4
Working hours	17.3	10.3
Employment	16.7	9.9
Working conditions	15.1	9.0
Discipline	9.7	5.8
Others	2.5	1.5
Total	167.7*	100.0

Note: *This total comes to more than 100 because on many occasions there was not one single reason to explain why a strike began.
Source: Dassa, 1978, p. 92.

Indications of the political significance of strike activity during the 1970s can however be found in the work of Mouriaux. He indicated four ways in which strikes may be linked to aspects of the political sphere. Firstly, political actors may intervene in support of certain strikes. Secondly, strikes may become political as a result of their own internal momentum. Thirdly, the greater the number of people involved in strike activity, the greater the level of politicisation. Finally, strikes may become more political at specific moments of the political calendar and notably at election times (Mouriaux, 1985, p. 140). The first and the last of these factors are the most interesting for an analysis of the relationship between trade union confederations and political parties. The first will be examined in the second part of the chapter and the last will be investigated here. Mouriaux noted that in years where there were legislative elections there was a reduction in strike activity, likewise for years in which there was a Presidential election. As was seen in Table 6.1, there was a marked reduction in the number of strikes in 1974 (a Presidential election year), a marginal reduction in 1978, but an increase in 1973 (legislative election years). However in terms of the number of firms affected, there was a major reduction in 1973 and 1974 and a marked reduction in 1978. The number of strikers declined in all three years. The number of days lost declined in 1974 and 1978 but increased slightly in 1973. One weakness in Mouriaux's argument lies in the fact that the strike figures refer to the whole calendar year, whereas the elections took place in the earlier part of the year, March in 1973, May in 1974 and March in 1978. The potential for the politicisation of strike activity was at its highest before the elections, and yet these strike figures refer to the whole calendar year. A more serious weakness lay in any evaluation of the figures for 1974, the year of the Presidential election. Unless the trade union confederations were extremely well appraised of Georges Pompidou's physical condition, it is difficult for them to know what strike strategy to follow prior to elections, when the Presidential elections were not due to be held until 1976. It was only Pompidou's untimely death in April 1974 that led to the elections in May, and it is stretching credulity a little to suggest that trade union attitudes to strike activity were dominated by concerns about the possible death of the President two years before the end of his term of office. A more useful way of attributing political significance to strike activity at election time is to compare a period prior to the legislative elections of 1973 and 1978 with a corresponding period in preceding years. One solution would be to take strike figures for January to March for 1973 and 1978 and compare them with figures for the same period during the other years.

Table 6.4 Monthly strike statistics (1970–73)

Month	Number of strikes and days lost	1970	1971	1972	1973
January	strikes	188	293	243	251
	days lost	56.7	165.0	77.1	148.0
February	strikes	324	604	371	279
	days lost	227.2	396.8	165.1	109.8
March	strikes	403	525	534	267
	days lost	190.6	278.4	289.1	138.4
Total	strikes	915	1422	1148	797
	days lost	474.5	840.2	531.3	396.2
(Number of days lost in thousands)					
1970/1/2 : 1973 1st quarter	total strikes	114	178	144	100
	days lost	120	212	134	100
1970/1/2 : 1973 Whole year	total strikes	79	115	92	100
	days lost	46	112	96	100
(100 = 1973)					

Source: Ministère du Travail

Table 6.4 shows that the total number of strikes and days lost in the first quarter was lower in 1973 than in all the previous three years. Strike activity did not stop just prior to elections. There were still enough reasons for going on strike. However workers were less likely to go on strike just prior to elections. Lessons had been learnt from the Events of May. Berteloot was not the only trade unionist concerned by the risks of industrial unrest just prior to political elections. These figures are all the more revealing since, as can be seen from the lower section of the table, there was less strike activity just prior to the 1973 legislative elections than in similar periods in previous years, but year on year there was a relatively larger number of strikes and days lost through strikes throughout the whole of 1973 than for example in 1970 and also in 1972.

Table 6.5 Monthly strike statistics (1975–78)

Month	Number of strikes and days lost	1975	1976	1977	1978
January	strikes	170	382	348	226
	days lost	69.4	222.0	158.3	73.3
February	strikes	342	518	453	268
	days lost	171.6	437.3	230.3	131.4
March	strikes	395	721	499	267
	days lost	213.1	722.6	366.9	414.1
Total	strikes	907	1621	1300	761
	days lost	454.1	1381.9	755.5	618.8
(Number of days lost in thousands)					
1975/6/7 : 1978	total strikes	118	213	171	100
1st quarter	days lost	73	223	122	100
1975/6/7 : 1978	total strikes	121	136	103	100
Whole year	days lost	176	228	166	100
(100 = 1978)					

Source: Ministère du Travail

If the same exercise is undertaken for the 1975–78 period (as shown in Table 6.5), the trend is similar. There were proportionately less strikes in the first quarter of 1978 than in the corresponding period for the other three years, and there were fewer days lost in 1978 than in 1977 and in 1976. The impact of these results is reduced slightly however by the fact that in general terms there were marginally less strikes and fewer days lost in strikes throughout 1978 than in previous years. Nevertheless the overall results from these tables support the argument that in the run-up to elections workers were sensitive to the demands of the political calendar. This leaves the following questions. Did this reduction in strike activity result from a policy decision taken within the trade union confederations themselves? Did they consider that 'social peace' was a precondition for political success at election time? Did trade union confederation allow the demands of the political sphere to impinge upon their activities in the industrial sphere?

Trade unions and strikes

French trade unions called strikes for a variety of reasons which were not always easy to disaggregate. They clearly called strikes in pursuit of industrial demands, wages, trade union rights, jobs, and working conditions etc. One of the major strikes in 1977 occurred at the Dubigeon shipyard in Nantes and was called because both the CGT and the CFDT were opposed to the introduction of clocking-in machines. In some ways this was the straw that broke the camel's back. There were other important contributory factors, and the ground had been prepared earlier in the year by a management decision to make a number of employees redundant.[8] The immediate political significance of this type of strike action was limited, but on other occasions the CGT and the CFDT called strikes in their campaigns for demands linked to the wider political economy. Politicisation was more evident, because the target of this action was often the government. National days of action complemented this particular strategy. At the time of its national day of action on 7 June 1972, the CGT made the following demands; no salary should be lower than 1000 francs per month, there should be a guarantee of increased purchasing power; the retirement age should be lowered to 60 and the pension should be 800 francs per month.[9] For the national day of action on 1 December 1977, the CGT and the CFDT, made a longer and more extensive list of demands; purchasing power should be maintained but priority should be given to the low paid, full employment should be guaranteed, the retirement age should be reduced, the working week should be reduced, working conditions should be improved, trade union rights should be respected and extended, apprenticeships should be granted as of right and employees' representatives should manage the social welfare system.[10] These lists took on the form of mini-manifestos and as such assumed political as well as industrial significance. Indeed, on occasions trade union leaders admitted to having political objectives also. At the time of the national day of action called by the CGT and the CFDT for 7 October 1976, Michel Warcholak, one of the CGT confederal secretaries, justified this strike action because of the need to wreck the austerity measures which were contained in the 'Plan Giscard–Barre–Ceyrac' (Ceyrac being the leader of the French employers' confederation, the CNPF). Moreover, this strike would reinforce workers' confidence and their aspirations for change.[11] Albert Mercier, one of the CFDT national secretaries, explained that this same strike would allow workers to demonstrate their resolute opposition to the latest government measures.[12]

The CGT was the driving force behind these national days of action, which took place normally once or twice a year, in addition to the normal May Day demonstrations.[13] Trade union confederations put forward industrial demands, but given the nature of these demands and the number of strikers involved, the political significance was unmistakable. Should there be any doubt, the CGT used the following slogan on demonstrations at that time – *'union, action, programme commun'*. The CGT was clearly prepared to use these national days of action to provide support for the political parties of the Union of the Left. When these parties joined in the demonstrations, as was the case on 6 December 1973 for example, then the political nature of strike activity was further reinforced. As for the CFDT, its strike strategy fluctuated. At the beginning of the 1970s it had a reputation for decentralised strike activity. At the time of the national day of action on 7 June 1972, it refused to take part because, according to a statement from the National Bureau, this form of strike activity represented a momentary and inconsequential expression of discontent.[14] An article in *La Croix* explained this strategy in the following terms: the strike victories at companies such as le Joint Français and at Penarroya and Girosteel had reinforced the confidence of CFDT activists who were convinced that local strike activity was more effective. These examples were more likely to mobilise workers than any national days of action with their contrived slogans.[15] However, the CFDT took part in the national day of action in December 1973, along with the political parties of the Left.[16] According to Dumont, this change took place, as a response to criticism from within and outside the trade union movement and from within the CFDT itself.[17] The CFDT was becoming more involved in the political sphere and more prepared to provide the political parties of the Union of the Left with support, and, as has already been seen, some months later it gave wholehearted support to François Mitterrand at the 1974 Presidential election. With the readiness of numerous members of the CFDT to participate in the *Assises du Socialisme* in the autumn of 1974, the mood was one of joint opposition to the government. Because of the unity of action strategy with the CGT and because of the readiness to participate in the political sphere, the CFDT was induced to change its policy towards strike action. Both confederations agreed on a national day of action for 23 September 1975 and for 13 May 1976.[18] After the break-up of the Union of the Left, a national day of action was organised for 1 December 1977. The CFDT also agreed to participate, even though it was beginning to contemplate a change in its political and industrial strategy. It was felt at that time in the CFDT that the possibilities for different forms of industrial action were more limited than ever and that trade unions needed to engage in strike action so as to avoid the demobilisation of the majority of workers, as a result of the break-up of the Union of the Left.[19] The CFDT was exhorting the political parties to act together, so it was not the time to be seen undermining unity on the trade union side. However by the beginning of 1978, it was clear that the Union of the Left was irretrievably lost, and has already been seen, the CFDT reverted to a strategy based on the industrial sphere. There was no place for quasi-political demonstrations, and the CFDT refused to participate in any other national days of action with the CGT.

During the 1970s both trade union confederations attempted to engage in a responsible form of strike action, and they tried to disassociate themselves from forms of strike action which were favoured by the extreme-left. Georges Séguy claimed that the CGT did not favour one specific form of strike action over all others, and was not opposed to the occupation of factories, a tactic used by extreme-left trade unionists. He claimed however that the CGT was opposed to factory occupations if they were decided upon by a minority of the workforce and if factory equipment was damaged in the process. In the wake of the Events of May, there had been a few cases of managers or employers being held captive by the workforce, and the CGT was opposed to this form of strike action (Séguy, 1975, p. 170). Nor was the CGT in favour of *grèves-bouchons*, where employees in one strategic stage of production went on strike, thus paralysing the whole production process. André Berteloot, one of the confederal secretaries, argued that this form of action would be manipulated by a minority, that is, the extreme-left.[20] Moreover, this form of strike action would set one set of workers against another.[21] The CFDT started to disassociate itself from violent minority strikes from March 1972 onwards.[22] At its 1973 national conference held in Nantes, the CFDT expressed its disapproval of acts of violence against people and of the sabotage of factory equipment. However it refused to condemn the workers involved themselves. It attempted to disassociate itself from local strike committees, *comités de grève*, which, it was claimed, should not be allowed to take over responsibilities from local trade union organisations. Moreover strike support committees, *comités de soutien*, were also viewed with circumspection.[23] By the time of the 1976 national conference the CFDT was actively criticising the creation of strike committees which, 'were the product of the manipulation of workers by a tiny minority'.[24]

Were the CGT and the CFDT responsible for the reduction in strike action in the run-up to political elections identified in the first part of this chapter? The trade union confederations were keen to provide support for the political parties at the time of the elections, but to neglect strike activity would leave them vulnerable to the suggestion that 'social peace' would be betraying workers' interests, a charge put by the extreme-left.[25] Ross noted that, 'the most obvious, and in many ways least controversial, direct political action of the CGT in recent years has been its consistent effort to squeeze down protest in the labor market during election campaigns' (Ross, 1979, p. 57–58). Soskice made a similar comment, in which he also implicated the CFDT.[26] The trade union confederations naturally rejected such suggestions. Speaking on behalf of the CGT some time before the 1973 legislative elections. Georges Séguy stated that the CGT was determined to pursue industrial demands energetically. The time remaining prior to the elections would allow the CGT to obtain concessions from the government and the employers.[27] However, this was rhetoric and was contradicted by comments made the following year. At the time of the 1974 Presidential election, the Executive Commission of the CGT published a statement to the effect that the CGT was aware of its responsibilities in terms of industrial demands. It was in the workers' interests that the elections should take place 'in a climate of serenity'. This did not mean that workers should give up legitimate claims but that 'any social unrest should make way for a rapidly negotiated, positive, solution'.[28] A week later Georges Séguy stated that if there had been no elections the second half of April would have been one of considerable strike activity,[29] which implies that in the CGT had indeed soft-pedalled on its strike activity at election time. In a special issue of *CFDT Aujourd'hui* on CFDT–CGT relations, Edmond Maire claimed that the CGT was particularly concerned with popularising the Common Programme at election time, and so it stifled strike activity, not because it wanted to spare management, but because it wanted to concentrate its attacks on the government. In this way the CGT seemed to be hanging back in terms of industrial conflict which, according to Edmond Maire, was as necessary before elections as after them.[30]

It is not easy to find examples where strike activity was aborted for electoral reasons. Trade unions were unlikely to admit that they had not fiercely defended employees' interests in the workplace, particularly given their avowedly apolitical stance and given the rivalry inherent in trade union pluralism. Georges Séguy was quoted as saying at the beginning of September 1977 that the CGT was not going to ease up strike activity in the pre-electoral period since 'workers' demands cannot wait'.[31] However Rioux claimed that the CGT was responsible for stifling strike activity in the dispute in the electricity supply industry at the end of 1977;

the CGT seems to be sensitive to public opinion, and if there are to be strikes they should be organised in a responsible fashion. The leaders of the CGT gave the impression that there would not necessarily be a defeat at the March elections and so as to prepare for the future prudence was necessary'.[32]

At the 40th conference held some months after the 1978 legislative elections, Georges Séguy admitted that the CGT's policy of support for the Common Programme had overshadowed its activities and that this, 'had negative consequences for industrial campaigns. These campaigns were linked to the perspective of political change and could have given the impression that the CGT's activities were too global, too politicised and too distant from workers' daily and immediate preoccupations'.[33]

The CFDT also strenuously denied that it had stifled industrial action at election time. According to Edmond Maire, speaking before the 1973 legislative elections, 'we do not intend to sacrifice any workers' interests for any electoral tactics'.[34] A little later he declared that the CFDT should not downgrade the importance of industrial action just because the elections were near.[35] It is worth remembering that the CFDT had shown less enthusiasm for the Union of the Left at this particular time and was anxious to demonstrate that political parties were not the only agents of political change. Even after the *Assises du Socialisme*, the message remained the same. Even with the possibility of the Left winning the next elections, there was to be no reduction in industrial action, because it was industrial action which was the principal motor of social transformation.[36] There were echoes here of the Popular Front. If the Left was to be elected, worker mobilisation would need to be at its most intense, since this was the only way of constraining the activities of the employers and of encouraging the government to continue with its reforms.[37] According to Edmond Maire, the October 1976 national day of action was 'to introduce wage-earners to the fight to defend purchasing power, industry by industry, office by office and firm by firm, without waiting for the Left's political victory',[38] the implication being that the CFDT was not willing to have its strategy in the industrial sphere compromised by the demands of the political sphere. However some of these comments were also made for rhetorical effect. By the time of the 1978 legislative elections, he explained that the break-up of the Union of the Left would have one advantage at least: trade unions could concentrate on industrial activities and they would not have to wait for the elections.[39] In spite of claims to the contrary, the CFDT had also been prepared to soft-pedal on industrial action and to wait for change via the ballot box.

The final point on trade union strike strategy refers to the ability to mobilise workers. It could be argued that the pattern of strike activity identified in the first part of the chapter occurred independently of the actions of the trade union confederations, because they were not capable of controlling the activities of their members and supporters. In general terms, there has always been doubt as to the ability of the trade union confederations to control strike activity. In his comments on wildcat strikes in France, Reynaud claimed that, 'France is unaware of this problem, to the extent that it has had to borrow the expression from the English language, not because there is more discipline, but because there is often none at all' (Reynaud, 1975, p. 166). Evidence suggests that Reynaud has exaggerated the point. One study demonstrated that there was a relative, although not perfect, agreement between workers and trade unions about the decision to take strike action. In only a minority of firms surveyed was the call to go on strike spontaneous and without the approval of local trade union organisations (Dubois, *et al*, 1971, p. 273–78). Hardly surprisingly, trade unions have always insisted on the democratic nature of strike action decision-making. According to Georges Séguy, the CGT had always advocated that branches should have the geatest room for manoeuvre so as to create the best conditions for trade unionists and other workers to be involved consciously and responsibly in strike action. He claimed that he was opposed to the centralisation of strike activity and to the idea of the leadership systematically taking the initiative (Séguy, 1975, p. 168–69). Speaking at the CGT Metalworkers' conference in 1976 at St-Etienne, he enumerated the problems inherent in the centralisation of strike organisation. It would lead to *attentisme et immobilisme* – a hesitant wait and see approach to strike activity.[40] Yet, there were contrary claims from within the CGT. According to Jean-Louis Moynot, the CGT was more interested in controlling strikes than launching them (Moynot, 1982, p. 95). This claim was reinforced by evidence from external sources. Durand and Dubois argued that CGT strike activity tended to be relatively centralised, and regional and national officials often intervened in strikes as advisors or even negotiators (Durand & Dubois, 1975, p. 118–19).

The CGT did not want to be associated with irresponsible strike activity, and at that time (1973), the CFDT leadership was also striving to disassociate itself from some forms of local strike organisation, in an effort to distance itself from the activities of the extreme-left. By the time of the next CFDT conference in 1976, Edmond Maire explained, that the role of the confederation in strike action should on the one hand be to ensure the coherence of all the activities of the organisations within the confederation and on the other to take on a certain number of initiatives of interest to the whole movement.[41] This would make it possible to have a greater control of strike action. In their study Rozenblatt *et al* showed that the CGT and the CFDT had differing attitudes to local strike organisation, but concluded that both trade union confederations were not prepared to be associated with strike committees over which they had no control, nor were they prepared to allow workers on their own to play a leading role in strikes.[42] Both trade union confederations clearly attempted to control strike activity. Although they were not always successful, evidence suggests that the pattern of strike activity in France during the 1970s reflected their strike objectives. These objectives were two-fold. On the one hand, trade union confederations sought to support workers in their attempts to protect and improve conditions in the industrial sphere. On the other, trade union confederations were prepared to use strikes as an adjunct to their activities in the political sphere. One further question remains – was trade union strike strategy determined by the objectives of the political parties of the Union of the Left?

Political parties and strikes

The political parties of the Union of the Left respected certain conventions of functional demarcation, if only by default, in that they made few statements on the subject of strike activity. There was no mention of strike activity in the Common Programme of Government and no indication of the response of a future government of the Union of the Left when faced with industrial unrest. Would strikes legitimate the government of the Left's claim to introduce wide-ranging reforms or would they undermine its overall economic policy? No specific response was given, but a hint of an answer was to be found in a comment made by François Mitterrand at the time of his election campaign in 1974. In her study, Colliard noted that one of his campaign themes was 'social peace', which would require 'the trade unions to tone down workers' demands' (Colliard, 1979, p. 87). However, the author did not explain how this would be achieved; nor did the candidate, presumably for fear of alienating valuable trade union support at election time.

For the French Communist Party, the issue was easy enough. It supported strike action, even when it was not necessarily in agreement with the form the strike took, because the prime responsibility for the conflict lay with the employer.[43] The PCF drew attention to strikes in its publications – particularly in *L'Humanité* and also in *Politique Aujourd'hui*. It participated in demonstrations accompanying national days of action. There is clear evidence to show that the PCF provided moral support, as for example with the strike at Renault in March 1975.[44] The PCF also provided material support, as for example with the strike at the Rateau plant in 1974.[45] However, according to Claude Poperen, at no time was there any order, whether from the national or local leadership, saying that a strike should take place – 'never, never, never, that would be completely out of the question'.[46] Aimé Halbeher claimed moreover that it was not the function of the PCF workplace branches to call strikes.[47] Given such emphatic statements of non-interference in trade union decisions to call strikes, it is not surprising that evidence to the contrary is difficult to find. However, Jean-Marie Mick, the Communist mayor of Pierre–Bénite, explained that the PCF had on occasions tried to take control of a strike movement at Péchiney–Ugine–Kuhlmann, the chemical plant within his constituency. However, if it was ever known that the PCF had attempted to control the strike, then there was the risk of 'breaking the movement', since this might 'frighten people off'.[48] Roy noted nevertheless that at the time of the strike at Renault quoted above, it was rumoured that the forklift truck operators' strike had actually been launched by the Communist Party cell.[49]

Further and more substantial evidence of PCF interference in strike activity may be found in the work of Badie (Badie, 1975). A central theme of his work is that the PCF, as the party of the working class, would want to control strike activity to ensure that the party's wider political strategy was not jeopardised. Strikes may break out without the agreement or even the knowledge of the party, but when they assume certain proportions, the local communist organisation would attempt to take them over and if possible lead them. He quoted the case of the strike of unskilled workers at Renault–Billancourt at the beginning of 1973. At first the communist section remained detached from the discussion over the original grievances, and the CGT actively campaigned for a rapid agreement to be reached. Once the strikers rejected the agreement, the CGT completely changed its position and backed the strike. Realising that the strike was likely to be important, the communist section immediately offered its support, in an attempt to wrest control from the extreme-left. Then the communist section attempted to establish its position at the head of the movement and broaden out the issues raised in the strike. If successful in taking over control of the strike, the local communist section had two options, either to channel or to stifle the movement, according to the demands of its own political strategy. For an example of channeling strike action, Badie referred back to the Events of May 1968. At first the PCF attempted to keep the students' movement distinct and separate from the preoccupations of the workers. However when it realised that the latter were anxious to express their solidarity with the students, the party changed tack. It then started to support the movement, launching a student-workers demonstration for 13 May and broadening the issues raised by the students' movement. This in turn seemed to raise the stakes, since this campaign had been well received throughout the country. As a result, the PCF changed tack yet again and attempted to give the strike movement a resolutely political dimension, claiming that workers wanted 'to do away with the Gaullist government', and 'install a democracy which would pave the way for socialism'. It then took on responsibility for increasing strike activity. Badie quotes the *Révolution Prolétarienne*, an extreme-left publication, which claimed that the PCF called the postalworkers out on strike, without even consulting the CGT. The PCF changed tack twice within a week and as a result was able to channel the strike movement. It had been able to impose its own mass strike model and its own political objectives on the industrial situation.

The PCF was also prepared to stifle strike action, (*à froid* – before much strike momentum had been developed), by simply ignoring workers' demands. This was the tactic assumed by the local communist party organisation at the time of the strike at le Joint Français in Saint Brieuc (Capdevielle, *et al*, 1975). Later when strike momentum had been built up, the problem was more complex. The PCF could not stifle a strike too brutally, since this would alienate workers. At the time of the Events of May it attempted to stifle strike activity on two occasions. In the first instance, the PCF supported the negotiations between trade union confederations, employers and State representatives which led to the temporary resolution of the conflict. However, the PCF had misjudged the combative mood of the strikers, and these measures were rejected. In the second instance, the PCF was more successful. In the run-up to the ensuing legislative elections which the PCF wanted to contest without being considered the party of civil disorder, it adopted an intransigent position in its statements but encouraged a more flexible approach to industry by industry negotiations. In conclusion to this part of his work, Badie noted that the PCF found itself in an ambiguous position. It actively intervened in strikes, it decided their direction, it channelled them and sometimes even stifled them effectively. On the other hand, it was constantly bound to a strategy which imposed on it the need to take grassroots aspirations into consideration, to direct and amplify them, even if these aspirations were in contradiction with certain aspects of its own political strategy. The PCF tried to use strikes to its own political advantage, but in order to be able to do so, it also had to be prepared on occasions to have its political strategy knocked off course somewhat. The PCF's strategy was predicated on its ability to articulate its views and objectives directly to the working population, not only through its own party organisation but also through the good offices of the CGT. Badie takes this articulation for granted. As has been seen in Chapter 1, the 'transmission belt' did not work effortlessly, particularly at the level of the workplace. Although some workplace branches were a major force, and Renault was the prime example, many only existed on paper, and in numerous firms there was none at all. How would the 90 per cent of CGT members, non-communists, obtain the communist message? Even in Renault at Boulogne-Billancourt, the bastion of communist support during the mid-1970s, with a CGT membership of just under 8,000 and PCF membership of 2,000,[50] many of the 37,000-strong workforce would still be impervious to the exhortations of the PCF, as was demonstrated at the time of the Events of May. As Jean-Marie Mick explained, some communist CGT members tend to act more as trade unionists than as members of a political party,[51] so on occasions the industrial demands of the CGT would be pursued rather than the political objectives of the PCF. Finally, as has been shown in Chapter 5, even amongst communist members of the CGT there were divergent opinions, and this would also have interfered with this process of articulation.

There has been less research into the Socialist Party's views on strikes. In the 1970s the Socialist Party was still a relatively new party, anxious to establish itself primarily as a political organisation and as an electoral force. Moreover it did not see itself exclusively as the party of the working class whose power historically lay with its ability to withdraw its labour. The only article on the subject was written by Jean-Paul Bachy, the assistant to the Secretariat for Social Affairs in the mid 1970s. He considered that the role of the Socialist Party was to popularise the solutions that the Left was proposing, notably those contained in the Common Programme, and to develop solidarity in all its forms (Bachy, 1975, p. 71–78). Clearly this explanation does little to advance our understanding of the issue. There is no evidence to suggest that the PS took an active interest in strike activity. It did however support strike activity on a number of occasions. It drew attention to strikes in its publications and provided moral support. *Combat Socialiste* was set up to highlight the importance of workplace activities and as part of this, strike activity, and *L'Unité* and *Le Poing et la Rose* featured regular articles on strikes. On occasions the PS offered material support and organised collections on behalf of striking workers.[52] At the time of the Renault strike in the Spring of 1975 it offered political support and called on local socialist organisations to take all necessary initiatives (described as the following; signing petitions, sending delegations to *préfectures* and local Renault organisations), so that the conflict could be rapidly resolved in the interests of the employees. In addition, a PS parliamentary delegation asked to be received by the Minister of Industry and by the management of Renault.[53] It participated in demonstrations accompanying national days of action. On a few occasions François Mitterrand intervened directly in support of striking workers, writing to Currus and Chauffour employees whose jobs were being lost since the firms were going into liquidation.[54] Socialist councils offered material support. At the time of the Currus strike, the local council provided meals for the strikers and the local party collected considerable amounts of money, according to Claude Germon.[55] During the 1977 strike at the Dubigeon shipyards in Nantes, the socialist-led local council also provided financial assistance for strikers.[56] The PS did not explain officially why it chose to act in this way. However, at the time of the 1975 Renault strike, Alain Rannou, the person responsible for workplace branches at the national level, claimed that the aim of this action was to ensure that negotiations took place as quickly as possible,[57] a sentiment reiterated by the former socialist mayor of Nantes, Alain Chenard.[58] For them, the emphasis was on the strike as an instrument of collective bargaining, and not as a form of political protest.

Both political parties of the Union of the Left provided moral and material support for strike activity, but were anxious to demonstrate their respect for functional differentiation between their activities and those of the trade unions. In theory it was the function of trade unions to call strikes in the first place, and then at a second stage the political parties could choose to support them or not. In practice, and in spite of statements to the contrary, there is some evidence to suggest that the PCF played a more direct role in this initial process. The PCF definitely had a more sophisticated and all-embracing strike strategy, and it attempted to use strike action for its own particular political goals. There is however some doubt as to the ability of the PCF to implement such a strategy. On the other hand, there is no evidence that the Socialist Party had a coherent strategy for industrial conflict, and, given its patchy coverage at the workplace and its more tenuous links with the trade unions, it would have had major problems of implementation. However on the occasions it was drawn into industrial conflict and did support strike activity. In this way it could demonstrate that it was sympathetic to the demands of the strikers who might be potential socialist voters and it could compete with the PCF on a terrain which was previously a communist preserve.

Conclusions

The study of strikes in France has made it possible to improve our understanding of the relationship between trade union confederations and the political parties of the Union of the Left. Strikes have their roots in the industrial sphere and workers go on strike primarily to improve their wages and working conditions, not for overtly political reasons. Strikes are not an alternative to representation within the political sphere, but an adjunct. They affect and in turn are affected by events in the political sphere. Strike activity declined during the 1970s as a result of industrial and political reasons: the repercussions of the oil crisis meant that unemployment posed a greater threat, and consequently workers were less likely to go on strike for fear of losing their jobs. In addition, the repercussions of the break-up of the Union of the Left left workers demoralised and less confident about their ability to shape the course of events. To claim, as does Dubois that the decline of strike activity during this period is due 'without any doubt' to the difficulties experienced in the Union of the Left, is to overstate the political case and to neglect other factors of an industrial nature. It is nevertheless the case that strikes were sensitive to the constraints of the political sphere. Strike activity declined markedly, although not absolutely, in the run-up to the two sets of legislative elections in 1973 and in 1978. In spite of unconvincing claims to the contrary, both the CGT and the CFDT were less prepared to engage in strike activity at sensitive moments of the political calendar, because they did not want strikes to detract from the possible electoral successes of the political parties of the Union of the Left. The trade union confederations were prepared to put the demands of the political sphere before those of the industrial sphere. There is other evidence to support this contention. National days of action were manifestations of opposition to the government of the day and, by extension, indications of support for the political parties of the Union of the Left. The global nature of the list of demands required government intervention in the political economy, and, if a government of the Right was unwilling or unable to satisfy these demands, the implication was that a government of the Left would. During the whole of the period of the 1970s, the CGT was particularly keen to engage in this form of industrial conflict. Moreover it was anxious to draw the CFDT into this approach. The CFDT, on the other hand, was initially opposed to the exploitation of industrial conflict for party political purposes, but it is a measure of its readiness to favour the political sphere during the period of the Union of the Left that it was prepared to change its strike tactics. In spite of its previous preference for local forms of strike activity, it changed to a strategy favouring national days of action, at least for the period 1973-77. Only after the break-up of the Union of the Left did the CFDT begin to revert to its former approach to strike activity. Although it would be misleading to overstate the case, it is true that both trade union confederations engaged in industrial conflict for political purposes during the period of the Union of the Left.

This politicisation of industrial conflict was accompanied by a parallel industrialisation of the political sphere and by a tiny shift in the balance of party-union relations. Although political parties were not prepared to provide the same level of support for trade unions in the industrial sphere as the latter provided in the political, they did on occasions provide moral and material support for strike action during this period. The French Communist Party was more enthusiastic and systematic about this than was the Socialist Party. In this way the PCF attempted to take control of industrial conflict and to use it for its own political purposes. However it is not at all certain that it was able to succeed on a large scale. Moreover in the process it was sometimes induced to sacrifice its own short-term political objectives. The PS seemed to have no overall position on strike activity, but responded on an *ad hoc* basis. The relationship between the trade union confederations and the political parties was such that the latter were only prepared to provide a limited level of support as a *quid pro quo* for the support they received in the political sphere.

Notes

1. Quoted in Caire, C., *La grève ouvrière*, Paris, Editions Ouvrières, 1978, p. 52.
2. Dubois, P. in Kesselman, M. & Groux, G., *Le mouvement ouvrier français*, Paris, Editions Ouvrières, 1984, p. 251.
3. For details, see Bridgford, J. 'The events of May – consequences for industrial relations in France', in Hanley, D & Kerr A. (eds), *May 68 : coming of age*, London, Macmillan, 1989, p. 100–16.

4. *Nouvel Observateur*, 1 January 1974.
 5. Dubois, P. in Kesselman, M. & Groux, G. *op cit*. p. 247. It is curious that this statement was dropped from the English language version.
 6. *Travail Informations*, 17–23 May 1976.
 7. For the CFDT, see *CFDT Syndicalisme*, 17 June 1976. The CGT now produces its own *Bilan Mensuel des Luttes*. For the employers, see the quote by François Ceyrac (the former leader of the CNPF, the French Employers' Association), in an article by Magniadas, J. 'Politique Contractuelle et Lutte de Classe', *Economie et Politique*, May 1970, p. 52.
 8. Tract, 'Retablir les faits', CGT–CFDT Dubigeon, no date.
 9. *Le Peuple*, 1–15 June 1972, p. 5.
10. *Le Peuple*, 15–30 November 1977, p. 2.
11. *Le Peuple*, 1–15 November 1976, p. 2.
12. *CFDT Syndicalisme*, 30 September 1976, p. 3.
13. For details, see *CFDT Syndicalisme*, 13 December 1973, p. 2–3.
14. *CFDT Syndicalisme*, 29 June 1972, p. 2.
15. *La Croix*, 11 May 1972.
16. *CFDT Syndicalisme*, 13 December 1973, p. 2.
17. *Le Monde*, 9 October 1974.
18. *Le Monde*, 22 April 1976.
19. *Le Monde*, 9 November 1977.
20. *Le Peuple*, 16–31 May 1973, p. 2.
21. *Le Monde*, 17–18 March 1974.
22. *CFDT Syndicalisme*, 20 March 1972, p. 2.
23. *CFDT Syndicalisme*, 15 March 1973, p. 70.
24. *CFDT Syndicalisme*, Supplément, 4 March 1976, p. 46.
25. See the article 'Pas de trève sociale pour les élections présidentielles', *Lutte Ouvrière*, 1–15 April 1974.
26. See the chapter by Soskice, D. in Flanagan, R. Soskice, D. & Ulman, L., *Unions, economic stabilisation and incomes policies*, Washington, Brookings Institution, 1983, p. 637.
27. *Le Monde*, 25 November 1972.
28. *L'Humanité*, 4 April 1974.
29. *L'Humanité*, 11 April 1974.
30. *CFDT Aujourd'hui*, January–February 1976, p. 39–40.
31. *Le Monde*, 9 September 1977.
32. *Nouvel Observateur*, 19 December 1977.
33. *Le Peuple*, 1–31 December 1978, p. 9.
34. *Le Monde*, 18 August 1972.
35. *Le Monde*, 26–27 November 1972.
36. According to Michel Rolant, one of the members of the Executive Commission of the CFDT, *Nouvel Observateur*, 12 April 1976.
37. According to Edmond Maire, *CFDT Syndicalisme*, 15 December 1977, p. 5.
38. *Nouvel Observateur*, 4 October 1976.
39. *Le Monde*, 17 December 1977.
40. Quoted in *Mouvement ouvrier et unité d'action*, Notes et Documents du BRAEC, April–June 1981, p. 33.
41. *CFDT Syndicalisme*, 3 June 1976, p. 14–15.

42. For details, see Rozenblatt, P, Tatatou, F & Tallard, M., *Analyse du conflit Lip et des repercussions sur les pratiques ouvrières et les stratégies syndicales*. Unpublished Doctorat 3e Cycle d'Economie Appliquée, Université de Paris IX Dauphine. Vol I, p. 120–21, 125–42, 172–74, 198.
43. Interview, Aimé Halbeher 21 February 1986.
44. *Le Monde*, 5 March 1975.
45. *Nouvel Observateur*, 11 March 1974.
46. Interview, Claude Poperen 26 March 1986.
47. Interview, Aimé Halbeher 21 February 1986.
48. Interview, Jean-Marie Mick 11 May 1987.
49. *Le Monde*, 5 March 1975.
50. Interview, Aimé Halbeher 21 February 1986.
51. Interview, Jean-Marie Mick 11 February 1987.
52. *Combat Socialiste*, December 1975, p. 11.
53. *Le Poing et la Rose*, May 1975, p. 12.
54. *Le Poing et la Rose*, May 1975, p. 13.
55. *Faire*, April 1976, p. 47.
56. Interview, Alain Chenard 1 April 1986.
57. *L'Unité*, 28 March 1975, p. 9.
58. Interview, Alain Chenard 1 April 1986.

Chapter 7

Collective Bargaining, Trade Union Confederations and the Union of the Left

In his comparative study of trade unionism and collective bargaining, Clegg noted that 'French trade unions, however, and especially the CGT, place far more weight on this type of political action (that is to change the social order), so that the French trade union movement as a whole is at least ambivalent between political action and collective bargaining as methods of trade union action' (Clegg, 1976, p 116). The implication is that participation in the collective bargaining process in the industrial sphere compromises union objectives in the political sphere, and it is the aim of this chapter to examine this ambivalence between political action and collective bargaining. It is worth recalling that the expression, collective bargaining, poses certain methodological problems, because it has diverse meanings and functions in different national environments (Bean, 1985, p 70–99). It should not be assumed that it occupies the same centrality in industrial relations in France as collective bargaining, 'in other countries where it appears as the fundamental vocation of trade unions, the best means of resolving disagreements between employees and employers and finally the favoured instrument of social progress'.[1]

There is a consensus that the system of collective bargaining in France is relatively underdeveloped. Trade unions have traditionally been reluctant participants in the collective bargaining process, but then so have employers who have often been unwilling to forsake their commanding position within the firm. In addition, it was not until 1936 that workplace representatives were formally recognised in law, and often much later in practice. Indeed it was not until 1968 that trade unions were accorded legal representation within the workplace. The French system provides more 'than mere consultation but less negotiation than in the Anglo-American sense of the term' (Adam, 1978, p. 420–51). Others would argue that in France, negotiation as such does not take place – 'it is a sham – propositions are made by the employer: employees subscribe to them or they do not' (Lyon-Caen, 1979, p. 351). McCormick has reviewed the applicability of collective bargaining theories to the French case and found them all wanting.[2] 'Convergence' theorists have claimed that all nations would develop similar social and political systems, and it would only be a matter of time before French trade unions and employers automatically developed common interests and sought a relationship which would favour the establishment of collective bargaining practices. Yet by the 1970s France had become a modern industrialised nation, and the major trade union confederations had still not embarked on a consensual approach to the resolution of industrial problems. 'Cultural' theorists have claimed on the other hand that it is not in the nature of the French to engage in face-to-face negotiations, and so it is not surprising that collective bargaining had failed to gain a firm foothold. This theory fails to explain why in certain circumstances trade unions and employers were nevertheless prepared to engage in discussions and also to sign collective bargaining agreements. A third theory, linked to the first, predicts that French trade unions would enter a more mature stage of development and automatically forsake 'revolutionary' trade unionism. They would then develop a natural interest in collective bargaining. This theory fails to explain why in the 1970s the CGT and the CFDT still considered themselves to be 'revolutionary' and yet they were prepared to engage in collective bargaining on occasions. Collective bargaining in France is *sui generis* and does not slot easily into a neat comparative theoretical framework.

It is the potential political significance of collective bargaining which is of particular interest in this chapter. Although observers have stressed the importance of the politicisation of strike activity, there has been little attention paid to the potential political significance of the lack of strike activity, due in part at least to the institutionalisation of industrial conflict. In one of the few works devoted solely to the study of collective bargaining in France, Reynaud makes little reference to the influence of the political on collective bargaining. He merely states in a footnote, with reference to the mid 1970s, that the political situation must have played a role, but unfortunately he gives no further explanation (Reynaud, 1978, p,52). The potential for the politicisation of collective bargaining is great, particularly given the relationship of wages, the central feature of collective bargaining, to economic policy and policy-making in general. This potential is even greater in the public sector, where size, cost and example to the private sector make it central to the success of government economic policies. This chapter aims to investigate the potential for the politicisation of collective bargaining in France and is divided into two major parts. The first analyses the existing data on collective bargaining during the 1970s, both in the public and private sectors, to see if a specific pattern of collective bargaining emerges for the period of the Union of the Left. The second section examines the attitudes of trade union confederations and political parties to collective bargaining in order to shed further light on the issue of party-union relations.

Collective bargaining in the 1970s

Collective bargaining did not develop naturally out of custom and practice, as it did in Great Britain, but was grafted on to a largely unwelcoming industrial relations system by legal means. French legislation was more concerned with establishing the content of agreements, their compulsory form and their scope of application, than encouraging the participants to engage in real negotiations. The 1950 law, amended in 1971 after a unanimous vote in the National Assembly, provided the basis for the legal framework for the period relevant to this study. Agreements were to be written: they were to contain the minimum terms of social legislation: non-union employees were also to benefit from the agreements: agreements could be extended to other parties: and all agreements were to be binding on their signatories. The law distinguished between *conventions collectives* and *accords d'établissement ou salariés*, national or regional agreements based on one particular industry, and plant agreements which were originally limited to the adaptation of national or regional agreements or the fixing of wages and fringe benefits. As a result, a varied group of agreements emerged, national multi-industry, national single industry, regional and *départmental* single industry and plant level agreements.[3] The agreements were expected to last one year, though the 1950 law made it possible for expired agreements to remain in force for a further year. So-called unlimited agreements were to last five years with the possibility that they could be terminated at the request of any one of the parties, who were defined as any association of employers or an individual employer on the one hand and one or more 'representative' unions, that is, belonging to one of the recognised national trade union confederations on the other. Although certain government-owned firms, Renault for example, came within the scope of these laws, industrial relations in the public sector were regulated differently. Public sector wage bargaining, in the electricity and gas supply industries, the railways, the coal industry and the civil service, was conducted separately. Wage increases were calculated as a function of developments in the national economy. From 1963 onwards this was known as the 'Toutée system', which was replaced, primarily as a reaction to the Events of May 1968, by a new form of public sector collective bargaining system. Jacques Chaban Delmas, Prime Minister from 1969 to 1972, was responsible for introducing new-style public sector wage bargaining agreements, which, as will be seen, led to a considerable burst of collective bargaining activity in the short term.

It could be argued that a legal, if not legalistic, approach to collective bargaining has had a negative effect on its development. If agreements could be extended not only in time but also to other groups of employees in the same industry or indeed in other geographical areas without further negotiation, then for some employers there was no need to engage in the arduous process of collective bargaining. If the signature of only one so-called 'representative' trade union confederation was necessary to conclude an agreement, then little credibility would be accorded to an agreement signed for example by the CFTC representing a small proportion of an already under-unionised workforce. If the terms of an agreement could be repudiated by one of the signatories, a frequent occurrence, then the initial agreement itself would be of little value. If the results of conciliation could not be imposed and if arbitration recommendations would only be valid once accepted by both parties, then little external pressure could be exerted on participants to negotiate in good faith. As Reynaud has explained, 'in spite of apparent legal continuity and the apparent strictness of the law, the French system (of collective bargaining) has been marked by extreme discontinuity and by poor control over events and change' (Reynaud, 1975, p.151).

Turning to the pattern of collective bargaining, it is clear that doubts hang over the accuracy and validity of the figures for signed collective bargain agreements presented by the Ministry of Employment. Not all agreements were logged with the relevant Ministry. It was not until the end of the 1970s and more specifically in the 1980s that the Ministry of Employment began to take the question of the overall collection of collective bargaining statistics more seriously.[4] The Ministry statistics offer some guidance, but they provide no information about the economic position of the enterprise, the type of workforce, the relative strength of the various trade unions and previous collective bargaining records. Equally it must be remembered that, 'the figures should not give the wrong impression; collective bargaining remains an intermittent, irregular and infrequent phenomenon',[5] and according to Jezequel, a senior official in the Ministry of Social Affairs, it is not possible to estimate the number of employees covered by collective bargaining agreements (Jezequel, 1981, p 462).

Collective bargaining in the private sector

Trade union confederations and the national employer's association, the *Conseil National du Patronat Francais* (CNPF), were involved in collective bargaining at the national multi-industry level. Agreements were signed by the CGT and CFDT on the following subjects: job security (1970), maternity benefits (1970), vocational training (1970), *mensualisation* – single status (1970), early retirement payments (1972), unemployment benefit (1974), short-time working (1975).[6] At the national industry level there was a considerable number of agreements signed throughout the entire period of the 1970s, as can be seen from Table 7.1. The sharp increase in 1972 came about, as a result of the fact that the 1971 legal amendment had made it easier to conclude agreements. There followed a short period of stability and then overall decline, which can be explained by the consequences of the economic crisis (Jezequel, 1981, p.463), or rather by 'the effects of the directives of the Barre Plan as regards wages'.[7] In addition, there is evidence to show that at that time the employers had become less willing to engage in collective bargaining. On occasions the leader of the CNPF, François Ceyrac, was reluctant to meet with the trade union confederations,[8] and in the mid 1970s Yvon Chotard, the Vice President of the CNPF, sent round a circular to his members demanding that no agreements should be signed with salary increases higher than the official cost of living index.[9] The usefulness of these aggregate figures is limited however. As was explained earlier in the chapter, it only needs the signature of one 'representative' trade union confederation for an agreement to be legally valid, and the Ministry's published statistics do not indicate which trade union confederations signed which agreements.

Can this decline in the number of agreements signed be explained by the demands of the political sphere? Did the CGT and the CFDT refuse to sign a number of national industrial agreements because they wanted

Table 7.1 Industry-wide collective bargaining agreements – France 1970–79

Year	Agreements	Year	Agreements
1970	1413	1975	1659
1971	1393	1976	1426
1972	1693	1977	1295
1973	1647	1978	1284
1974	1621	1979	1487

Source: Jezequel, 1981, p. 462.

to foment dissatisfaction in the industrial sphere and thus engender dissatisfaction in the political sphere? Is it possible to argue like Jezequel that, 'a certain electoral wait and see policy could also have played a role in the decline in the number of signed agreements in 1977'? Although no major study of collective bargaining in the private sector has ever been undertaken, it is possible to gain some insight into the readiness of the CGT and the CFDT to sign agreements, as a result of an internal exercise carried out by the French Ministry of Employment. However this data should be handled with great care. Of the 406 national agreements in force in April 1981, 104 were originally signed in the period between the signing of the Common Programme of Government and the legislative elections in 1978. Whilst the largest proportion of agreements was signed by FO (86 per cent), which, given its commitment to collective bargaining, is not surprising, 76 per cent of the agreements were signed by the CGT and just over half of them (56 per cent) were signed by the CFDT. Clearly the CGT, and to a lesser extent, the CFDT, were not prepared to desert the industrial sphere, and leave it to FO.[10] Statistics relating to local agreements demonstrate that trade unions respond to varying local industrial conditions. In the metal-working industry, for instance, where there was no national collective bargaining agreement, most regional and departmental agreements were not signed by the CGT nor the CFDT. However there were some exceptions. They both signed agreements in the following *départements* – Morbihan, Ille-et-Vilaine, Bouches-du-Rhône, Calvados, Manche, Mayenne and the Haut-Rhin.[11] Further evidence of local variation is to be found in a survey of collective bargaining in the Rhône-Alpes region. In the metal-working industry, the CGT and the CFDT were relatively willing to sign agreements in the Ain, but not in the Isère and in the Loire they did not sign any. Moreover they signed relatively few in Haute-Savoie, Rhône, Drôme and Ardèche. In all these cases local circumstances determined union activity (Bunel & Abdou, 1980, p.125–45).

The Ministry of Labour commissioned a limited study of collective bargaining which noted that 'around the mid 1970s collective bargaining became more infrequent and gave way to more direct clashes between employers and employees or to decisions which were *faits accomplis*'. The decline in strike activity was explained in terms of a series of mutually reinforcing factors: economic restructuring which had broken down 'labour collectivities' and had led to the weakening of collective trade union power: trade union disunity and deunionisation exacerbated by the general political context which was characterised by the failure of the Left in the 1978 legislative elections and by the break-up of the Union of the Left; an employers' strategy which avoided negotiations in the normal institutional frameworks, as well as a certain centralisation of the employers' social policy'. Of the 89 national agreements appertaining to the metal-working industry, 25 were signed during the period of the Union of the Left, and of these nine were signed by the CGT and eight by the CFDT.[12] These figures are testimony to the pragmatism of the trade unions in the industrial sphere. One particular agreement was not signed by the CGT and the CFDT, and one of the employers said that this had occurred, 'for political reasons. At that time they (the CGT and CFDT) did not want to sign any agreement'. (This view was also put by the national association of employers in the engineering industry; in *l'Anneé Metallurgique,* the annual journal of the *Union des Industries Métallurgiques et Minières,* it was stated that, 'the CGT and the CFDT put obstacles in the way of the collective bargaining process because they were seeking to undermine economic revival in the hopes of bringing about a political crisis'.[13]) The authors of the ministerial report considered however that on this occasion the breakdown in collective bargaining procedures had occurred for reasons that lay firmly within the industrial sphere, that is, employers had done away with certain paid holiday entitlements for monthly paid staff. At plant level, in one particular engineering company, the authors identified three specific periods (1950–61, 1962–77 and 1977–81) for collective bargaining purposes. These periods did not correspond to the demands of the political calendar, but to changes in ownership of the firm. The first change corresponded to the takeover by Alsthom and the second to the takeover by Creusot-Loire.

In another monograph, on the clothing industry, the collective bargaining process broke down again because of the demands of the industrial sphere.[14] At the local level, in the Cholet, which straddles four *départements*, Maine-et-Loire, Vendée, Deux-Sèvres and Loire-Atlantique, the most significant variables conditioning collective bargaining were the consequences of the economic crisis, deunionisation, the lack of trade union coordination and the victimisation of the workforce. The employers were loathe to negotiate at a regional level since, with a wide variety of different firms, there was a risk of all employees demanding what was on offer in the wealthier firms. There was no mention of wider political perspectives. From 1975 onwards in the metalworking industry in the Rhône-Alpes region, wage bargaining became rarer and gave way to unilateral recommendations by the employers, with the result that even the 'reformist' trade unions, such as FO, were less inclined to sign agreements, because wage indexation clauses had been abandoned. Moreover, from 1975, the responsibility of negotiating the salaries of the low paid was virtually handed over to the State, because of the provision of the minimum legal wage, the SMIC. The austerity measures introduced by the Prime Minister Raymond Barre were the final nail in the coffin of wage bargaining (Bunel & Abdou, 1980, p. 125–45).

In the private sector industrial criteria were paramount. According to McCormick:

Specific industrial characteristics encourage employer unity perceived as necessary to the economic survival of the industry: high investment costs, greater industrial concentration, and an organised work force are the major stimuli for employer cohesion. Given the legal structure, legal cohesion is a precondition for industry-wide collective bargaining. In industries whose structure is more dispersed, capital investment lower, and the work force less organized, employer unity is more difficult: as a result, so is collective bargaining. The legal and industrial structures are the primary determinants of the character of a particular industrial relations system.

She concludes:

If collective bargaining has had a different fate in the cement and semi-finished wood product industries, this is not due to more positive cultural attitudes or ideologies; the ideological CGT and CFDT are the major negotiators for workers. Nor is it directly because these industries are more modern. Instead, collective bargaining is more institutionalized in these industries because they are sufficiently well-organized and motivated to establish their own collective bargaining procedures, and to overcome the barriers set by the French legal framework.[15]

Again there is no mention of the demands of the political sphere. Whilst the picture is not totally clear, it would seem that the French trade unions were not ambivalent about their readiness to participate in the collective bargaining process. They were prepared to sign a variety of different agreements, and evidence suggests that collective bargaining in the private sector was dominated by the demands of the industrial sphere.

Collective bargaining in the public sector

Public sector bargaining is exposed to a greater level of potential politicisation. Given the importance of the public sector within the broader economy, governments need to exert tight control over public sector wage bargaining in order to ensure the success of their general economic policies. In the aftermath of the Events of May 1968 the French Prime Minister Jacques Chaban Delmas aimed to achieve this with the creation of a 'new society', and he aimed to create a process of collective bargaining which would ensure the participation of the trade union confederations. When the first new-style public sector wage agreements were signed, he proclaimed victoriously (and also prematurely); 'today a revolution has taken place, without blood being spilt, without a town or a civilisation being destroyed. For the next two years or more exactly twenty one months, it can be considered that there will be no more strikes'.[16] This ill-judged statement helped to reinforce the politicisation of public sector bargaining. It also represented a challenge to the trade union confederations. If they participated in the this new-style public sector bargaining process, they would be legitimising the actions of a government to which they were opposed.

Writing at the end of 1974, Jobert identified three phases of public sector bargaining. October 1969 to December 1970 was the initial period when all the trade union confederations, except the CGT, were prepared to sign agreements. The second period, 1971, was a year of consolidation, when all the trade union confederations, including the CGT, were prepared to sign agreements. 1972 onwards was a 'mutilated' period, when, 'the political began to take precedence over the industrial, which explained to a large extent why the CGT and the CFDT refused to sign subsequently' (Jobert, 1974, p.397–410). In terms of readiness to sign public sector bargaining agreements, there was a distinction between the 'revolutionary' trade union confederations, the CFDT and the CGT, and the 'reformist' trade union confederations. FO readily signed agreements in the Civil Service, the railways (SNCF), the electricity and gas supply industries (EDF/GDF) and in the Paris metro (RATP), at least until 1976. Although the CGT and CFDT were less enthusiastic about collective bargaining in general, they did not systematically refuse to sign agreements in the public sector. For the period 1969–73, they signed just under half of the agreements in the electricity and gas supply industries, the coal industry, the railways, the Paris metro and Renault, taken together. They were prepared to sign agreements until 1976 in the electricity and gas supply industries. After the signing of the Common Programme in 1972, the CGT was still prepared on occasion to sign agreements, in the Potassium Mines of

Alsace, the Paris Airport and in the aeronautical industry (SNECMA), whereas the CFDT was prepared to sign in these industries, and also in the atomic energy authority (CEA).[17] As in the private sector, the CGT and the CFDT did not have a totally systematic approach to collective bargaining and the signing of agreements. They were anxious not to leave the industrial sphere to FO and the other 'reformist' trade union confederations. A further period was discernible at the end of 1976, at the time of the introduction of the Barre Plan and the de-indexing of wages in the public sector. As Roy explained, public sector bargaining broke down at this time not because of the demands of the trade union confederations, but specifically as a result of government policy.[18]

The initial success of public sector bargaining has been explained by the fact 'there was something in it for everyone'. On the one hand, trade unions that signed agreements could argue that they were demonstrating a sense of responsibility, whilst the others could maintain their halo of intransigence. On the other hand, the State was able to pursue its policies without having to do battle with its own employees. At the beginning of the decade national trade unions belonging to the CGT and the CFDT were primarily attracted by the gains to be made in the industrial sphere. In certain industries, they could point to increases in real wages as a result of these agreements. From 1971 agreements provided for index-linked wage increases. In 1971 it was agreed that real wages in the public sector should increase by 2 per cent on average (1.7 per cent in the civil service and 2.5 per cent in the electricity and gas supply industries). Real wages increased more in the 1969–72 period in the civil service, the electricity and gas supply industries and the coal industry than in the 1964–67 period (on the other hand, real wages grew marginally less quickly in the railways and in the Paris metro) (Dubois, 1974, p.126,137). Other commentators have stressed the importance of interconfederal rivalry for the success of public sector bargaining. According to Berthier, if the agreements had a real impact on wages and working conditions, it would be invidious for the CGT, for example, to be the only trade union not to sign. It would look as if it was abandoning the industrial sphere to the others. However, if the CFDT refused to sign, then the CGT would feel less compelled to sign, since it would be less isolated and would fear being vulnerable on its left flank.[19] It was only when both confederations were unenthusiastic about signing agreements that it was safe to abstain; and even then, FO could take the credit for negotiating improved wages and conditions.

Interesting exceptions to the general pattern of public sector bargaining are to be found in the electricity and gas supply industries. Both the CGT and the CFDT signed these agreements until 1976, a time when they had already ceased to sign agreements in other public sector industries. There was one major exception however; the CGT refused to sign the 1970 agreement. According to Jobert, the reasons were political. The CGT's refusal to sign was influenced as much by its opposition to the 'new society' advocated by Jacques Chaban Delmas, as it was by the actual content of the agreement (Jobert, 1974, p.403). On the other hand, according to Echevin, the reasons were industrial. The CGT took an active part in the negotiations and did not engage in systematic opposition to bargaining as such. It refused to sign primarily because it was opposed to the clause requiring a period of notice before a strike could be called. Moreover, it held a ballot, and employees in the industry recommended that the agreement should be rejected (Echevin, 1970, p.93–95). Echevin's argument seems more convincing. This offending clause was dropped the following year, and the CGT signed the agreement and subsequent ones, as did the CFDT. The attraction of gaining substantial industrial benefits, particularly in terms of increases in real wages, outweighed the potential disadvantage of legitimising government policy at that time.

In the 1970s there was a significant level of collective bargaining in France, both in the private sector, and a significant level of trade union participation in the bargaining process. Not surprisingly, given the diversity of each bargaining situation, trade unions were not able to act in a totally coherent and systematic fashion. In the private sector the CFDT, and particularly the CGT, signed a considerable number of different agreements, at national industry level and also at the local level. In the public sector, the CGT and the CFDT participated in the bargaining process, particularly at the beginning of the 1970s and were prepared to sign a certain number of agreements. However as the decade wore on, the demands of the political sphere became more pressing and the benefits of public sector wage bargaining became less attractive, so the CGT and the CFDT were less prepared to sign agreements and to legitimise this process.

Trade union confederations and collective bargaining

'Revolutionary' trade union confederations like the CGT and the CFDT were torn between the political and industrial spheres. They were anxious not to give the impression that, in signing agreements, they approved of the prevailing economic and social order and of the policies of a Right-wing government, but on the other hand they were keen to show that they were instrumental in improving the wages and working conditions of workers in general and of their members and potential supporters in particular. They were particularly conscious of the fact that participation in the collective bargaining process could lead to identification with the prevailing political and economic system. Jean-Louis Moynot explained that the CGT had refused to sign certain agreements, not because the CGT was opposed to the government, but because the content did not satisfy CGT demands and also because there was a risk of 'integration' which he defined as 'allowing the employers or the government to realise their objectives with the support or agreement of the trade unions'. For Edmond Maire, 'the government was aiming to make public sector bargaining an instrument of participation in the prevailing system . . . for the Prime Minister negotiating meant that the CFDT should rally to the goal that he had defined in order to reinforce the system'.[20] However, as has been seen in the first part of this chapter, this did not stop the CGT and the CFDT from signing agreements at the beginning of the 1970s. At a later date the CGT claimed however that those trade union confederations that were still prepared to sign agreements (for instance FO) were forcing workers to put up with the consequences of the crisis; in presenting these agreements as progressive these same trade union confederations were keeping up the illusion that it was possible to amend a system which needed to be changed.[21]

This did not mean that the CGT and the CFDT refused to take part in negotiations with the government and the employers on principle. According to Jean-Louis Moynot, the CGT had never thought that there was a contradiction between, on the one hand, fighting for general political perspectives and, on the other, signing agreements.[22] Moreover, according to Georges Séguy collective bargaining was desirable, as long as it led to social progress and did not impinge on trade union freedom.[23] In an article devoted to the issue of collective bargaining, Georges Séguy explained that:

we've always thought of public sector bargaining as an aspect of the relations between employers and employees which must by necessity exist in a system like ours . . . we shall continue to exploit all the possibilities of negotiated solutions and we shall sign what we think is advantageous for the workers.[24]

Both the CFDT and the CGT were aware of the importance of public sector bargaining for the success of the policies of the political parties of the Right in government. According to Edmond Maire, Chaban Delmas knew that the continuation of his 'reign' depended on the success of public sector bargaining.[25] In a retrospective study of collective bargaining in the public sector, Raymond Barberis of the CGT Public

Sector Workers' Union claimed that those confederations (that is, the others) that had signed public sector agreements had given support to and even encouraged the overall retrograde and antisocial philosophy inherent in government policy.[26] When negotiations broke down in the RATP, the Paris Transport Authority, in 1977, the CGT stated that to have signed such an agreement would have been tantamount to giving official approval to the austerity policy against which workers had campaigned since October of the previous year.[27] The CGT and the CFDT did not refuse to have dealings with the government, even though it was made up of members of the political parties of the Right. Indeed, on numerous occasions, the CGT and the CFDT called on the government to begin negotiations. Just after the signing of the Common Programme of Government, the CFDT, for instance, wrote to Pierre Messmer, the Prime Minister of the time, and Edgar Faure, his Minister of Social Affairs, asking for negotiations to take place.[28] At a later date, the CFDT wrote to Raymond Barre when Prime Minister asking for negotiations to start up.[29] Both Georges Séguy and Robert Bono, one of the CFDT's confederal secretaries, wrote to the government asking for negotiations to be resumed in the 1974 dispute in the postal service,[30] and at that same time delegations from the CGT and the CFDT met and issued a joint statement calling on the government to start up negotiations again.[31] However, meetings between the leaders of the CGT and the CFDT on the one hand and the representatives of government on the other were infrequent and *ad hoc*.

The trade union confederations refused on occasions to sign collective bargaining agreements for other reasons. They opposed the curtailment of their activities. As Georges Séguy wrote, 'we won't sign anything restrictive, constraining, illusory or insufficient'.[32] The CFDT was anxious to ensure that the period for which the agreement was meant to last was as short as possible.[33] According to René Bidouze, the general secretary of the CGT Public Sector Workers Union, one of the reasons why the CGT did not sign agreements in the Civil Service and in the Post and Telecommunications industry was because the agreement was to last for an excessive period of time.[34] The CGT and the CFDT were unwilling to sign agreements putting a limitation on trade union rights, and particularly the right to strike. They both expressed the view that the government wanted to use public sector bargaining agreements to reduce the level of strike activity.[35] The CGT stipulated that agreements should contain no limitation on trade union rights nor on the right to strike,[36] and the CFDT demanded that agreements should not contain no-strike clauses.[37] In addition, both trade union confederations were concerned by the ramifications of collective bargaining for trade union rivalry. According to the CFDT, only 'representative' trade unions should be allowed to participate,[38] that is, the CGT, CFDT, FO, CGC, CFTC, FEN, and not the small company unions such as the *Confédération Française du Travail* (CFT) or the *Confédération des Syndicats Libres* (CSL). Indeed, some of the 'representative' trade union confederations, particularly the CFTC and on occasions FO, had a tenuous claim to representativity, because of their extremely low membership figures in certain areas. At its 39th conference in 1975, the CGT demanded that no agreement should be implemented unless signed by organisations representing the majority of the workforce[39] – this would not only legitimate the agreement but also put the CGT, as the largest trade union confederation with the best grassroots support, in a powerful position.

It is not surprising that both trade union confederations were anxious to ensure that the government did not use collective bargaining as an instrument of wage control.[40] They were opposed to the notion of public sector cash limits. This would mean that wage bargaining would only centre on the way in which the total sum was to be shared out, and in this the trade unions would primarily be engaged in championing the sectional interests of competing groups of workers.[41] Given that during the early and mid–1970s the CGT and the CFDT had differing views on the question of wage differentials, it is clear that negotiating within a framework of cash limits could only exacerbate relations between the two trade union confederations. In addition, they were both opposed to the way in which these cash limits were calculated, that is, in terms of the overall success of the nationalised industry or of the national economy,[42] since they did not want wage increases to be dependent on the prosperity of the capitalist economy. In general terms the CFDT was opposed to the establishment of a link between wages and productivity, and, according to Georges Séguy, linking wages to the success of the industry was like, 'being free, but being inside a cage'.[43] The CGT, in particular, disagreed with the government over the mechanism for triggering wage increases in the public sector. It favoured an automatic inflation-related wage provision.[44] Indeed the CGT claimed that it had signed the 1971 wage agreement on the railways specifically because of the clause relating to index-linked wage increases.[45] The CGT was commited to an automatic link between wages and the rate of inflation and at its 38th conference in Nîmes in 1972 it called specifically for wage guarantees.[46] There was also concern over the time at which these increases would be triggered. If, these increases were only granted once a year, then employees would be disadvantaged during the period immediately preceding the increase in wages (particularly in a period of high inflation). The CGT also disagreed with the government over the official calculation of the cost of living index, a crucial feature for deciding when increases in the minimum legal wage were to be made.[47] The CGT claimed that the official figure underestimated the increases in the cost of living in the real economy and so from 1972 onwards it established its own index. It was difficult for a trade union confederation to sign an agreement in which increases in nominal wages were eroded by the debatable accuracy of the official price index calculations.

Both the CGT and the CFDT participated in the process of collective bargaining, and, in spite of considerable misgivings on occasions, signed a variety of different agreements. At the beginning of the 1970s, both trade union confederations were wary of participating in public sector bargaining, because they were loath to be identified with the prevailing social and economic order, and because they were also conscious of the fact that this would give support to the Right-wing government. However they did so, because they could not afford to abandon the industrial sphere to the other trade union confederations, particularly FO, and because they were able to obtain real benefits without compromising their freedom for manoeuvre. In addition, the demands of the political sphere were less pressing at that time. The political parties of the Union of the Left had not yet signed the Common Programme of Government and had thus not yet established themselves as a credible alternative government. However, as the 1970s progressed, there was less to be gained in the industrial sphere from public sector bargaining. Pierre Messmer, Jacques Chirac and Raymond Barre were less prepared to support public sector bargaining than had been Jacques Chaban Delmas. The memory of the Events of May 1968 was beginning to fade. Moreover, as has been seen in previous chapters, both trade union confederations were becoming increasingly committed to their activities in the political sphere. The CGT maintained that not only social and economic but also political conditions should be taken into consideration when agreements were being negotiated.[48]

With the break-up of the Union of the Left and the failure of the Left to win the legislative elections in 1978, it was clear that trade union objectives were not going to be attained by means of participation in the political sphere. Backmann noted that, after the second round of the 1978 legislative elections, the major trade union confederations expressed one unanimous demand, the desire to negotiate.[49] The general secretary of the CFDT wrote to the President of the Republic asking for a meeting so as 'to start up negotiations'.[50] The CFDT claimed that starting up negotiations would restore confidence in trade union action and help to set up a favorable power relationship with employers after the defeat of the political parties of the Left.[51] Edmond Maire advocated a new approach to collective bargaining itself. When asked about the necessity of compromise in bargaining, he claimed that it depended on what was meant by 'necessary'. 'This should not be automatic, as was the case with FO, but the possibility of compromise between social forces with different or opposing social objectives could not be discounted. If the CFDT was to ignore this, it would not be an effective social movement.'[52] After the failure of its political strategy, the CFDT was clearly rethinking its views on collective bargaining. The CGT also saw the 1978 legislative elections as a watershed and immediately afterwards asked for negotiations to start up.[53] Lucien Chavrot explained that ideology had no role to play in collective bargaining. If the CGT considered an agreement positive, it would sign.[54] At the national CGT conference in the autumn of the same year, Georges Séguy intimated that the CGT's approach to collective bargaining had been unproductive. He asked whether the tendency to link everything to the election of a Left-wing government had not led the CGT to underestimate the concessions that could have been extracted from employers. He claimed that trade union action could impose concessions and that the value of a compromise was to be measured in terms of economic realities. Moreover in terms of trade union rivalry, it was not a good idea to let the other trade union confederations gain all the credit any concessions obtained.[55] After the 1978 legislative elections, negotiations started up in the private sector, and a major landmark was achieved. In the metalworking industry, a national wage agreement was signed for the first time by both the CGT and the CFDT.[56] However, similar developments did not take place in the public sector. Moreover, it was not long before trade union leaders were complaining bitterly that negotiations with the employers' associations had more or less run into the ground.[57] Whilst the trade union confederations had seen the need to change their attitude to collective bargaining, the government and the employers felt that their approach had been vindicated and that there was no obvious reason to change.

Political parties and collective bargaining

Collective bargaining is the prerogative of the trade union confederations, a fact implicitly acknowledged by the political parties of the Union of the Left who showed little interest in this issue whether in the private sector or, more surprisingly given its underlying potential for politicisation, the public sector. In the previous chapter it was noted that the French Communist Party had a clear strategy for strike action. The same could not be said of collective bargaining. Moreover, its position was further obscured by the fact that, of the few contributions to party publications on this subject, most were written by Communists who were simultaneously well-placed members of the CGT. Jean Magniadas falls into this category. At the beginning of the decade, he was to criticise the speech made by the Prime Minister, Jacques Chaban Delmas, in which the latter saw a 'new society' dawning, as a result of the new-style public sector bargaining agreements. For Magniadas these agreements would simply encourage class collaboration. Signing 'insufficient and unacceptable' agreements demonstrated the readiness of the other confederations to support government policy. The PCF supported the CGT in its attempts to persuade the government to drop a certain number of restrictive clauses in these agreements.[58] There is little evidence of a consistent position throughout the 1970s. At the beginning of the 1970s the public sector wage bargaining agreements, were seen as an attempt to proscribe the type of strike action seen in May 1968. It was thought that the aim of these agreements was to subordinate any improvement in living and working conditions to the demands of productivity. The PCF was of the opinion that only a class-conscious organisation like the CGT had not been deceived and so had not signed agreements like the one in the Civil Service. When the CGT did sign, however, as for instance in the electricity and gas supply industries, the PCF explained that the terms of the agreement were advantageous for the employees. That was also why the CGT was prepared to sign the agreement in the railways. According to the PCF, the battle led by the CGT had borne fruit.[59] The PCF had no specific strategy of its own. If the CGT signed an agreement, the PCF supported it. Equally, if the CGT reversed its position and decided not to sign an agreement, then the PCF supported this too. In some ways this gives some credence to the argument that the PCF was to support the CGT as a *quid pro quo* for the latter's support in the political sphere.

However, Soskice saw this relationship in a different light.[60] He concluded in his work on the French political economy in the 1970s that for the PCF the role of the CGT lay in preserving the hostility of the workforce towards employers and government. This would be threatened by the development of collective bargaining, which would legitimise the employer as a social partner and thus hold out the possibility of social progress under a non-communist regime. Interestingly, as was seen in the first part of this chapter, the CGT signed a considerable number of collective bargaining agreements, and if Soskice's view is accepted, then this can only mean that the PCF was unable to exert sufficient control over the CGT. It seems more likely that the PCF had a less rigorous approach to the issue of collective bargaining. Badie's study of the PCF's attitude to industrial conflict does not shed much light on the party's attitude to the avoidance of conflict or the resolution of conflict through the procedures of collective bargaining. He does not explain how the PCF would maximise, channel or stifle strike action, if it did not have a strategy for avoiding or resolving conflict. Two brief allusions are made to the PCF's attempts to become involved in collective bargaining, both at times when the PCF wanted to stifle strike activity; in 1967 at the time of the strikes surrounding the debate on social welfare, and in 1968 at a time when some groups of workers were still on strike just prior to the elections (Badie, 1975, p. 98–99, 102–105). To be able to switch successfully from one mode to another, from conflict to resolution of conflict, and to pass on the message so that it is understood and acted upon, requires an extraordinary level of political and industrial sophistication, an issue which Badies does not address.

As for the Socialist Party, there is even less evidence of an interest in collective bargaining. An article in *La Croix* at the time of the 1974 Presidential election noted that François Mitterrand, if elected, might be prepared to call a tripartite meeting between the government, the trade union confederations and the employers' association, but no further details were given.[61] This omission could be explained in terms of the readiness of the PS to respect functional differentiation. However it could also be seen as a measure of the lack of preparedness to govern. Equally, such vagueness could be explained in terms of electoral tactics. Francois Mitterrand wanted to attract support from the widest possible constituency, from members of the CGT and CFDT, but also of the other trade union confederations, such as FO and FEN, which were more prepared to sign collective bargaining agreements. The Socialist Party's dilemma was underlined by François Mitterrand at a press conference in 1975. He asked why some thought that it was class collaboration when the FEN signed a wage agreement, but not for instance when the CGT negotiated with government and employers at the time of the Events of May 1968.[62] A little more light is shed on a socialist approach to collective bargaining by two articles by Jacques Delors, who had been the adviser on social affairs to Jacques Chaban Delmas in 1969 but who had subsequently joined the Socialist Party in 1974. He blamed the lack of collective bargaining on the government and on the employers, but made no mention of the strategy that trade unions and the Socialist Party should take.[63] In a further article written after the 1978 legislative elections, Delors made a plea for the resurrection of collective bargaining. He bemoaned the fact that from 1972 onwards public sector bargaining had only been concerned with pay bargaining and with setting one trade union confederation against the other. Delors observed that since 1974 public sector bargaining had become an empty ritual, and employers and employees had met infrequently. Collective bargaining was not only a process for periods of economic growth, as proclaimed by certain employers, nor a question of extremes with no middle ground, 'hence the search for temporary compromises so as to be able to live together'. Collective bargaining should be less secretive and there should be an 'articulated' network of negotiations, at different levels. He considered that there should be a way of combining a reasonable increase in wages with an anti-inflation campaign, whilst giving high priority to the low paid.[64] Delors was signaling his previously held belief that collective bargaining was an acceptable form of resolving conflict. It is not clear whether the rest of the Socialist Party was in tune with his thinking at that time.

Conclusions

Collective bargaining in France has been described as 'intermittent, irregular and infrequent', but this should not disguise the fact in the 1970s collective bargaining occurred at all levels, both in the private and public sector. The CGT and the CFDT were somewhat ambivalent about collective bargaining as a means of trade union action, to take up Clegg's phrase, but considerably less so in the private sector than in the public sector. In the private sector, they were prepared to participate in the bargaining process, and throughout the 1970s the CFDT, and particularly the CGT, signed a number of different agreements, at national multi-industry level, national industry level and also at the local level. In the public sector, an arena where the demands of the industrial sphere were more obviously accompanied by the demands of the political sphere, the CGT and the CFDT participated in the bargaining process, particularly at the beginning of the 1970s, and were prepared to sign a number of agreements. However as the decade moved on, the CGT and the CFDT were less prepared to sign agreements and to legitimise public sector wage bargaining. In the mid 1970s, the threat to the existing social and economic order posed by the Events of May had receded, and the employers and the different governments became less committed to the concept and practice of integrating the trade union confederations into the process of collective bargaining. In addition, the consequences of the oil crisis, and particularly the high rate of inflation and high level of wage claims, had a destabilising impact on the practice of collective bargaining. The successful attempt by Raymond Barre to de-index wages and thereby to reduce their real value put an end to meaningful collective bargaining, and the trade union confederations could not expect to obtain real benefits for their members. This coincided with a clearer commitment by the CGT and the CFDT to engage in the political sphere. The CGT and the CFDT could still demonstrate their readiness to negotiate, which would ensure that they would not be accused of neglecting the industrial sphere, knowing that the employers and the government would be less willing to agree to their demands. Moreover, when collective bargaining did not succeed, they could put the blame on the employers and the governments of the Right, thus aiding their political objectives. In the late 1970s, once it was clear that trade union objectives were not going to be achieved through political means, the CFDT attempted to switch its strategy back to the industrial sphere. The CFDT, and even the CGT, implied that a tendency to rely on change in the political sphere had encouraged them to undervalue the benefits of collective bargaining. Consequently, they were to develop a renewed interest in collective bargaining, which was however to meet with a limited response from employers in the private sector and no response at all from the government in the public sector. By the end of the 1970s the CGT and the CFDT were faced with a double disappointment. Their political strategies had not borne fruit, and their newly developed interest in an industrial strategy based increasingly on collective bargaining had failed to find an echo with employers in the private and public sectors.

Notes

1. Rapport Adam, 'La négociation collective en France'. *Droit Social*, November 1978, p.385–91.
2. McCormick, J. 'Gaullism and collective bargaining: the effect of the Fifth Republic on French industrial relations' in Andrews, W. & Hoffman. S., *The impact of the fifth republic on France*, Albany, SUNY, 1981, p. 199–201.
3. Information on the content of the laws is drawn from CIR, *Worker participation and collective bargaining in Europe*. Study 4. HMSO. p.41–43.
4. Interview, Germain Ferec, 22 February, 1985. Since 1982, the *Bilan annuel de la négociation collective* has been produced by the relevant Ministry.
5. Rapport Adam. 'La négociation collective en France'. *op cit.*, p.386.
6. Data from the *Ministère de l'Emploi*.
7. Rapport Adam, 'La négociation collective en France', *op cit.*, p.386.
8. *Le Monde*, 5 August, 1976.

9. *Le Figaro,* 26 November, 1976.
10. Unpublished data from the *Ministère de l'Emploi.*
11. Unpublished data from the *Ministère de l'Emploi.*
12. *La négociation collective dans l'industries métallurgique de l'Isère (1972–1981),* 1983, unpublished report Ministère de l'Emploi. p.21–28, 81–83.
13. *L'annee métallurgique.* Paris. Union des Industries Métallurgiques et Minières. 1985. p.37.
14. *La négociation collective 1972–1981 Habillement,* 1ère Partie unpublished report *Ministère de l'Emploi.*
15. McCormick, J. 'Gaullism and collective bargaining: the effect of the Fifth Republic on French industrial relations', *op cit.,* p.199–201.
16. *Le Monde,* 17 September, 1969.
17. Data from *Ministère de l'Emploi.*
18. *Le Monde,* 12–13 December, 1976.
19. *Les Echos,* 26 December, 1972.
20. *Projet,* November 1970, p.1040. *Les Echos.* 15 June, 1971.
21. *Le Peuple,* 1–15 June, 1975, p.2.
22. *Projet,* November 1970, p.1037.
23. *La Vie Française,* 29 January 1971.
24. *L'Humanité,* 25 February 1972.
25. *Combat,* 28 February 1972.
26. *Dix ans de politique contractuelle dans le secteur public et nationalisé – bilan,* CGT, Etudes et Documents Economiques, 1982, p.5.
27. *L'Humanité,* 8 July 1977.
28. *CFDT Syndicalisme,* 20 July 1972, p.1.
29. *CFDT Syndicalisme,* 7 November 1976, p.4.
30. *L'Humanité,* 20 November 1974. See also article by Dumont in *Le Monde,* 23 March 1977.
31. *L'Humanité,* 23 November 1974.
32. *L'Humanité,* 25 February 1972.
33. *CFDT Syndicalisme,* 15 March 1973, p.72.
34. *Le Peuple,* 15–30 November 1974, p.6.
35. For the CGT, see Séguy, G., *L'Humanité,* 7 January 1971, and for the CFDT, see Moreau, J., *L'Unité,* 31 March 1978, p.22.
36. *Le Peuple,* 1–31 May 1972, p.61.
37. *CFDT Syndicalisme,* 30 December 1971, p.2.
38. *CFDT Syndicalisme,* 7 June 1973, p.19.
39. *Le Peuple,* 1–31 July 1975, p.58.
40. *CFDT Syndicalisme,* 22 July 1976, p.3-4. *Le Peuple,* 15 February 1976, p.2.
41. For the CFDT, see *CFDT Syndicalisme,* 10 June 1971, p.2. For the CGT, see Moynot, J-L., 1970, p.1040.
42. See the statement by the CFDT public sector unions, *Le Monde,* 24 December 1974.
43. *L'Humanite,* 14 January 1971.
44. See quote by Georges Séguy in Dubois, P., 1974, *Mort de l'etat-patron,* Paris, Editions Ouvrières, p.205.
45. According to Georges Séguy, *L'Humanité,* 7 January 1971.
46. *Le Peuple,* 1–31 May 1972, p.61.

47. *Le Peuple*, 1–15 February, 1977, p. 2. For the CFDT's position, see Edmond Maire, *Le Monde*, 7 April, 1976.
48. *Le Peuple*, 1–31 May, 1972, p. 62.
49. *L'Unité*, 24–30 March, 1978, p. 15.
50. *CFDT Syndicalisme*, 30 March, 1978, p. 3–4.
51. *CFDT Syndicalisme*, December 1978, p. 21.
52. *CFDT Syndicalisme*, 20 April, 1978, p. 2–3.
53. *Le Monde*, 21 May, 1978.
54. *Projet*, November 1978, p. 1046–48.
55. *Le Peuple*, 1–31 December, p. 9–10.
56. For details, see *L'Année Métallurgique*, 1978, p. 42–43. For the background to the negotiations, see *Le Monde*, 9–10 July, 1978.
57. See statement by Edmond Maire, *Le Monde*, 7 November, 1978.
58. Magniadas, J. 'Politique contractuelle et lutte de classe', *Economie et Politique*, May 1970, p. 43–60.
59. Gelly, R. 'De quoi est malade la politique contractuelle?', *L'Humanité*, 8, February, 1972.
60. For details see Flanagan, R., Soskice, D & Ulman, L., 1983, *Unions, economic stability and income policies*, p. 648.
61. *La Croix*, 23 March, 1974.
62. *Le Monde*, 14 October, 1975.
63. *Le Monde*, 24–25 May, 1977.
64. *L'Unité*, 31 March, 1978, p. 23–24.

Conclusions

French trade union confederations and political parties have developed complex and dynamic sets of relations which have significant consequences for party politics, trade unionism and industrial relations. Trade unions and political parties carried out different functions, but in practice the parameters of this functional differentiation were often difficult to establish, because these spheres of activity were interrelated. In order to compensate for their relative weakness in the industrial sphere French trade unions needed to become active in the political sphere. This did not mean that they entered into a neocorporatist relationship with the government, which during the whole period of the 1970s was dominated by the political parties of the Right. Instead, they were drawn into a relationship with an alternative government made up of the political parties of the Left.

The fragmented and ideological nature of the political Left and of the trade union movement in France has produced a multi-dimensional pattern of party–union relations which in itself is not unusual in Western Europe. However its nature is distinctive. Relations between the CGT and the PCF were radically different from those between the CFDT and the PS, and both were different from party–union relations to be found in other countries. At first sight there are similarities between the French and Italian cases, but on closer inspection significant differences emerge. In Italy trade union density was higher, and unity of action was more developed. Moreover there was no Italian counterpart of the CFDT and no appropriate equivalent in France of the large Christian Democrat trade union confederation *Confederazione Italiana dei Sindicati Lavoratori* (CISL). The political situation was also different. The Communist Party in Italy was stronger and more influential than its French counterpart which was gradually being overhauled by the Socialist Party. In addition the Italian Communist Party was a committed advocate of Eurocommunism, whereas the PCF was initially less enthusiastic and later positively hostile to this notion, a fundamental divergence which had significant consequences for party–union relations.

Although well represented throughout the structures of the PCF, members of the CGT formed only one of a series of groups vying for influence within the party. On the other hand, PCF members were especially well represented within the CGT, particularly in key positions within its decision-making structures, and so were able to establish a dominant position within the confederation, its national unions and its local organisations. This does not necessarily mean, however, that during the 1970s the PCF was able to assume total control of the activities of the CGT or to oblige the confederation to act solely in terms of its political objectives. The PCF did not use the CGT as a transmission belt, neither did it bestow relative autonomy on the CGT. During the 1970s CGT–PCF relations entered a new and different phase characterised by the fact that the PCF was prey to a certain factionalism and thus less able to provide a clear and unequivocal lead. In addition, because of the climate of unity on the Left, the CGT was vulnerable to a variety of pressures from other organisations, which drew it away from the PCF. As a result, the PCF temporarily lost its total hold over the CGT, a fact which became all the more noticeable towards the end of the decade, when it actively sought to re-establish a greater level of control.

On the non-communist Left party-union relations were qualitatively different. The PS and the CFDT were autonomous but committed to a perspective of political change which brought them together during the period of the Union of the Left. The Socialist Party was primarily interested in attracting the support of a broad based political constituency, a strategy which did not require the same level of relationship with one particular trade union confederation. Whilst many members of the PS were members of a trade union, many were not. Within its ranks the CFDT generally had the highest level of representation, and its relative position was further reinforced during the period of the Union of the Left, as a result of the decision taken by members of the CFDT, both individually and collectively, to reinforce the PS. The CGT also had members in the PS, as did FEN, the teachers' union, and FO, the other major trade union confederation. In this way the PS had access to a broader political constituency but as a result was unable to establish a coherent line on party–union relations, for fear of alienating one particular group of supporters or another. Few active members of the different trade union confederations were to be found in the higher echelons of the PS, and there is no suggestion that French trade unions had the same relationship with the PS as did their counterparts with social democratic parties in other countries. There is no evidence to suggest that one organisation was able to control the activities of the other or to exploit informal patterns of influence within the other. Personnel links between the CFDT and the PS were less intense and less exclusive than those between the CGT and the PCF. The period of the Union of the Left saw the CGT move slightly away from the PCF and, on the other hand, the CFDT draw closer to the PS. Nonetheless, these were temporary phenomena and, after the break-up of the Union of the Left, the PCF was to re-establish a greater level of control over the CGT, and the CFDT was to drift away from the PS.

Both trade union confederations rejected a narrow industrial interpretation of trade unionism. They refused to be solely concerned with the regulation of employment and insisted on their right to participate in the political sphere. The CGT campaigned vigorously in support of the manifesto of the Union of the Left, the Common Programme of Government, and in support of the Left at the legislative and Presidential elections in 1973 and 1974. The CFDT's initial position was somewhat different. Claiming a certain functional distinctiveness, it refused to support the Common Programme of Government, and launched a low key campaign on behalf of the entire Left at the time of the legislative elections in 1973. Nonetheless, the following year saw a switch in strategy, and the CFDT overtly entered the political sphere. It was increasingly drawn into the logic of the Union of the Left, campaigning wholeheartedly on behalf of François Mitterrand at the time of the 1974 Presidential elections, and so attempting to strengthen the Socialist Party. When the Union of the Left broke up in 1977, the two trade union confederations were unable to insulate themselves from the vicissitudes of inter-party rivalry. The CGT became increasingly critical of the PS and its policies, aligning itself more openly with the PCF. In the run-up to the 1978 legislative elections, the CGT called ritualistically for the victory of a Union of the Left that no longer existed, but indicated a distinct preference for the PCF. When it became clear that the PCF was in political and electoral difficulties, communist members of the CGT, and its general secretary Georges Séguy, rallied behind the party. In this way CGT autonomy was undermined, and CGT-PCF alignment was reinforced. As for the CFDT, its response was remarkable. In spite of its initial lack of enthusiasm for the Common Programme of Government, it produced a compromise set of policy proposals with the aim of bringing the PCF and the PS together and thus saving the Union of the Left. However, once it became apparent that the parties were not going to be reunited, the CFDT abruptly changed tack and reverted to a strategy emphasising the primacy of the industrial sphere. At the 1978 legislative elections, it nevertheless called on its members to vote for the political parties of the Left. The failure of the Union of the Left was a reminder to the CFDT of the dangers of embarking on a trade union strategy which allowed the political to gain precedence over the industrial.

Events in the political sphere had significant consequences for the development of French trade unionism. There is no doubt that the agreement between the PCF and the PS had a beneficial impact on trade union unity of action. Interconfederal relations were more harmonious and intense during the period of the Union of the Left then they had been before or have been since. The CGT and the CFDT issued a vast number of joint statements and devised joint strategies for the attainment of their industrial demands. Given the state of party-union relations in France, trade union unity of action would be unthinkable without party unity. However to see it solely in terms of the Union of the Left is misleading, since the trade union confederations also actively participated in establishing a climate of unity which was to permeate the entire Left. It must not be forgotten however that trade union unity of action was influenced by other factors, albeit to a lesser extent; ideological positions, employment trends, international links, workplace rivalries and patterns of membership. When the Union of the Left broke up in September 1977, the unitary practices of the trade union confederations did not disappear overnight, and unity of action was to continue haltingly for some years. However, once the dynamic of political unity had been broken, the ever present centrifugal pressures within the industrial sphere came to the fore, and CGT-CFDT unity gradually disappeared. The bitterness and disappointment engendered swamped the CGT and the CFDT, and they have not attempted subsequently to repair the damage.

Events in the political sphere also impinged on the internal politics of the trade union confederations, causing factionalism within the CGT and the CFDT. It is significant that opposition did not occur as a result of disagreements over industrial issues, but rather as a result of differing political perspectives. Within the CGT there was no opposition to the notion of trade unions being active in the political sphere, nor to the idea of providing support for the Union of the Left. Opposition to the confederal line was first expressed by socialist members of the CGT, who were dissatisfied with the CGT's overt alignment with the PCF. Shortly afterwards, a further wave of opposition appeared. On this occasion it emanated from an unusual quarter, from communist members of the

CGT, a further indication of the fact that control of the activities of the CGT had slipped temporarily from the grasp of the PCF. These dissident communists were opposed to the decision taken by orthodox communists to re-establish control over the activities of the CGT and to draw it into a more sectarian phase. As for the CFDT, opposition to the confederal line was more disparate and more widespread throughout the entire period of the 1970s. At the beginning of the 1970s some members opposed the decision to engage in unity of action with the CGT, but equally at the end of the decade others bemoaned the demise of trade union unity. There was disagreement over the refusal to support the Common Programme of Government and over the lack of commitment to a strategy of support for the non-communist Left; yet later there was opposition to the Moreau Report which advocated withdrawal from the political sphere. This opposition emanated from two identifiable groupings; on the one hand, a fragmented group of Trotskyists and Maoists on the extreme left which had a certain, albeit declining, presence within the CFDT during this period: and, on the other, a 'rolling' group of national and local unions linked to a movement, 'Contribution' with no overt party political affiliation. Opposition was rife, and differences over major elements of trade union strategy so great that it is remarkable that the CFDT did not implode during this period.

Events in the political sphere also influenced aspects of French industrial relations, which underlines the importance of investigating both the political and industrial aspects of party–union relations. Although strikes had their roots in the industrial sphere and employees went on strike primarily to improve their wages and working conditions, they affected and in turn were affected by political events. The decline in strike activity during the 1970s cannot be explained by one single variable, but must be ascribed to a combination of factors, both industrial (the repercussions of the oil crisis) and political (the break-up of the Union of the Left). In spite of unconvincing claims to the contrary, both trade union confederations were less prepared to engage in strike activity at sensitive moments of the political calendar (for instance, prior to the 1973 and 1978 legislative elections), not wishing to harm the electory chances of the Union of the Left. At other times, the CGT, and on occasions the CFDT, were also prepared to use specific forms of strike activity for political purposes, and national days of action, in particular, served to focus opposition to the government and provide vicarious support for the Union of the Left. This politicisation of industrial conflict was accompanied by a small shift in the balance of party-union relations, since political parties were prepared to provide moral and material support for trade unions and strikers, particularly at a local level.

However, in doing so, the French Communist Party was anxious to use industrial conflict as an instrument to further its own political objectives. Evidence suggests that it was not necessarily able to succeed on a large scale.

Collective bargaining clearly had its roots in the industrial sphere, but could not be divorced entirely from the political sphere. In the public sector, the CGT and the CFDT participated in the bargaining process, particularly at the very beginning of the 1970s, and were prepared to sign a certain number of agreements which offered distinct advantages, for example, in terms of index-linked wage increases. However, as the decade progressed, successive governments became less inclined to engage in meaningful collective bargaining, and the trade unions were less prepared to sign agreements which were less and less attractive. Moreover the trade unions were increasingly aware of the political ramifications of legitimising public sector bargaining. They did not want to help right-wing governments succeed in the area of wage bargaining. On the other hand, collective bargaining in the private sector was removed from the glare of overt politicisation and also from the direct control of the leadership of the confederations. In these circumstances, the organisations of both trade union confederations were more prepared to participate in the bargaining process and sign agreements, at a number of different levels. It is noteworthy that, after the evident failure of their political strategies, both the CFDT and the CGT admitted that a tendency to rely on change in the political sphere had led them to underestimate the value of collective bargaining.

Party–union relations were in disequilibrium, with priority being given to the political sphere. Both the CGT and, to a lesser degree the CFDT, provided significant support for the parties of the Union of the Left. In addition, events in the political sphere had a clear impact on French trade unionism, conditioning the politics of inter- and intra-confederal relations. Yet political parties did not compensate for this by providing a commensurate level of support in the industrial sphere. Indeed the PCF attempted to use the industrial sphere to pursue its own political objectives, whilst the PS remained on the margins for the most part. Moreover, on occasions, the trade unions used their position within the industrial sphere to provide further support for the political parties of the Union of the Left.

A further dimension to party–union relations was added in the 1980s when the political parties of the Right were voted out of office, and the trade unions were faced with a government of the Left. The socialists and communists were in an excellent position to restore the balance in party–union relations and to provide the trade union confederations with a belated *quid pro quo* in the industrial sphere for the support that the political parties had previously received in the 1970s in the political sphere. They started with the best of intentions, passing a series of laws designed to improve employees' rights and to reinforce the position of the trade unions in the workplace, increasing the wages of the low paid and introducing a number of significant social reforms. When put to the test, however, their commitment to French trade unionism buckled. The government was dominated by the Socialist Party which, as has been seen, had tenuous links with the world of trade unionism. Its economic policies led to thousands of redundancies in major industrial sectors, thus further weakening the membership base of the trade unions. As part of its anti-inflation policy the government introduced a wage freeze in 1982 which helped to undermine the collective bargaining process and to marginalise the trade unions. The French trade unions were faced with a familiar dilemma. Should they defend the interests of their members and supporters in the industrial sphere or support their allies in the political sphere? Even after the political disappointments of the 1970s, their reflexes were still political. They were loath to provide the parties of the Right with political ammunition, and so they chose to support their political allies, thus further reinforcing the widely held belief that trade unions concentrate on their activities in the political sphere to the detriment of their effectiveness in the industrial sphere, a reason often given for leaving – or failing to join – a trade union. Of course, the decline in membership in the 1980s meant that trade unions were weaker and less able to mobilise workers in the pursuit of their interests in the industrial sphere. This crisis of French trade unionism can be explained by developments in the industrial sphere, notably changes in the labour market, but also by events in the political sphere and more specifically the legacy of party-union relations from the period of the Union of the Left.

Appendix I
Union and Party Structures

Structures of the *Confédération Générale du Travail*

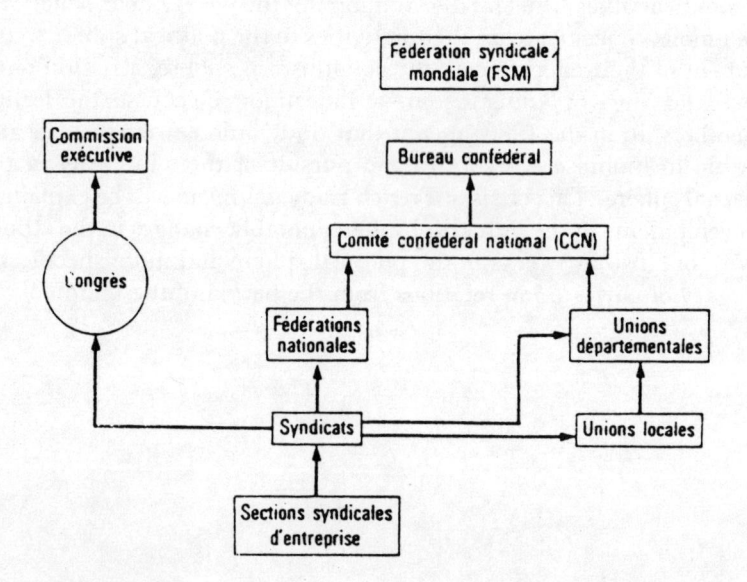

```
                                    Fédération syndicale
                                    mondiale (FSM)
                                          ↑
   Commission                       Bureau confédéral
   exécutive                              ↑
       ↑                    Comité confédéral national (CCN)
                                    ↑              ↑
    ⎛      ⎞              Fédérations          Unions
    ⎜Congrès⎟             nationales           départementales
    ⎝      ⎠                   ↑                    ↑
       ↑                                       Unions locales
       └──────────────── Syndicats ──────────────→  ↑
                              ↑
                       Sections syndicales
                       d'entreprise
```

Structures of the Confédération Française Démocratique du Travail

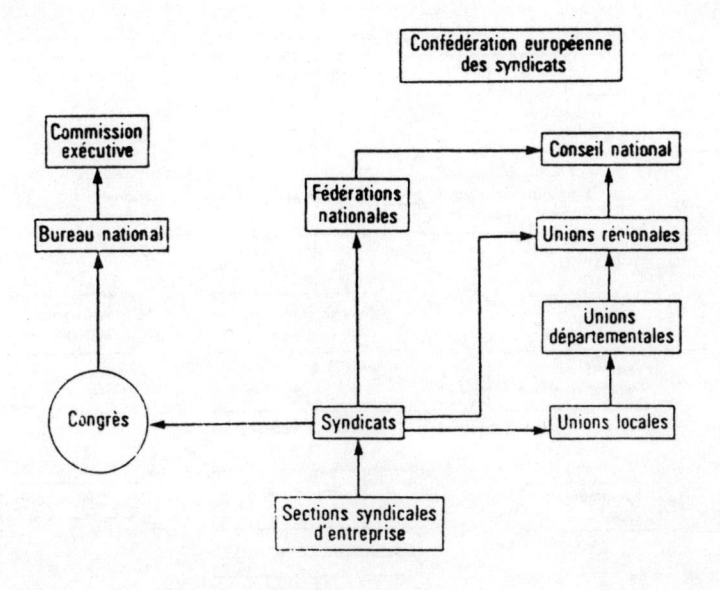

```
                              Confédération européenne
                                  des syndicats

    Commission                                      Conseil national
    exécutive
        ↑                    Fédérations                 ↑
                             nationales            Unions régionales
    Bureau national              ↑                       ↑
        ↑                                           Unions
                                                    départementales
                                                        ↑
    ( Congrès ) ←──────── Syndicats ──────────→   Unions locales
                              ↑
                         Sections syndicales
                          d'entreprise
```

Source: Mouriaux, 1984, p. 41–42.

184 Appendix

Structures of the Socialist Party

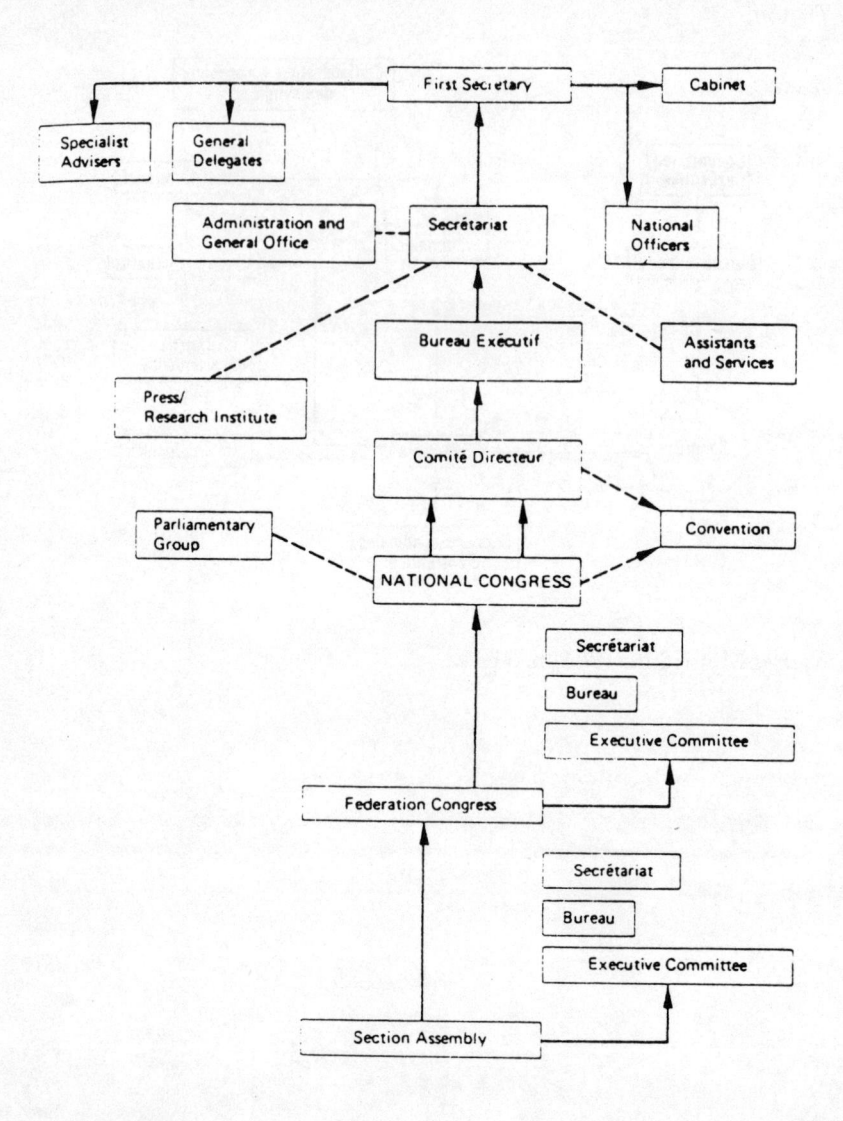

Structures of the French Communist Party

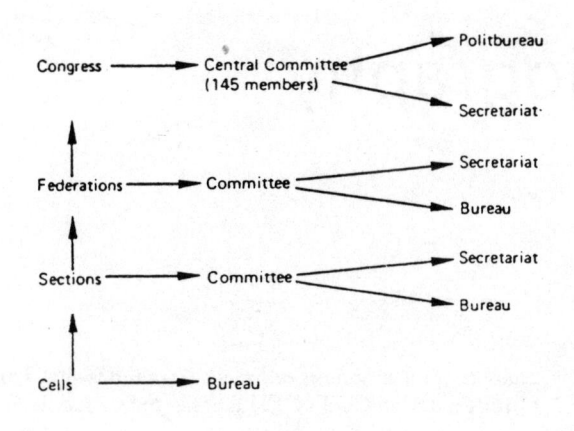

```
Congress ──────▶ Central Committee ──▶ Politbureau
                  (145 members)    ──▶ Secretariat
          ▲
          │
Federations ────▶ Committee ──▶ Secretariat
                             ──▶ Bureau
          ▲
          │
Sections ──────▶ Committee ──▶ Secretariat
                             ──▶ Bureau
          ▲
          │
Cells ─────────▶ Bureau
```

──────▶ indicates election channel

Source: Nugent & Lowe, 1982, p. 67, 114.

Bibliography

Adam, G., 1964, *Atlas des elections sociales en France*, Armand Colin, Paris
Adam, G., 1967, L'unité d'action CGT–CFDT, *Revue Française de Science Politique*, June : 576–90.
Adam, G., 1968, Eléments d'analyse sur les liens entre le PCF et la CGT, *Revue Française de Science Politique*, June : 524–41.
Adam, G., 1978a, La négociation collective en France, *Droit Social*, November : 385–91.
Adam, G., 1978b, La négociation collective en France, *Droit Social*, December : 420–51.
Adam, G., 1983, *Le pouvoir syndical*, Dunod, Paris.
Adam. G., et al., 1970, *L'ouvrier français en 1970*, Armand Colin, Paris.
Adam. G., & Reynaud, J-D., 1978, *Conflits du travail et changement social*. PUF, Paris.
Andrews, W. G., & Hoffmann, S., 1981, *The Fifth Republic at twenty*, State University of New York Press, Albany.
Andrieux, A. & Lignon, J., 1973, *Le militant syndicaliste d'aujourd'hui*, Denoel, Paris.
Andrieux, A., & Lignon, J., 1981, La CFDT, un phénomène original, *Projet*, November : 1065–79.
Bachy, J-P., 1974, Les syndicats et l'election présidentielle, *Nouvelle Revue Socialiste*, 3 : 57–66.
Bachy, J-P.,1975, Théorie et pratique des relations partis-syndicats, *Nouvelle Revue Socialiste*, 12–13 : 38–53.
Bachy, J-P., 1976, La contribution des syndicats au renouveau socialiste depuis 1958, *Nouvelle Revue Socialiste*, April : 55–68.
Bachy, J-P., 1980, L'état et les conflits. *Revue Française des Affaires Sociales*. 1 : 123–76.
Bacot, P., 1979, *Les dirigeants du Parti Socialiste*, Presses Universitaires de Lyon, Lyon.
Badie, B., 1975, *Le PCF et la grève*, Doctorat d'Etat. IEP. Paris
Barbet, D., 1977, Partis et syndicats. *Nouvelle Revue Socialiste*, 23 : 39–46.
Barjonet, A., 1968, *La CGT*, Seuil, Paris.
Barralis, R., et al., 1981, *Le débat ignoré*, CERC. Paris.

Baudouin, J., 1980, Les phénomènes de contestation au sein du parti communiste français, *Revue Française de Science Politique*, February : 78–111.
Baumfelder, E., 1968, La revendication – élément de la pratique syndicale. *Sociologie du Travail*, April–June : 149–67.
Bean, R., 1985, *Comparative industrial relations*, Croom Helm, London.
Bell, D., & Criddle, B., 1984, *The French socialist party*, OUP, Oxford.
Belloni, F., & Beller, D., 1978, *Faction politics : political parties and factionalism in comparative perspective*, ABC-Clio, Santa Barbara.
Bergeron, A., 1975, *Lettre ouverte à un syndiqué*, Albin Michel, Paris.
Bergeron, A., 1976, *Ma route et mes combats*, Ramsay, Paris.
Bergounioux, A., 1975, *Force Ouvrière*, Seuil, Paris.
Bergounioux, A., 1982, *Force Ouvrière*, PUF, Paris.
Bergounioux, A., 1983, Typologie de rapports syndicats-partis en Europe occidentale', *Pouvoirs*, 26 : 17–29.
Blackmer, D., & Tarrow, S. (eds.), 1975 *Communism in Italy and France*, Princeton University Press, Princeton.
Boggs, C., & Plotke, D., 1980, *The politics of eurocommunism*, Southend Press, Barton.
Branciard, M., 1982, *Syndicats et partis*, Vol I & II, Syros, Paris.
Breum, W., et al., 1981, *Die Gewerkschaften in der BRD*, VSA.
Bridgford, J., 1988, Back from the brink – the French Communist Party and the 1988 elections, *Modern and Contemporary France*, October : 34–46.
Bridgford, J., 1989, The Events of May : consequences for industrial relations in France, in Hanley, D., & Kerr, A.P., *May '68 : coming of age*, Macmillan, London : 100–116.
Bridgford, J., 1990, French trade unions : crisis in the 1980s, *Industrial Relations Journal*, Summer : 126–135.
Bridgford, J., & Stirling, J., 1985, Ideology or pragmatism? : trade union education in France and Britain, *Industrial Relations Journal*, Winter : 234–43.
Brierley, W. (ed.), 1987, *Trade unions and the economic crisis in the 1980s*, Gower, Aldershot.
Brown, B. (ed.), 1979, *Eurocommunism and eurosocialism: the Left confronts modernity*, Cyrco Press, New York.
Brun, J., 1971, Les communistes et l'action syndicale, *Cahiers du communisme*, May : 66–79.
Buffin, D., & Gerbaud, D., 1981, *Les communistes*, Albin Michel, Paris.
Bunel, J. & Abdou, M., 1980, La négociation collective de branche dans la région Rhône-Alpes, *Annales de l'Université Jean Moulin*, XVII : 125–45.
Butler, D., & Stokes, D., 1971, *Political change in Britain*, Pelican, London.
Caire, G., 1978, *La grève ouvrière*, Editions. Ouvrières, Paris.
Capdevielle, J., 1970, la CFDT depuis 1968, *Projet*, November : 1077–85.
Capdevielle, J., 1973, CFDT – un congrès pour quoi faire, *Projet*, June–August : 856–59.
Capdevielle, J., et al., 1975, *La grève du joint français*, Presses de la Fondation Nationale des Sciences Politiques, Paris.
Cayrol, R., 1974, Les militants du parti socialiste, *Projet*, September–October : 935–42.
Cayrol, R., 1975, L'univers politique des militants socialistes, *Revue Française de Science Politique*, February : 45–51.

Cayrol, R., 1978a, La direction du parti socialiste', *Revue Française de Science Politique*, April : 201–19.
Cayrol, R., 1978b, Le parti socialiste à l'enterprise, *Revue Française de Science Politique*, April : 296–312.
Clegg, H., 1976, *Trade unionism under collective bargaining*, Basil Blackwell, Oxford.
Clerc, J-M., 1973, Les conflits sociaux en 1970 et 1971, *Droit Social*, January : 19–26.
Cohen, M., 1977, La politique de l'enterprise et le droit du travail, *Revue Pratique de Droit Social*, December : 361–76.
Colliard, S., 1979, *La campagne présidentielle de François Mitterrand en 1974*, PUF, Paris.
Colpin, J., 1976, L'enterprise au coeur de la strategie du parti, *Cahiers du Communisme*, February–March : 247–49.
Colpin, J. (ed.), 1979, *Communistes à l'entreprise*, Editions, Sociales, Paris.
Cox, A. & Hayward, J., 1983, The inapplicability of the corporatist model in Britain and France, *International Political Science Review*, 2 : 217–40.
Creigh, S & Makeham, D., 1982, Strike incidence in industrialised countries : an analysis, *Australian Bulletin of Labour*, 3 : 139–49.
Crouch, C. (ed.), 1978, *State and economy in contemporary capitalism*, Croom Helm, London.
Crouch, C. & Pizzorno, A. (eds.), 1978, *The resurgence of class conflict in Western Europe since 1968*, 2 vols., Macmillan, London.
Dassa, S., 1978, *Les grèves de 1976 (étude quantitative)*, CNAM, Paris.
De Angelis, R., 1982, *Blue collar workers and politics: a French paradox*, Croom Helm, London.
Delamotte, Y., 1983, *Le droit du travail en pratique*, Editions d'Organisation, Paris.
Descamps, E., 1971, *Militer*, Fayard, Paris.
Dubois, P., 1974, *Mort de l'Etat-Patron*, Editions Ouvrières, Paris.
Dubois, P., et al, 1971, *Grèves revendicatives ou grèves politiques?*, Antbropos, Paris.
Denantes, F., 1978, Le ressort syndical de l'identité communiste, *Projet*, November : 1095–102.
Derville, J., 1975, Les communistes de l'Isere, *Revue Française de Science Politique*, February : 53–71.
Desseigne, G., 1971, CGT, CFDT vers un syndicalisme unique?, *Politique Aujourd'hui*, October : 3–12.
Durand, C. & Cazes, S., 1970, La signification politique du mouvement de mai, *Sociologie du Travail*, 12 : 293–308.
Durand, M., & Dubois, P., 1975, *La grève*, Fondation National de Sciences Politiques, Paris.
Durand, M, & Harff, Y., 1977, Panorama statistique des grèves, *Sociologie du Travail*, October–December : 356–75.
Durrieu, Y., 1974/5, Le PS au rendez-vous de l'autogestion, *Autogestion et Socialisme*, October–January : 85–100.
Echevin, P., 1970, Des coupures de courant aux contrats de progrès, *Projet*, January : 93–95.
Echevin, P., 1977, Les syndicats et la crise de la gauche, *Projet*, December : 1241–45.
Elleinstein, J., 1976, *Le PCF*, Grasset, Paris.

Evin, K. & Cayrol, R., 1976, Les partis politiques dans les entreprises, *Projet*, June : 633–43.
Evin, K., & Cayrol, R., 1978, 'Comment contrôler l'union' *Projet,* January 1978.
Eyraud, F., 1983, La négociation salariale dans la metallurgie, *Sociologie du Travail*, 3 : 295–312.
Fabre, R., 1978, *Toute vérité est bonne à dire*, Fayard, Paris.
Fajon, E. (ed.), 1975, *L'union est un combat*, Editions Sociales, Paris.
Fauvet, J., 1964 & 1966, *Histoire du Parti Communiste Français*, Fayard, Paris.
Feretti, R., 1976, Les militants de la fédération du Bas-Rhin du PS – elements d'une sociologie', *Nouvelle Revue Socialiste*, 14/15 : 8–16.
Filo della Torre, P, et al., 1979, *Eurocommunism : myth or reality?*, Penguin, London.
Fiszbin, H., 1980, *Les bouches s'ouvrent*, Grasset, Paris.
Flanagan, R., Soskice, D. & Ulman, L., 1983, *Unions, economic stability and income policies*, Brookings Institute, Washington.
Frachon, B., 1967, *Au rythme des jours*, vols. 1 and 2, Editions. Sociales, Paris.
Franklin, M., 1985, *The decline of class voting*, Clarendon Press, Oxford.
Gallie, D., 1978, *In search of the new working class*, CUP, Cambridge.
Gallie, D., 1983, *Social inequality and class radicalism in France and Britain*, CUP, Cambridge.
Gaullier, X., 1968, Syndicats et partis politiques, *Projet*, March : 257–62.
Giesbert, F-O., 1977, *François Mitterrand* Seuil, Paris.
Girault, J., 1989, *Benoît Frachon Communiste et Syndicaliste*, Presses de la Fondation Nationale de Sciences Politiques, Paris.
Goguel, F., 1970, *Géographie des elections françaises sous la Troisième et la Quatrième République*, Armand Colin, Paris.
Groux, G., & Mouriaux, R., 1989, *La CFDT*, Economica, Paris.
Halbeher, A., 1976, Tout dépendra de l'activite du parti à l'entreprise, *Cahiers du Communisme*, February–March : 268–70.
Hammond, T., 1957, *Lenin on trade unions and revolution 1893–1917*, Columbia University Press, New York.
Hamon, H. and Rotman, P., 1982, *La deuxième gauche*, Ramsay, Paris.
Hanley, D., 1986, *Keeping left? CERES and the French Socialist Party*, Manchester University Press, Manchester.
Hanley, D., & Kerr, A., 1988, *The events of may – twenty years on*, Macmillan, London.
Hardouin, H., 1978, Les caractéristiques sociologiques du Parti Socialiste, *Revue Française de Science Politique*, April : 220–55.
Harmel, C., 1970, Les organes directeurs de la CGT, *Etudes Sociales et Syndicales*, January–February : 18–23.
Harmel, C., 1975, Les syndicalistes à la direction du parti socialiste, *Etudes Sociales et Syndicales*, March–April : 22.
Harmel. C., 1982, *La CGT*, PUF, Paris.
Harmel. C., & Tandler, N., 1982, *Comment le parti communiste contrôle la CGT*, Bibliothèque d'Histoire Sociale, Paris.
Harrison, M., 1973, *Trade unions and the Labour Party since 1945*, George Allen & Unwin, London.
Hayward, J., 1981, *Surreptious factionalism in the French Communist Party*, Hull Papers in Politics, Hull.

Hincker, F., 1981, *Le Parti Communiste au carrefour*, Albin Michel, Paris.
Hyman, R., 1972, *Strikes*, Fontana, London.
Jeanson, A., 1971, Les syndicats, nouveaux acteurs politiques, *Projet*, June : 694–708.
Jenson, J., & Ross. G., 1984, *The view from inside*, University of California Press, Berkeley.
Jezequel, C., 1981, Aperçus statistiques sur la vie conventionnelle en France, *Droit Social*, June : 462–65.
Jobert, A., 1974, Vers un nouveau style des relations professionnelles, *Droit Social*, September–October : 397–410.
Johnson, R.W., 1981, *The long march of the French left*, Macmillan, London.
Jourdain, H., 1974, La politique dans l'entreprise, *Cahiers du Communisme*, October : 80–91.
Jourdain, H., 1982, *Comprendre pour accomplir*, Editions. Sociales, Paris.
Juquin, P., 1977, *Programme commun: l'actualisation à dossier ouvert*, Editions. Sociales, Paris.
Kergoat, J., 1983, *Le Parti Socialiste. De la commune à nos jours*, le Sycomore, Paris.
Kesselman, M. & Groux, G., 1984, *Le mouvement ouvrier français*, Editions. Ouvrières, Paris.
Kindersley, R. (ed.), 1981, *In search of eurocommunism*, Macmillan, London.
Korpi, W. & Shalev, M., 1979, Strikes, industrial relations and class conflict in capitalist societies, *British Journal of Sociology*, 2 : 164–87.
Krasucki, H., 1972, *Syndicats et socialisme*, Editions Sociales, Paris.
Krasucki, H., 1980, *Syndicats et unité*, Editions Sociales, Paris.
Kriegel, A., 1968, *Les communistes français*, Seuil, Paris.
Krumnow, A., Detraz, A. & Maire, E., 1975, *La CFDT et l'autogestion*, Cerf, Paris.
Lagroye, J. et al., 1976, *Les militants politiques dans trois partis français*, Pedone, Paris.
Landier, H., 1981, *Demain, quels syndicats?*, Pluriel, Paris.
Lange, P., Ross, G. & Vannicelli, M., 1982, *Unions, change and crisis*, George Allen & Unwin, London.
Lash, S., 1984, *The militant worker*, Heinemann, London.
Laurens, A. & Pfister, T., 1977, *Les nouveaux communistes aux portes du pouvoir*, Stock, Paris.
Lavau, G., 1978, The changing relations between trade unions and working class parties in France, *Government and Opposition*, Autumn : 437–57.
Lavau, G., 1981, *A quoi sert le Parti Communiste Français?*, Fayard, Paris.
Lesire Ogrel, H., 1967, *Le syndicat dans l'entreprise*, Seuil, Paris.
Lestienne, B., 1979, CGT – retour au social?, *Projet*, March : 376–79.
Lorwin, V., 1954, *The French labour movement*, Harvard University Press, Cambridge.
Lyon-Caen, G., 1979, Critique de la négociation collective, *Droit Social*, September–October : 350–56.
Maciness, N., 1975, *The communist parties of Western Europe*, OUP, Oxford.
MacShane, D., 1982, *François Mitterrand*, Quartet, London.
Magniadas, J., 1970, Politique contractuelle et lutte, *Economie de Politique*, May : 279–82.
Maire, E., 1973, La CFDT et l'union de la Gauche, *Preuves*, 1 : 15–26.
Maire, E., 1980, *Reconstruire l'espoir*, Seuil, Paris.

Maire, E. & Julliard, J., 1975, *La CFDT aujourd'hui*, Seuil, Paris.
Marchais, G., 1973, *Le defi démocratique*, Grasset, Paris.
Marchais, G., 1980, *L'espoir au présent*, Editions Sociales, Paris.
Mercier, A., 1976, La négociation, *CFDT Aujourd'hui*, May–June : 16–20.
Michelat, G. & Simon, M., 1977, *Religion, class and politics, comparative politics* October 159–186.
Minkin, L., 1974, The British Labour Party and the trade unions: crisis and compact, *Industrial and Labor Relations Review*, October : 7–37.
Minkin, L., 1978, The party connection: divergence and convergence in the British labour movement, *Government and Opposition*, Autumn : 458–83.
Minkin, L., 1980, *The Labour Party conference*, Manchester University, University Press, Manchester.
Mitterrand, F., 1969, *Ma part de vérité*, Fayard, Paris.
Mitterrand, F., 1973, *La rose au poing*, Flammarion, Paris.
Mitterrand, F., 1975, *La paille et le grain*, Flammarion, Paris.
Mitterrand, F., 1977, *Politique*, Fayard, Paris.
Mitterrand, F., 1980, *Ici et maintenant*, Fayard, Paris.
Mitterrand, F., 1981, *Politique 2*, Fayard, Paris.
Mouriaux, R., 1982, *La CGT*, Seuil, Paris.
Mouriaux, R., 1984, *Les syndicats dans la société française*, FNSP, Paris.
Mouriaux, R., 1985, *Syndicalisme et politique*, Editions Ouvrières, Paris.
Moreau, J., 1977, L'impact des propositions CFDT sur le PCF et la CGT, *CFDT Aujourd'hui*, September–October : 46–57.
Moreau, J., 1981, Syndicalisme et politique, *Projet*, November : 1080–89.
Morel, C., 1975, Physionomie statistique des grèves, *Revue Française des Affaires Sociales*, October–December : 183–95.
Moynot, J-L., 1973a, Luttes syndicales et bataille politique, *Nouvelle Critique*, October : 11–17.
Moynot, J-L., 1973b, Dialogue entre les syndicats, *Projet*, November : 1037–55.
Moynot, J-L., 1982, *Au milieu du gué*, PUF, Paris.
Nugent, N. & Lowe, D., 1982, *The left in France*, Macmillan, London.
Oppenheim, R., 1975, La question du cumul des mandats politiques et syndicaux à la CFDT, *Revue Française de Science Politique*, April : 317–37.
Parti Communiste Français, 1972, *Changer de cap: Programme pour un gouvernement démocratique d'union populaire*, Editions Sociales, Paris.
Parti Communiste Francais, 1978, *Programme commun de gouvernement actualisé*, Editions Sociales, Paris.
Parti Communiste Français and Parti Socialiste, 1972, *Programme commun de gouvernement*, Editions Sociales, Paris.
Parti Socialiste, 1975, *Syndicalisme et politique*, PS, Paris.
Parti Socialiste, 1975, *Quinzes thèses sur l'autogestion*, PS, Paris.
Parti Socialiste, 1978, *Le programme commun de gouvernement de la gauche: propositions socialistes pour l'actualisation*, Flammarion, Paris.
Platone, J. & Subileau, F., 1975, Les militants communistes à Paris: quelques données sociologiques, *Revue Française de Science Politique*, October : 837–69.
Poperen, J., 1976, *L'unité de la gauche*, Fayard, Paris.
Prost, A., 1964, *La CGT à l'epoque du Front Populaire 1934–39*, Armand Colin, Paris.
Rand Smith, W., 1981, Paradoxes of plural unionism – CGT–CFDT relations in France, *West European Politics*, January : 38–53.

Rand Smith, W., 1984, Dynamics of plural unionism in France: the CGT, CFDT and industrial conflict, *British Journal of Industrial Relations,* March : 15–33.
Rand Smith, W., 1987, *Crisis in the French labour movement,* Macmillan, London.
Ranger, J., 1969, Les liens entre le PCF et la CGT, éléments d'un débat', *Revue Française de Science Politique,* February : 182–86.
Reynaud, J-D., 1975, *Les syndicats en France,* 2 vols., Seuil, Paris.
Reynaud, J-D., 1978, *Les syndicats, les patrons et l'etat: tendances de la négociation collective en France,* Editions Ouvrières, Paris.
Reynaud, J-D., 1980, Industrial relations and political systems: some reflections on the crisis in industrial relations in Western Europe, *British Journal of Industrial Relations,* 1 : 1–13.
Reynaud, J-D., Dassa, S., Dassa, J. & Maclouf, P., 1971, Les événements de mai et juin 1968 et le système français de relations professionnelles, *Sociologie du Travail,* January–March : 73–97 and April–June : 191–209.
Ridley, F., 1970, *Revolutionary syndicalism in France,* CUP, Cambridge.
Robertson, D., 1976, *A theory of party competition,* Wiley, London.
Robrieux, P., 1981, *Histoire intérieure du Parti Communiste,* 4 vols., Fayard, Paris.
Ross, G., 1979, The Confedération Générale du Travail and Eurocommunism, *Politics and Society* : 33–60.
Ross, G., 1982, *Workers and communists in France,* University of California Press, Los Angeles.
Rozenblatt, P., et al, 1982, Analyse du conflit Lip et des repercussions sur les platiques ouvrières et les stratégies syndicales. Unpublished doctorate, Université de Paris IX, Paris.
Salomon, A., 1980, *PS la mise à nu,* Robert Laffont, Paris.
Savatier, J., 1977, Les activités politiques dans l'enterprise, *Droit Social,* June : 231–36.
Schifres, M., 1972, *La CFDT des militants,* Stock, Paris.
Séguy, G., 1975, *Lutter,* Stock, Paris.
Shalev, M., 1980, Industrial relations theory and the comparative study of industrial relations and industrial conflict, *British Journal of industrial relations,* 1 : 26–43.
Shorter, E. & Tilly, C., 1974, *Strikes in France 1930–1968,* CUP, Cambridge.
Subileau, F., 1979, Les communistes parisiens en 1977, *Revue Française de Science Politique,* August–October : 791–810.
Sur, S., 1977, *La vie politique en France sous la Ve République,* Editions Montchrestien, Paris.
Tiersky, R., 1974, *French Communism 1920–1972,* Columbia University Press, New York.
Tincq, H., 1975, Un an de rapports CGT-CFDT, *Projet,* September–October : 958–62.
Verdier, E. et al., 1981, *La presse syndicale,* CRESST, Paris.
Verdier, R., 1976, *PS-PC une lutte pour l'entente,* Seghers, Paris.
Vieuguet, A., 1971, Avec le programme de gouvernement: élever l'activité politique du parti à l'entreprise, *Cahiers du Communisme,* December : 21–62.
Von Beyme, K., 1978, The changing relations between trade unions and the Social Democratic Party in West Germany', *Government and Opposition,* 4 : 398–415.

Walsh, K., 1982, Industrial disputes in France, West Germany, Italy and United Kingdom: measurement and incidence, *Industrial Relations Journal*, 4 : 65–72.

Weiss, D., 1979, *Politique, partis et syndicats dans l'entreprise*, Editions d'Organisation, Paris.

Wilson, F., 1987, *Interest group politics in France*, Cambridge University Press, Cambridge.

Wright, V., 1983, *Government and politics of France*, Hutchinson, Second Edition, London.

Index

Acquier, André 22
Alézard, Gérard 109
Assises du Socialisme 21, 22, 28, 45, 65, 118, 119, 139, 142

Bachy, Jean-Paul 147
Barralis, Roger 107
Barre, Raymond 46, 85, 96, 98, 131, 160, 167, 172
Bérégovoy, Pierre 9
Berteloot, André 25, 131, 137, 140
Bidouze, René 165
Bobillier, Camille 120
Bompart, Jean-Pierre 118
Bonnevialle, Roger 28
Bono, Robert 165
Bourne, Jean-Paul 122
Braaksma, Michael 121
Bredel, Gilbert 116
Brunier, Joseph 116
Buhl, René 111, 113, 114

Caille, Marcel 41
Carassus, Pierre 21, 22, 109, 110, 112, 115, 124
Caudron, Dinah 112
Centre d'Etudes, de Recherches et d'Education Socialistes (CERES) 13, 45, 50
Ceyrac, François 157
Chaban Delmas, Jacques 73, 156, 161, 163, 164, 167, 169, 170
Charter of Amiens 2, 7
Charzat, Michel 18, 23
Chavrot, Lucien 168
Chenard, Alain 148

Chérèque, Jacques 9
Chesnel, Alain 120
Chevènement, Jean-Pierre 23
Chirac, Jacques 167
Chotard, Yvon 157
Coffineau, Michel 22
Collective bargaining 153–174
Colpin, Jean 11, 19
Committed autonomy 28, 30
Common Programme of Government 33–57
Compagnie Française des Pétroles — CFR-Total 38, 46, 48
Compagnie Générale d'Electricité 37
Confédération Française Démocratique du Travail (CFDT)
    and collective bargaining 163–168
    and elections 59–68
    and factionalism 115–124
    and personnel links with political parties 26–29
    and relations with the CGT 82–103
    and response to the Common Programme of Government 42–44, 50–53
    and strikes 138–149
    and voting behaviour 68–77
Confédération Générale du Travail (CGT)
    and collective bargaining 163–168
    and elections 59–68
    and factionalism 106–115
    and personnel links with political parties 23–26
    and relations with CFDT 82–103
    and response to the Common Programme of Government 39–42, 47–50
    and strikes 138–149

and voting behaviour 68–77
Confédération Générale du Travail-Force Ouvrière (FO) 1, 3, 19, 20, 21, 22, 23, 70, 72, 73, 77, 83, 105, 111, 160, 161, 164, 166, 167, 168, 170
Confédération Générale du Travail Unitaire (CGTU) 104
Confederazione Italiana dei Sindacati Lavoratori (CISL) 174
Corradi, Jean 107, 110
Couderc, Jeanne 122

Dassault 37
Declercq, Gilbert 90
Defferre, Gaston 4, 36
De Fouchier, Hervé 106
Deiss, Ernest 113
Delors, Jacques 170, 171
Descamps, Eugène 83, 86, 90
Detraz, Albert 42, 43, 44, 63
Dion, Léon 121
Duclos, Jacques 4
Defaud, Georges 116, 122
Duhamel, René 9

European Trade Union Confederation (ETUC) 85

Fabre, Robert 41, 46
Factionalism 104–128
Faure, Edgar 165
Fédération de l'Education Nationale (FEN) 20, 21, 63, 72, 73, 83, 95, 111, 170
Feuilly, Pierre 108, 112
Frachon, Benoît 25, 26, 39
French Communist Party (PCF)
 and collective bargaining 168–171
 and Common Programme of Government 33–54
 and elections 58–79
 and personnel linkages with trade union confederations 18–20
 and strikes 144–149
 and workplace branches 10–13
Frischmann, Georges 66

Garnier, Luc 121
Garrigne, François 118
Gaumé, Gérard 24, 111, 113
Germon, Claude 22, 106, 107, 108, 109, 110, 111, 112, 124, 148
Gilles, Ghristiane 112, 113, 114, 124
Giscard d'Estaing, Valéry 61, 73, 74

Got, Daniel 116
Goubier, Géo 121
Guntz, François 120

Halbeher, Aimé 16, 145
Halgand, Jean-Paul 121
Hembert, Patrick 118
Hennion, Françoise 118
Héritier, Pierre 23, 116
Hoiroux, Michèle 17
Honeywell-Bull 37
Hue, Claude 120
Huet, Rémy 121

Incerti, Louis 116
International Confederation of Free Trade Unions (ICFTU) 85
ITT-France 37

Jacquet, Gérard 9
Jeanson, André 22
Jévodan, Robert 112
Jourdain, Henri 16, 40
Joxe, Pierre 20, 110

Kerdraon, Jean-Noël 118
Krasucki, Henri 17, 24, 28
Krivine, Alain 62
Krumnow, Frédo 125

Laguiller, Arlette 62
Lambert, Jacqueline 113, 114
Lanoue, Georges 66
Laroze, Jean-Claude 25, 110
Laurent, Jean-Luc 116
Le Guen, René 66
Leroy, Roland 45
Ligue Communiste Révolutionnaire (LCR) 62, 117, 123, 124
Lip watch factory 62
Lomber, Jean-Pierre 117
Lutte Ouvrière (LO) 62

Maire, Edmond 9, 27, 28, 45, 50, 51, 53, 60, 62, 63, 64, 67, 84, 91, 94, 98, 116, 117, 120, 121, 125, 141, 142, 144, 164
Mantault, Dominique 107
Marangé, Jean 22
Marchais, Georges 9, 11, 19, 36, 37, 41, 43, 45, 46, 61, 67
Mercier, Albert 139
Mermaz, Louis 15
Messmers, Pierre 165, 167

Mexendeau, Louis 110
Mick, Jean-Marie 26, 145, 147
Migeon, Claude 118
Mitterrand, François 4, 9, 23, 33, 35, 36, 37, 41, 44, 45, 46, 48, 60, 61, 62, 63, 72, 73, 74, 93, 106, 118, 119, 139, 144, 148, 170, 177
Monmousseau, Gaston 26
Moreau, Jacques 9, 43, 51, 64
Moreau Report 52, 53, 97, 121
Moussy, Jean-Pierre 122
Mouvement des Radicaux de Gauche (MRG) 33, 35, 59, 60, 63, 65, 95, 118
Moynot, Jean-Louis 24, 105, 112, 113, 115, 124, 143, 164

Noly, Dominique 118, 122

Overney, Pierre 92

Parent, Jeanine 112
Parti Communiste Revolutioannaire (Marxiste-Léniniste) (PCR-ML) 123, 124
Parti Socialiste Unifié 27, 28, 29, 42, 60, 63, 64, 72
Pastre, Aimé 106
Péchiney-Ugine-Kuhlmann 37, 145
Peperen, Jean 36
Peugeot-Citroën 46, 48
Piaget-Charles 62
Political party functions 2, 10
Pompidou, Georges 36, 44, 63, 79, 136
Poperen, Claude 145

Questiaux, Nicole 110

Ramos, Alain 117
Rannou, Alain 15, 148
Relative autonomy 5, 26
Rhône-Poulenc 37, 43
Robert, Guy 117
Rocard, Michel 27, 45
Roussel-Uclaf 37, 41

Royer, Jean 70, 73

Sainjon, André 66
Saint Gobain-Pont à Mousson 37
Saint-Martin, Joseph 122
Sardrais, Claude 122
Sarre, Georges 14
Savay, Alain 36
Séguy, Georges 8, 9, 17, 23, 24, 25, 26, 28, 39, 40, 42, 48, 49, 50, 60, 65, 66, 67, 82, 84, 85, 86, 90, 93, 94, 97, 98, 99, 106, 108, 109, 110, 113, 140, 141, 142, 143, 163, 164, 168, 177
Socialist Party
 and collective bargaining 168–171
 and Common Programme of Government 33–54
 and elections 58–79
 and personnel linkages with trade union confederations 20–23
 and strikes 144–149
 and workplace branches 13–15
Strikes 129–150
Szpirko, Roland 117

Thomson-Brandt 37
Troublet, Jacques 114
Toutain, Roger 116
Trade union functions 2, 9–10
Transmission-beltism 5, 25, 56

Usinor-Vallourec 38

Varlet, Jean-Pierre 116
Vernet, Claude 121
Vieuguet, André 11, 15
Vitot, Roland 116

Warcholak, Michel 66, 139
Wellhof, François 120
Wendel-Sidérlor 38
World Federations of Trade Unions (WFTU) 85